POPULAR CRAFTS

GUIDE TO PAPER CRAFTS

Other books in the Popular Crafts series:

Popular Crafts Guide to Pottery	Alan & Gill Bridgewater
Popular Crafts Guide to Weaving	Alan & Gill Bridgewater
Popular Crafts Guide to Making Wooden Toys that Move	Alan & Gill Bridgewater
Popular Crafts Guide to Soft Doll Making	Pam Wheatley
Poular Crafts Guide to Enamelling	Karen Theilade & Lyn Collins
Popular Crafts Guide to Quilted Appliqué	Val Freeman

POPULAR CRAFTS

GUIDE TO PAPER CRAFTS

ALAN & GILL BRIDGEWATER

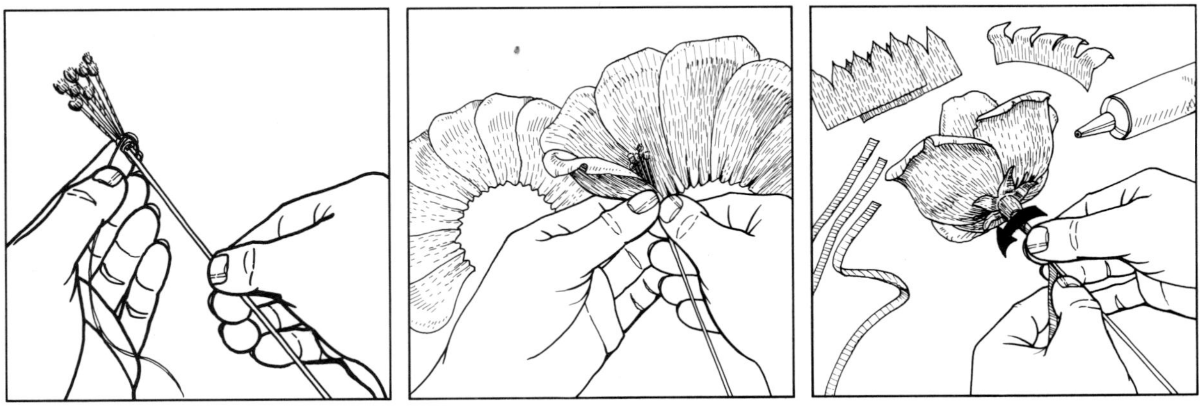

ARGUS BOOKS

Argus Books Limited
1 Golden Square
London W1R 3AB

ISBN 0 85242 907 X

Phototypesetting by Input Typesetting Ltd, London
Printed and bound by R. J. Acford, Chichester

CONTENTS

INTRODUCTION

INTRODUCTION

It has been said that paper is everything or nothing, depending on the person dealing with it. Sheets of silvery sharp-edged translucent tracing paper, rustling brown wrapping papers that protect and conceal, strong hand-made Japanese papers that are as light as air, crêpe papers in bright primary colours, eye catching foils, smooth creamy ivory boards, and crinkly wrinkley feather-weight tissues. Paper in its many and varied forms must surely be a uniquely beautiful and versatile material!

Take a crisp clean immaculate white sheet of paper, hold it in your finger tips and see how the rays of light catch its perfect smooth

A sheet or two of coloured paper, a small pair of fine-point scissors, and you are well on the way to making a Polish paper cuts frieze – not a bad way to spend a wet and windy winter's evening?

A paper cut worked in the naive folk Swiss style; this particular cut was worked by our son Glyn, who was only about ten years old at the time.

purity — you have in your hands a material that has unlimited art and craft potential. A cut or two with a razor sharp scalpel and you have a strong three dimensional paper sculpture. A few hours spent snipping away with a pair of fine-point scissors and you have a delicate lacey Swiss paper-cut. Folding, tearing, bending, creasing, drawing, ripping, pulping, painting, gluing, and cutting; greetings cards, garlands, pictures, cut-outs and portrait silhouettes – this book is about all of these and much much more.

For many centuries, craftsmen and artists have decorated and explored this most exciting man-made material. Furniture makers in the seventeenth and eighteenth centuries worked the most subtle découpage designs and motifs. In the nineteenth century naive folk artists produced paper cuts of great sensitivity, and of course closer to our own time Alexander Calder made his paper mobiles, and Buckminster Fuller created his inspired paper and cane geodesic domes.

A Japanese fan, a Chinese kite, a frieze – paper is all things to all people. And so it is with this book that we have drawn our inspiration from world wide ethnic, folk, traditional and modern sources. Art Deco paper sculptures, papier-mâché decorated with bold canal art motifs, under varnish découpage, origami, quilling, and paper flowers – this book will show you the way. With a text that is by turn, witty, pretty, solid, authoritative and revelational, and with a great many working drawings, inspirational illustrations and step-by-step details, we show you how you can make the most amazingly beautiful items. You don't need a workshop crammed with expensive equipment, nor do you need to buy in vast quantities of wet, bulky, difficult to handle materials. Young or old, strong or weak, athletic, bedbound, rich or poor, papercrafts are for you.

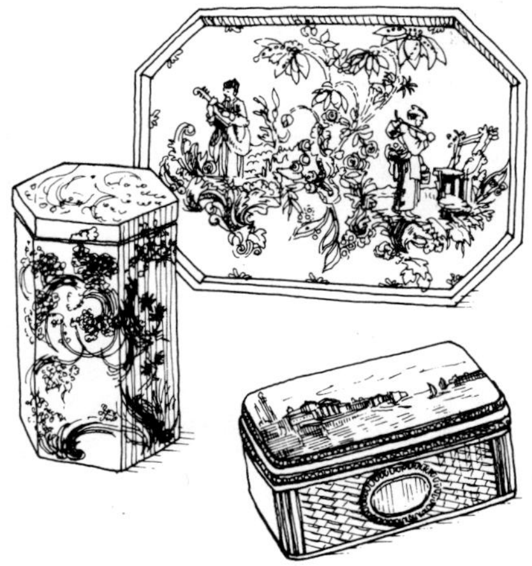

Découpage is the traditional craft of decorating a surface with illustrations cut from paper – an easy and inexpensive way of making a really beautiful and desirable item. Three découpaged items (a) a small biscuit tin (b) a tea caddy. (c) a small tea tray.

PAPERCRAFTS DATA

TOOLS, TECHNIQUES, MATERIALS, DESIGN AND WORKSHOP

Adhesives See glues, gums and adhesives.

Brushes. Papercrafters need brushes. Set yourself up with several good quality ones – go for the best, look after them and they will last a lifetime.

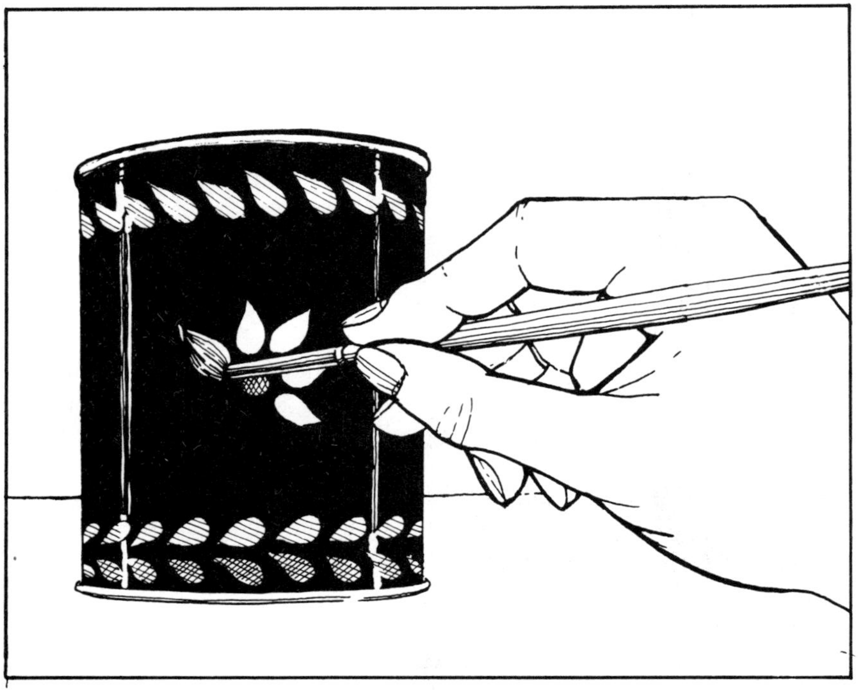

Art Deco. Papercraft inspiration can be drawn from just about any style or tradition – if you like working with a pencil, compass and a ruler, then why not have a go at an Art Deco type motif?

Art deco A style of design and decoration that was at its height in the 1930s, it is characterized by geometrical shapes, stylized natural forms, and symmetrical utilitarian design. Art Deco design, patterns and motifs might be used as inspirational material.

Brushes These come in a great many shapes and sizes – we use large and small, soft, long haired, fine-point artists brushes. Brushes of this type and character improve with use, so buy the best, keep them dry and clean, and always store them bristle up.

Cardboard A relatively inexpensive stiff bodied material that might be made from rags or wood fibre – a general term for just about any board that is thicker than paper.

Cartridge paper A printing paper that comes in a variety of thicknesses and qualities in colours that range from buff to white. A good quality cartridge paper can be used for sketching, water-colour work, ink drawings, and paper sculpture. When you are buying such a material, or any other card or paper come to that, request that it be packaged in its flat state.

Coated paper and board A board of this character is considered to be the highest grade. It has a very shiny glossy smooth surface and such a material might be used for making special greetings cards, presentation boxes, paper sculpture and such like. The paper and card have the same working and textural qualities, the only difference is the weight/thickness.

Cover boards and papers. Make contact with a paper supplier and get to see samples – always request that paper and card be packaged in its flat state.

Compass or a pair of compasses A two legged instrument used to draw out circles and arcs – yes you can make-do with pins, pencils and bits of string, but as likely as not you'll find yourself going round in circles. Ideally you will need a long legged pencil-holding compass, and a small screw operated compass.

Cover boards and papers Board and paper are classified and sold by weight. Paper weight starts at about 110 grams per square metre and ranges through to boards at about 500 grams per square metre. There are all manner of textures, qualities, structures and finishes – if in doubt as to the qualities of such-and-such a material, ask for a sample.

Gluing. There are any number of special glues and adhesives – we favour quick-dry petroleum gum type glues that can be spread with scraps of card – such a glue sets quickly, doesn't stain and can be removed with a solvent. Note – there are several non-sniff glues that have similar characteristics.

Crayons and markers There are pencil crayons, pastel sticks, wax crayons, watercolour pencils, and so on. We try to avoid messy, smudgy colours, so we tend to use best quality wood covered pencil crayons.

Crêpe paper A thin crinkled brightly coloured tissue-like paper, used primarily for decorations. Crêpe paper has a pronounced grain and texture, and it can be cut, stretched and moulded.

Cutting board Meaning a piece of plywood, blockboard or some such smooth portable surface on which you can use a knife – don't cut on your drawing board.

Découpage The art craft or process of decorating a surface with shapes or illustrations cut from paper – anything produced by this technique might be described as a Découpage.

Designing Meaning to work out the structure or form by making a sketch, outline, pattern or prototype. We usually start designing by visiting a museum, gallery or old bookshop – take plenty of sketch paper and coloured pencils. After working through a series of sketches, make a protype using inexpensive scrap off-cut materials.

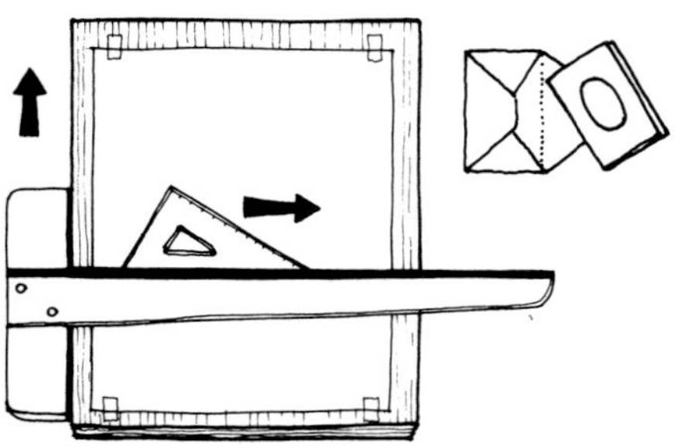

Drawing board. If you reckon on making items with good clean crisp, well worked lines, you will need a drawing board, a T-square and a set-square.

Detail paper A very thin inexpensive tissue-like translucent paper, which can be used for tracing and for working up a master drawing.

Drawing board Meaning a smooth surfaced board with at least one good straight edge – a board to be used for right angled and detailed marking out. You will also need, sooner or later, a T-square and a Set-square.

Drawing papers and boards Rag papers/boards, meaning boards and papers that are designed to be used for good class water-colour work.

Embossed paper A material that has a pronounced surface texture; the patterns, motifs and designs are made by running the paper through rollers.

Felt tip pens Meaning the ordinary inexpensive felt tip pens – they are brightly coloured and come in large packs. Don't use these pens for fine presentation work because they bleed – very useful for making quick sketches. Note – some museums and galleries prefer you not to use such pens on their premises.

Fixative Usually packaged in an easy-to-use aerosol, fixatives are used to spray over and protect works that might smudge – say a soft pencil drawing, a water colour and so on.

Foils Paper and boards with a metallic finish. Some foils are made entirely from plastic, or metal.

Glues, gums and adhesives There are hot glues, rubber glues in cans and tubes, rubber and petroleum based gums, easy-to-use adhesives in 'pens', contact adhesive, clear glues, and so on. A good all purpose glue is polyvinyl acetate, or PVA for short. PVA's are strong but not heat proof or waterproof, they set in about an hour, can be wiped off

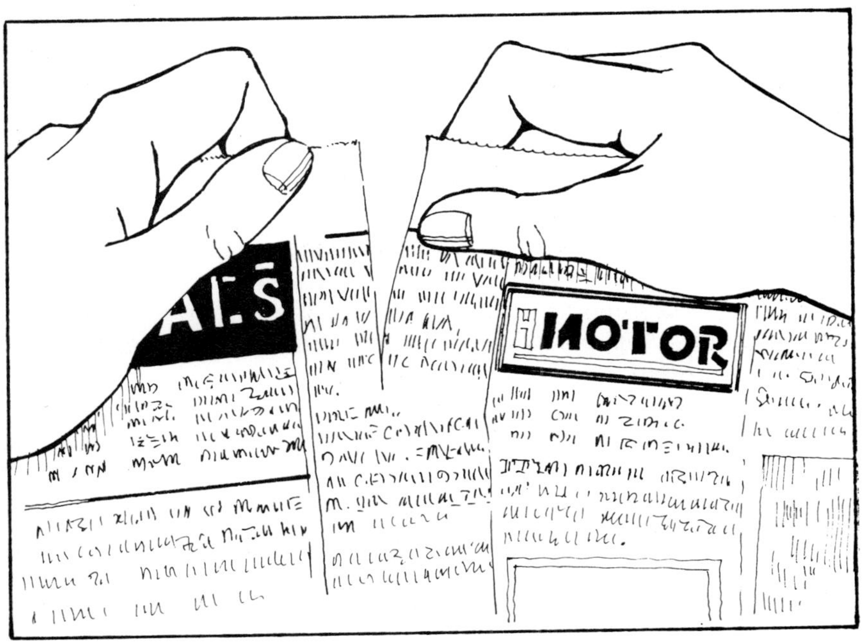

Papier Mâché. When you are making papier mâché, first tear the newspaper with the grain so as to make long strips; aim to reduce the paper to stamp-sized pieces.

Pliers. Several of the projects require that you use a pair of pliers – we favour long nose pliers, a pair that has a wire nipping slot.

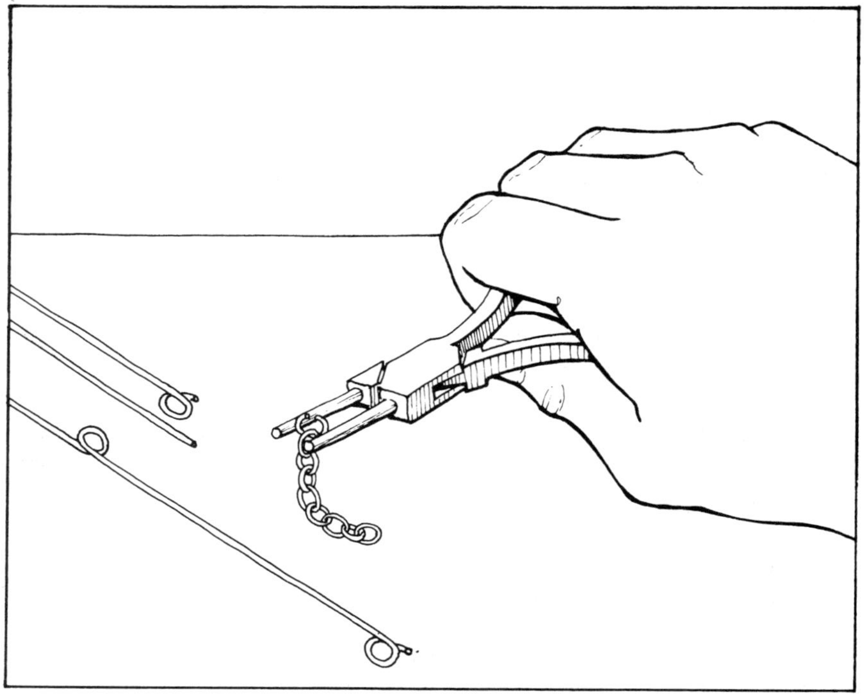

with a damp cloth when still tacky and are usually packaged in easy-to-use squeezy bottles.

Grids Meaning scaled grids that are placed over working drawings. You can buy grid paper, or you can draw up your own. If you want to change the size of a project, use a gridded paper and rework our designs a square at a time. So for example if you choose a project that has say one square to 1 inch, all you do is take a piece of grid paper that has 1 inch squares, and then transfer our design square by square. Once you have scaled up in this way, then you can trace direct.

Hand-made papers Papers that are made by hand – such papers tend to have non-mechanical textures and structures and are very expensive.

Ink Meaning black indian and various coloured good quality artists inks.

Ingres paper A paper with a hair-fibre finish or texture – a good material to use for quality paper sculpture.

Inspirational material Meaning magazine clips, photographs, museum exhibits and such like which you can use as the jumping off point for fresh ideas.

Ivory Board A good quality laminated paper/board with a beautiful white finish.

Japanese papers Hand-made – characteristically made from long and strong natural fibres like mulberry. Such papers resist tearing, have a good texture, are visually very attractive and exciting, and have a good wet strength.

Japanese paper sculptures Hand made paper items that relate to and draw their inspiration from the Japanese paper folding tradition. Japanese kites, fans, screens, in the context of this book, are all sculptures.

Jumping jack A toy figure of a man with jointed limbs that can be moved by pulling attached strings.

Kraft paper A strong wrapping paper made from wood pulp. Such a paper comes in a variety of colours and weights. Kraft papers might be used for making kites, prototypes and so on.

Laid papers A paper with a regular impressed mesh texture – the wire-pressed lines only run in one direction.

Modifying and adjusting If you like a particular project, but want to make it larger, smaller or whatever, first have a good look at the working drawings and then make your own prototype. Do you need thicker card or paper? Is the larger item still structurally and functionally sound? Will you need to use different tools and materials? These points all need to be carefully considered if you want to modify a project.

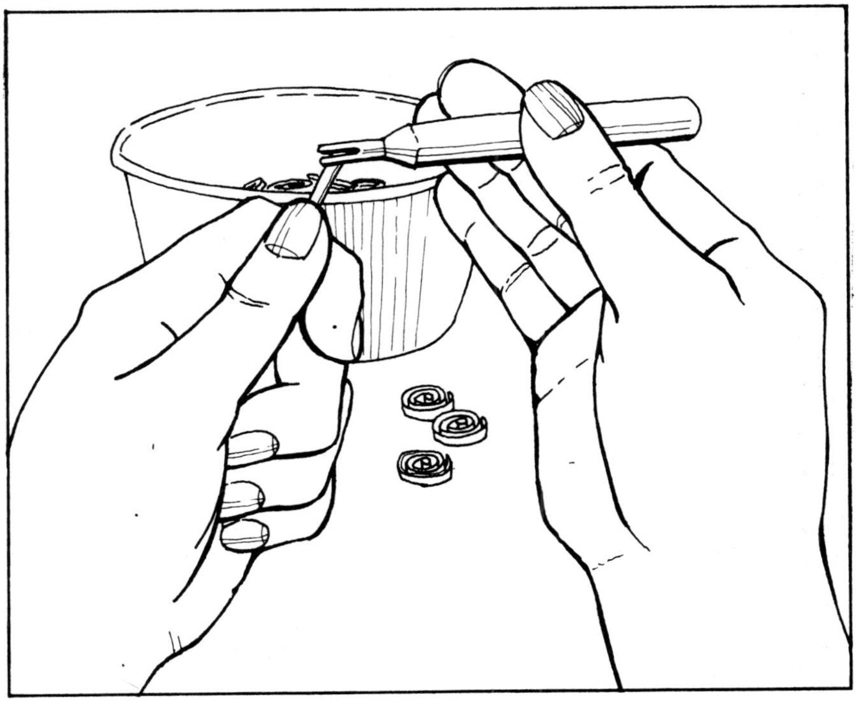

Quilling. Quill ribbons are made with thin strips of paper, which are worked and rolled with a small inexpensive slot-ended tool.

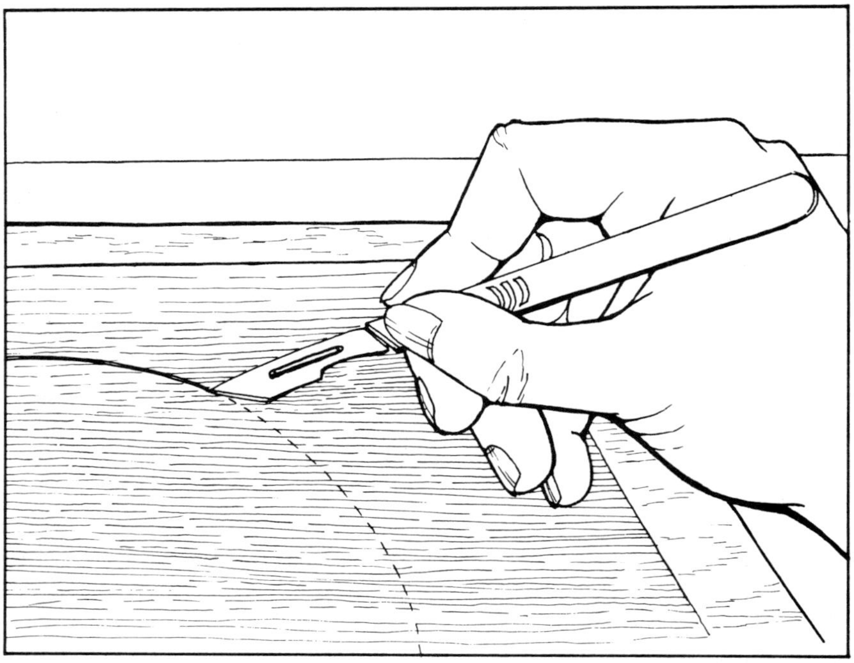

Scalpel. Use a fine-point razor-sharp scalpel when you want to achieve clean, crisp cuts – always work on a cutting board.

Manilla paper A strong flexible brown and off-white paper, usually made from hemp.

Marbled paper and board A paper/board with a marble-like paint finish which can be used for end papers in book binding or for any decorative work.

Masking tape A tape used to mask round areas that are to be painted, or a tape used to fix drawing paper to the workboard.

Measure That is to say a wooden ruler, a tape measure or a steel ruler – best to use a steel ruler.

Mobile A sculpture suspended in mid-air with delicately balanced parts that are set in motion by air currents.

Origami The art or process, originally from the Japanese, of paper folding. The term comes from the two Japanese words 'ori' meaning folding, and 'kami' meaning paper.

Paints There are water based paints, oil paints, enamels, paints with cellulose and so on. Generally water based paints are best with paper and card. We tend to use acrylics, paints from a paint box and powder paint mixed with water.

Papier-mâché A hard strong material made of paper pulp or layers of paper mixed with paste, size etc, and moulded when moist – from the French, chewed paper.

Paste A wallpaper type paste, a flour paste, a starch paste or a paste contained in an easy-to-use pen-like container. Be wary of using pastes, use them only when directed and use as little as possible.

Pencils Don't take pencils for granted, they are most important – we use a good quality soft 2B for designing and workouts, a 3B for line-in and tracing, and finally we do the pencil press transfering with a 2H. From 'soft' to 'hard' pencils are graded 6B 5B 4B 3B 2B HB 2H 3H and so on.

Poster paper A paper that is coloured on one side and plain mitt or gloss on the other – a good paper for prototypes, origami, paper-cuts and box making.

Pliers A small pair of long nosed combination wire snips and pliers – very useful.

Prototype The initial working model or maquette upon which the final design is based. So for example if you want to modify one or other of the projects, or you aren't quite sure how such and such a design works, then you will need to knock up a prototype. For example when we were making the mobile, we weren't quite sure as to the size, weight and fitting, so we made a rough with scrap card, pins and bits of string.

Silhouette. Silhouettes need not be simple profile outlines; see how we have achieved various textural effects.

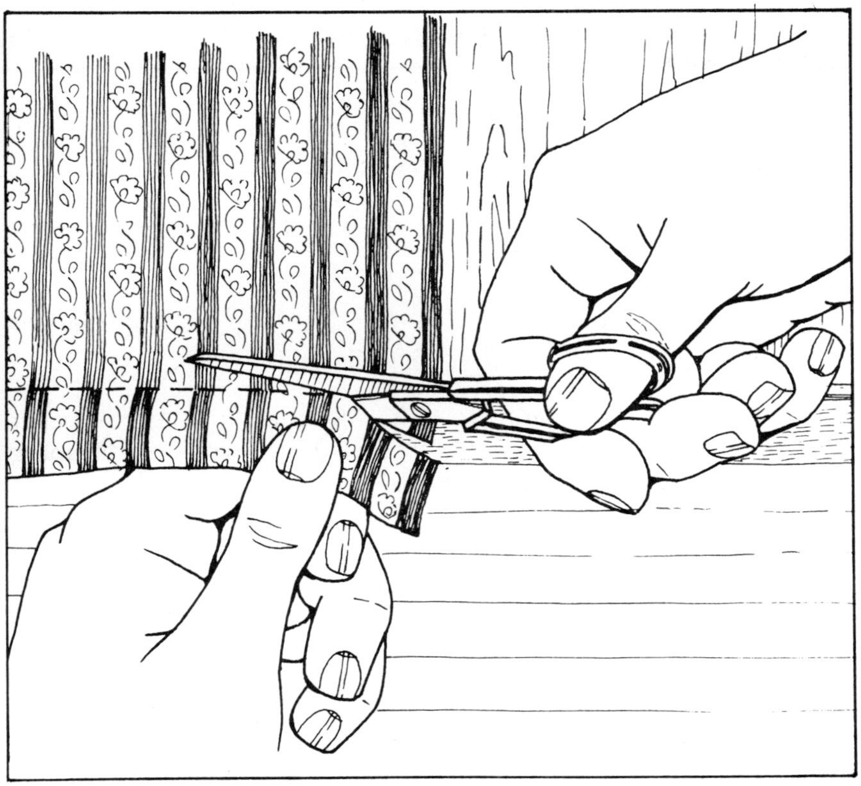

Scissors. You will need several pairs of scissors – make sure that they cut to their points, the handles fit your fingers and only buy the best non-rusting type.

Pulp board inexpensive smooth faced boards, they come in a wide range of weights and colours.

Punch Sooner or later you will need a hole punch. Best to get yourself either a selection of tube punches (to be used with a wooden block and a hammer), or one of the multi-size plier type punches.

PVA Glue Polyvinyl Acetate (PVA) (see glue).

Quilling Is the craft of rolling thin strips or ribbons of paper and then mounting and decoratively displaying them in such a way that the paper is seen edge-on.

Resin glue A very strong two-part quick setting adhesive that can be used for paper, card, paper-to-wood and such like – needs to be used with caution.

Rubbers There are ink rubbers, plastic rubbers, special rubbers and so on – we use a putty rubber for shiny papers, and a soft type generally.

Scalpel or craft knife There are fat handled general purpose knives, slim knives with retractable blades, model makers knives, and scalpels – we favour metal handled scalpels.

Scissors Every paper crafter needs at least two pairs of good quality

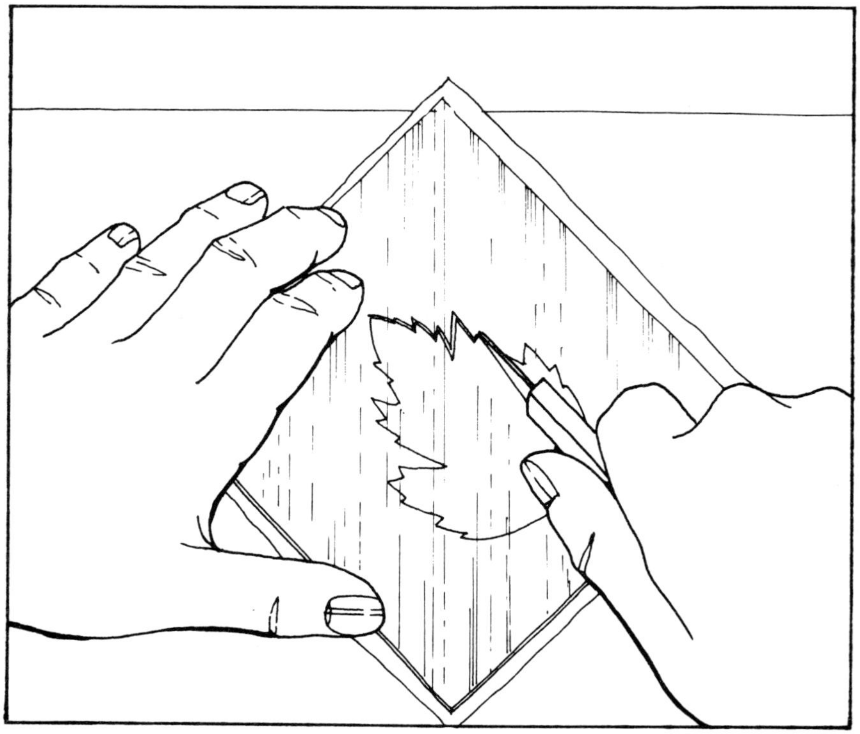

Stencil paper. When you cut stencil paper, use a super-sharp scalpel, for perfect, crisp edges. It is best to work on a sheet of stout glass.

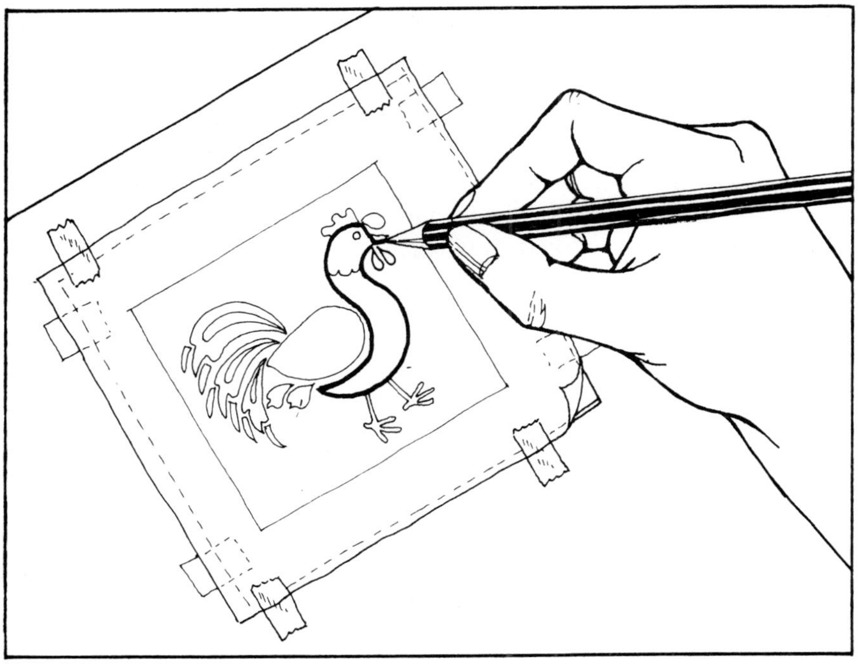

Tracing. Use a soft pencil for the actual tracing, and then use a hard pencil to press transfer – see how we use strips of masking tape to hold the work secure.

scissors. We have three pairs – a massive pair for chopping out prototypes, a pair of wallpaper scissors for thin card, and a little pair of curve-bladed nail scissors for delicate paper-cuts.

Silhouette An outline drawing filled in with black, often a profile portrait cut out of black paper and mounted on a light ground.

Stencil paper/card A stiff wax oil or varnish covered paper used for making templates and stencils.

Straight-edge Meaning a metal safety edge as used when cutting paper or card on a cutting board with a scalpel.

Strawboard The cheapest roughest board which tends to be brittle.

Tissue paper A thin soft delicate paper used to wrap fragile goods and for decoration – comes in a wide range of colours and qualities and can be matt or glazed.

Tracing paper A strong translucent paper used for tracing, which can be used for ink or pencil. We always use a good quality tracing paper of the grade 'smooth' and the weight '112'. We work up a master drawing or illustration, trace the drawing, line-in the reverse side of the tracing and finally use a hard pencil to press the lines of the design through to the working face of the paper/card. We have tried using poorer grades of wrapping tissue and the like, but have come to the conclusion that good quality tracing papers are the cheapest in the long run.

Wallpapers A paper usually printed or embossed with patterns and motifs, for pasting onto walls. Such papers can be used for all manner of papercrafts.

Working drawings Meaning well worked out scaled and detailed drawings – try not to scribble ideas and museum details down on scraps of paper, much better to have a sketch pad or a folder. When you have a nicely worked drawing, don't hack it up and use it as a pattern, but rather take a tracing.

Working face Meaning the side of the paper or card on which you have drawn the folding and cutting lines. If you are using a special delicate, colour-faced or textured material, then the working face might well be the 'wrong' side, then if you make a mistake you won't mark the special surface.

Workout paper/card When you are working out or modifying a project, you will need a great deal of scrap workout paper/card – we get ours from a local printers, but also use grocery cartons.

Workshop/working area In the context of this book, a good papercrafts workshop or working area might be anything from a spare room, the kitchen table, a tray on your knee, through to a nicely designed purpose built studio. As to the ideal working area, we would say that paper crafts are best managed in a clean, warm, well lit area of about 50 sq ft. Papercrafts tend to be a clean and dry craft, although from time to time you will need to use paints, paste and glue, but generally speaking it's a craft that can be managed quite comfortably alongside say cooking, sewing and general household activities.

As to special working conditions and equipment, apart from the items mentioned in the glossary, really you need no more than a clean worksurface, a display area and storage. So you will need a table or bench, best if it has an easy-to-clean surface, and shelves, draws, boxes and pinboard. Of course if you have got the space, then it would be a good idea to have a plan chest for card and paper storage, a guillotine, a sink – however for starters, the dining room or the spare room will do fine.

PROJECT ONE

POLISH FRIEZE

PROJECT PICTURE
Two traditional Polish paper cut motifs – see how they are built up from a number of layered cuts.

INTRODUCTION

THOUGHTS ON THE PROJECT

On high days and holidays in rural Poland, villages were traditionally decorated with the most beautiful folk art. On these festival and celebration occasions, almost every aspect of peasant life was enriched with colour and pattern. Painted wagons were brought out, items of carved and painted furniture were displayed, patterns were painted and stencilled on walls, doors and porches were bedecked with hanging paper decorations – in fact the whole environment was embellished and adorned with examples of naive folk art. And of all these folk arts – arts that have been described as, harmonious in their essential simplicity, rhythmic, aesthetic, and the perfect coming together of form, material and technique, perhaps the most beautiful and characteristic were the paper cuts. Cut-outs were pasted on ceilings, paper cuts were used to decorate white washed walls and every school room, church and cottage had its own special display of traditional motifs and patterns. Peacocks with huge tails, welcome wreaths, roosters, doves of peace, ribbons, banners, flags, hats, and wall friezes, all made out of folded and cut coloured paper.

As to the state of the art at the present time, of course since the nineteenth century, cheap, factory-made, mass produced objects have tended to replace folk made arts and crafts, but fortunately this trend has not swept through the whole of Poland. Somehow or other, in many rural areas, the craft of paper cutting still persists, and could even be said to be flourishing. An example of this folk art renewal or revival, is in Cracow and Lowicz where vast paper cut tapestries and banners are now used to decorate the interiors of public buildings. Poland has a unique and distinctive paper cutting tradition, and happily this tradition lives on.

CONSIDERING THE PROJECT

One of the joys of working paper cuts in the Polish tradition is the fact that the techniques can be adjusted and modified as the project goes along. The design concepts are beautifully flexible – for example, when you are working this project, if the mood takes you, you can change the motif emphasis, you can rework colours and patterns, you can keep overlaying the appliqué cut outs, and so on. If you enjoy designing and working in a manner that is free and intuitive, then Polish paper cuts are for you.

Start by taking a long look at the various working drawings. See how initially the motifs need to be broken down into a set of big bold knife-cut shapes, and see also how by cutting through a stack of papers of a different colour it is possible to make near identical multiples of the same form. This is not to say that the technique is in any way boringly repetitive, because once a supply of base or ground forms have been cut, then the various components can be scissor-worked, and individualized.

INSPIRATIONAL
The Polish motifs tend to relate to various traditional folk tales and customs – doves of peace – cockerels that symbolize light and so on. See how these characteristic motifs are worked from built-up fold and multiple cuts.

When you have folded, cut and worked the details – the wings, the tails, and such like, then they can be built-up into powerful, large scale appliqué pictures. This being so, the technique is ideally suited to the making of wall pictures. Have a look at the working drawings and see how we designed this project so as to make a nursery or playroom frieze. Note – cuts of this type and character make good group projects, and are just perfect for school, club, and playgroup situations.

TOOLS AND MATERIALS

For this project you need – a large roll or sheet of paper for the ground, eight large sheets of coloured paper, go for bright primary colours, and choose a paper that is fine, hard and colour-fast, a pair of small fine-point scissors, a stout bladed fine-point craft knife, a pencil and ruler, tracing paper, a special paper-to-paper adhesive/gum, a work

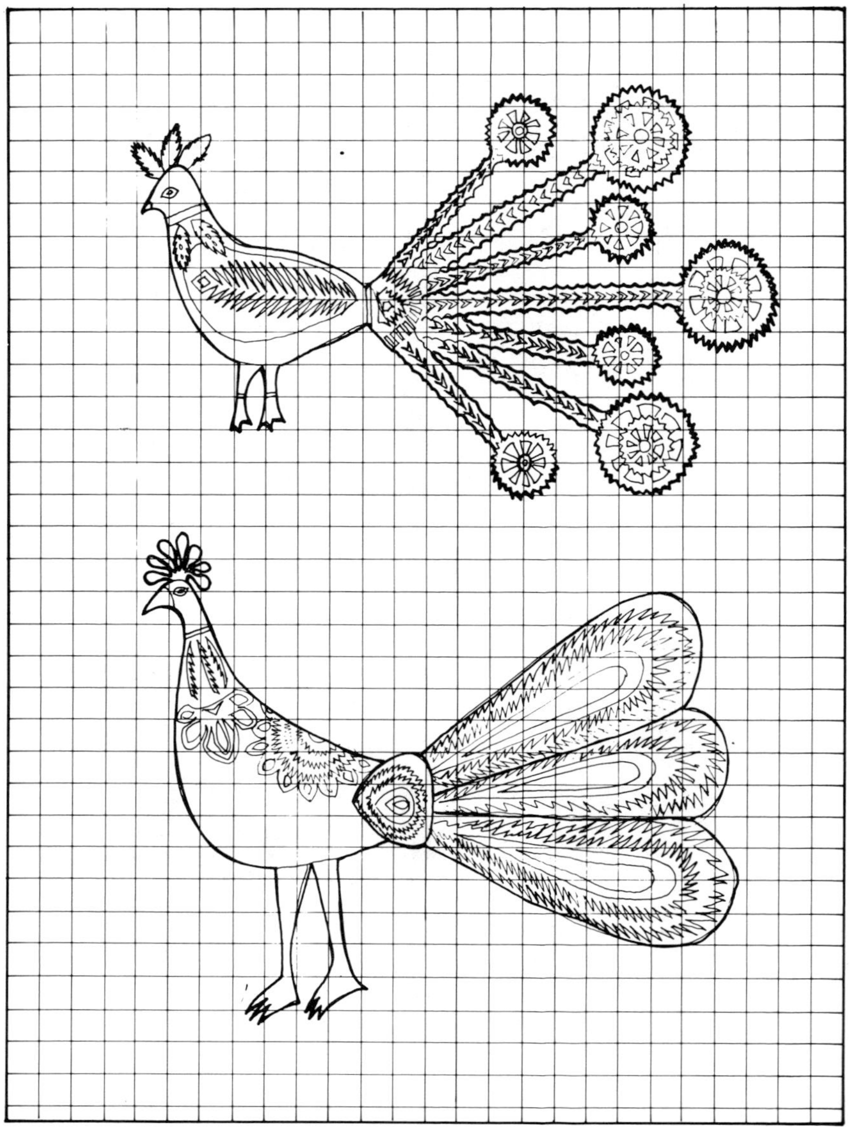

WORKING GRID
The scale is about two grid squares to 1 inch. See how the motifs are made up from a basic ground shape and various repeated and layered multiples.

board, and a cutting board. Note – Use a designers/photographers adhesive, and avoid water based pastes.

DESIGNING

Once you have taken note of all the technique implications, have a look at our working drawing motifs, and the inspirational designs, then perhaps rethink the theme so that it fits into your scheme of things. For example, if you want to make a frieze for your toddlers room, then you need to consider suitable patterns and motifs, you need to make decisions as to the overall size of the work and to the colours, and lastly of course, you need to relate the motifs to your own likes and dislikes. Meaning, you might want to stay with the

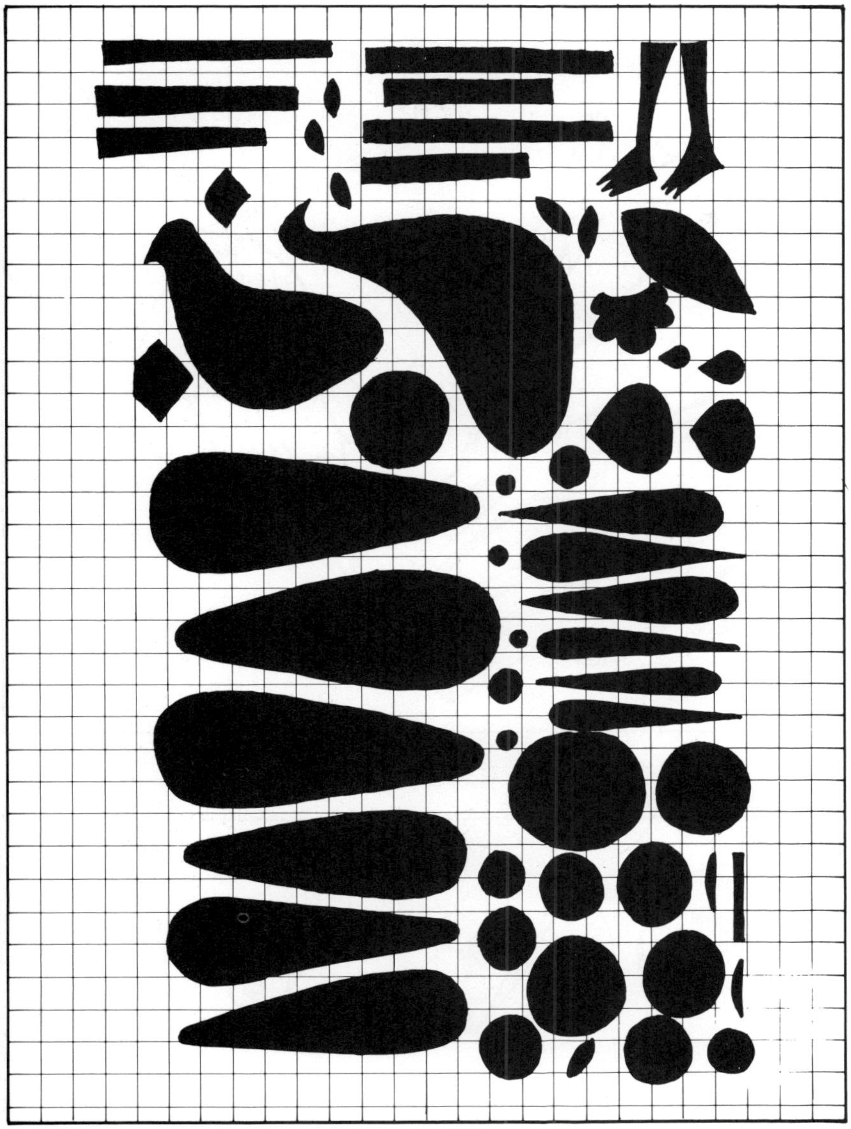

CUTTING GRID
The scale is about two grid squares to 1 inch. Draw the templates to size and trace them off.

traditional Polish imagery, or want to update the designs and have say, cars, and modern costumes. When you have decided just how you want your design to be, then work out a series of motifs, and finalise all the colour, form and size details.

Finally, break the motifs down into their component parts, work them to size, and then take some tracing paper and draw up a sheet of master templates. Note you will need templates for all the main elements – the bodies, tails, wings, feathers and so on.

KNIFE WORK

Once you have drawn the templates to size and traced them off, then take one of the sheets of coloured paper, and pencil press transfer the

Use a stout bladed scalpel to cut through the stack of coloured papers, hold the knife with one hand, and turn and guide the papers with the other.

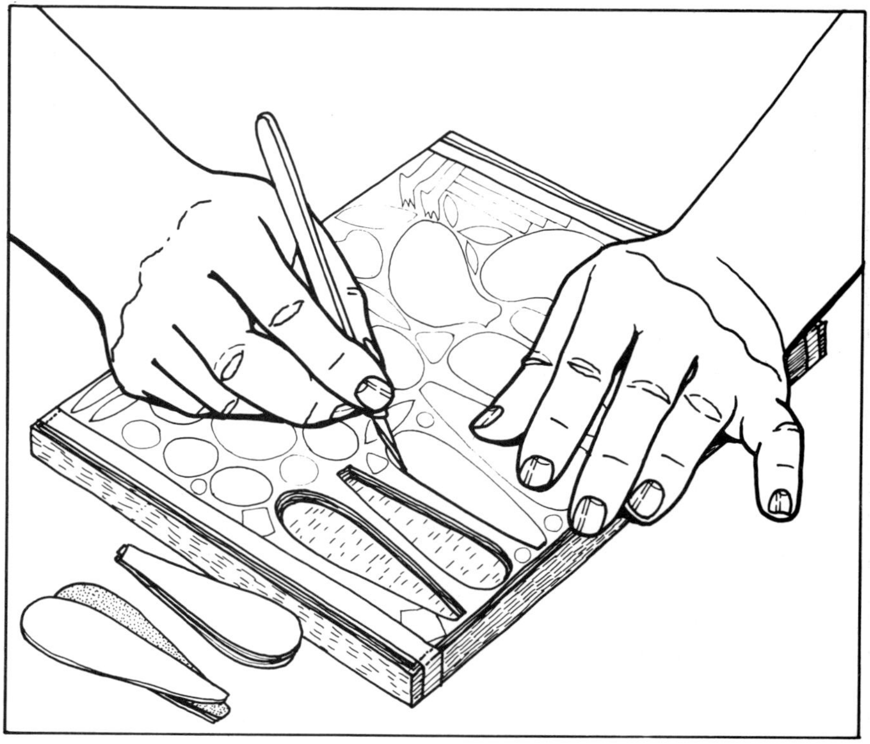

The tail motifs are made up from 'four-fold' circles – you will be cutting through eight paper thicknesses.

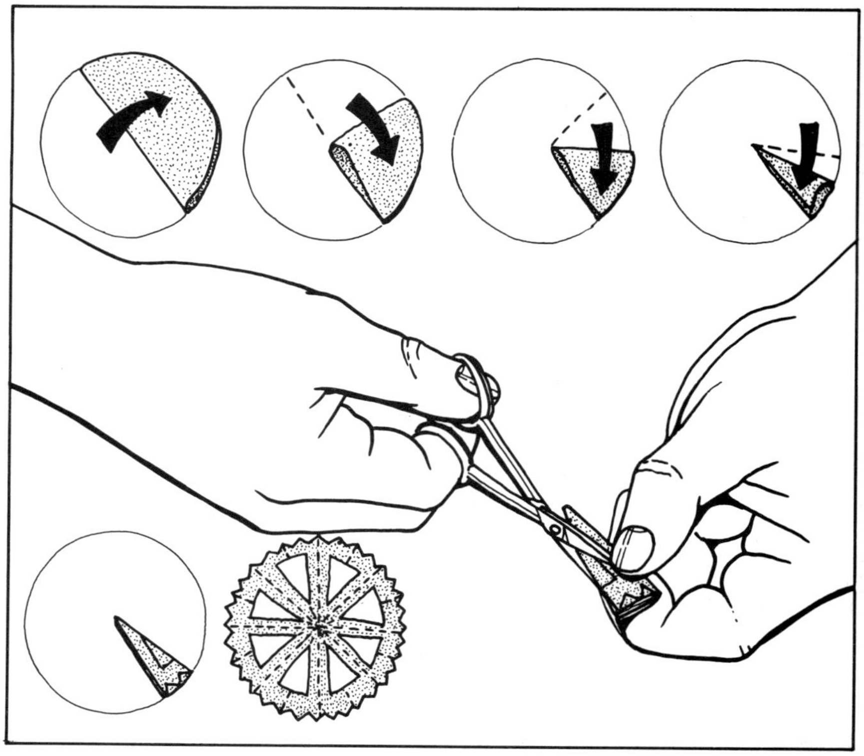

traced designs. Aim to fit the traced forms onto the coloured paper so as to avoid wastage. When all the traced lines have been transferred, then stack the eight different colour sheets so that the template sheet is uppermost. Now place the papers on the cutting board, secure the stack with straps of sticky tape, then clear the worksurface and take up your stout bladed scalpel.

Aim to work each of the forms with smooth uninterrupted cuts and try if possible to cut through all eight sheets of paper at a single stroke. Cut the paper, motif at a time, and gradually work out from the centre of the board.

Finally, when you have worked all the forms, then remove the tape, store the cut outs, and save the offcuts.

SCISSOR WORK

Before you start the scissor work, stop a while, and have a look at the various inspirational designs and see how, in the main, the scissor-cut forms are all either just folded in half, or as with the tail discs, folded four times. Start with one or other of the more basic forms, say one of the long tail strips. Simply fold the paper in half, then work up the fold removing scissor-cut nicks, and back along the open edges cutting little scoops. And so you continue, folding and cutting the crest feathers, cutting the tails discs, and so on, until you have scissor-worked all the knife-cuts forms.

Note – by the time you have cut and worked all the templates, that

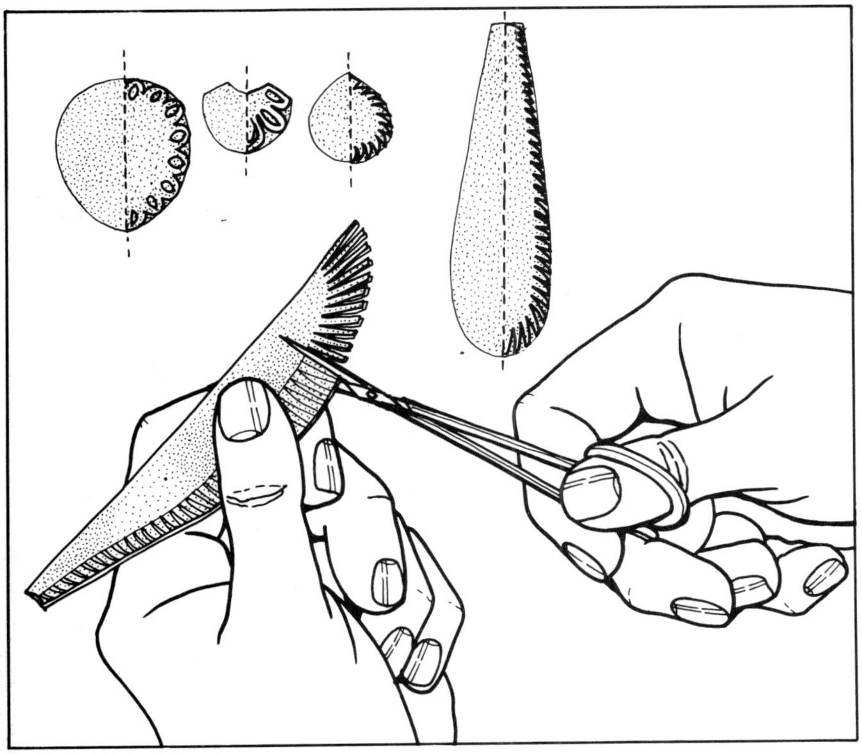

Most of the layered motifs are very simple and made from once folded pieces of paper – use a small pair of sharp fine-point scissors.

Spread out your stockpile of cut shapes, set out the main form and then layer up the various different coloured motifs.

is to say two birds on eight sheets of paper, all as illustrated, then you should have enough materials to make up sixteen individual multi-coloured peacock designs.

BUILDING THE FRIEZE

When you have knife and scissor worked all the elements that go to make up the peacocks, then is the time to start putting the whole frieze together. First clear the worksurface, then spread out the ground paper and set out your stockpile of cut shapes and the paper-to-paper adhesive. Now, working on one bird form at a time, glue and place the body, the head, and the legs – make sure that these primary elements are well placed in relationship to the total design, then start building up the details and the trim. That is to say, place and glue the tail strips, set the tail discs, cover up the tail-to-body join, and generally take a feather of this colour and a detail of that colour, until the bird design begins to take shape. And of course, when you have built up one bird, then you start on another, until you have filled out the whole frieze.

Finally, when you have placed and glued all the main scissor-worked trim, then you can cut, place and glue your own idiosyncratic appliqué work. Meaning, you can take fragments of offcuts and start to give the forms individual characteristics. For example, you might want to give the birds names, you might decide to enlarge a wing here, or enrich a crest there – continue until you consider the frieze finished.

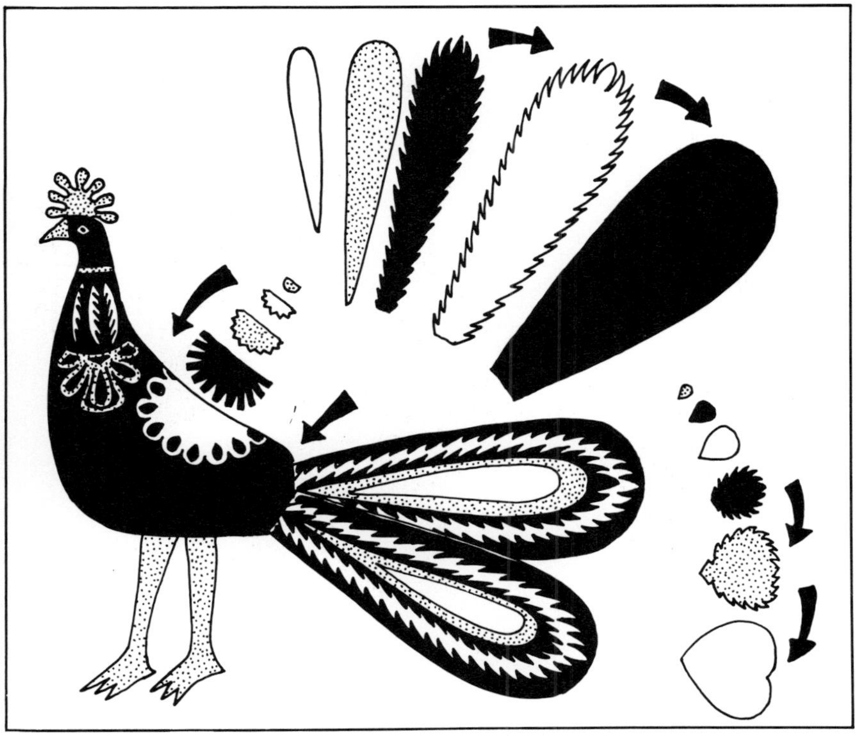

Finally when you have achieved a good design, then finish off with the little pieces of trim, use off-cuts to make your own modifications.

AFTERTHOUGHTS

When you are choosing your papers, go for thin, hard, fine, fast-colour papers. We have chosen to use eight matt papers, each of a different colour; but that is not to say that you can't use patterned papers, paper backed foils, coloured sweet papers and such like.

Be sure to use a good paper-to-paper adhesive – go either for a spray-on, or an easy to use adhesive contained in an twist-and-dab retractable container.

Try to cut through the eight sheets of paper at a single stroke, watch out for your fingers, and if you do have problems cutting through all the layers, then modify the project and use say a six-paper stack, or choose thinner papers.

Noting that your palette consists of eight different colours, don't use all the brightest colours on the first three or four motifs – have several colour try-outs at the pre-glue stage.

PROJECT TWO

CHINESE GREETINGS CARD

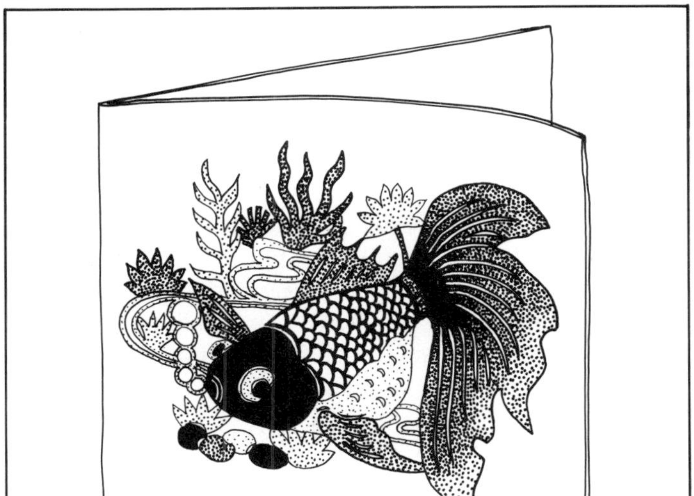

PROJECT PICTURE
A traditional Chinese fish motif, see how the design has been delicately colour tinted.

INTRODUCTION

THOUGHTS ON THE PROJECT

No one can say exactly when and where, in China, the craft of paper cutting originated, all we know for sure is that it has a very long history. That said, it follows that as the craft cannot of course predate the invention of paper, and as paper is thought to have been invented by a certain Tsai Lun around AD 100, then we can be pretty certain that the craft is well over a thousand years old. Some experts say that paper cuts were first used as burial tokens, that is to say little pictures of earthly possessions, while others consider that there are positive links between paper cuts and the crafts of block printing and stencil cutting.

All that apart, the craft of paper cutting is very popular in present day China, with peasants, and intellectuals working all manner of traditional and modern designs and motifs. In some regions paper cuts are still known as huang-hua, hua-yang, or 'window flowers', even if the cuts are not based on flower motifs. This dates back to days before the invention of glass, when oiled papers were used as a window covering, and paper cuts were used to decorate the covering. This tradition still survives in many rural homes with paper flowers being pasted onto glass windows. With the bright sunlight shining through the cut design, the effect is of bold silhouettes and vibrant colours, rather like western stained glass windows. In other parts of China, the papercuts are used as embroidery patterns or guides, that is to say, the cuts are pasted directly onto the item of dress to be decorated, then the cut is overworked with embroidery silks. And then again, in other parts of China the designs are worked in fine tissues, and then the tissues are tinted with subtle colours and mounted as wall pictures, or presented as festival cards.

Worked with very basic tools, scissors, knives, and fine chisels, Chinese paper cut designs range from straight forward everyday objects, cars, little figures and such like, through to traditional symbolic motifs. Dragon designs for power, rain and eternity, rice motifs for prosperity, and so on; goats, dogs, bamboo, butterflies, fish and flowers are all worked into the craft as a sort of decorative, good luck, sign language.

INSPIRATIONAL
Traditional Chinese paper cuts of this type and character make good greetings card motifs.

CONSIDERING THE PROJECT

Chinese paper cutting is an easy-to-do, inexpensive paper craft. With a minimum of tools and materials it is possible to achieve the most beautifully subtle and sensitive works. And of course you don't have to present the cuts in a greeting card form, you might prefer to use them as decorative mobiles, as fabric-work guide patterns, as stencils, and so on. However, no matter how you decide to use the technique, it's always a good idea to start by sitting back with a sketch pad and colours and working up a few colour and design try-outs. See our working drawings and inspirational designs, and note how, rather

WORKING GRID
The scale is four grid squares to 1 inch. Note how two identical motifs might be used to achieve a more complex design.

like a stencil plate, small 'bridges' of paper delicately link the various parts of the design so as to give the work strength.

Consider all the design and usage possibilities, and perhaps also make your own collection of inspirational clips – bits from magazines, old postcards, and such like. Finally, pull all your ideas together by taking a trip to the nearest craft centre or museum, get to see as many traditional paper cuts as possible, but concentrate your researches on those made in China and Japan.

INSPIRATIONAL
A traditional Chinese cut that illustrates the Great Wall Of China.

TOOLS AND MATERIALS

For this project you need, a fine-point scalpel or craft knife, a drawing board, a cutting board, a small pair of fine-point scissors, a few sheets

Trace off the master design and then pencil press transfer the lines of the tracing through to the working face of the tissue.

Support the tissue with a couple of sheets of backing paper, then fix the tissue on a cutting board with four tabs of masking tape.

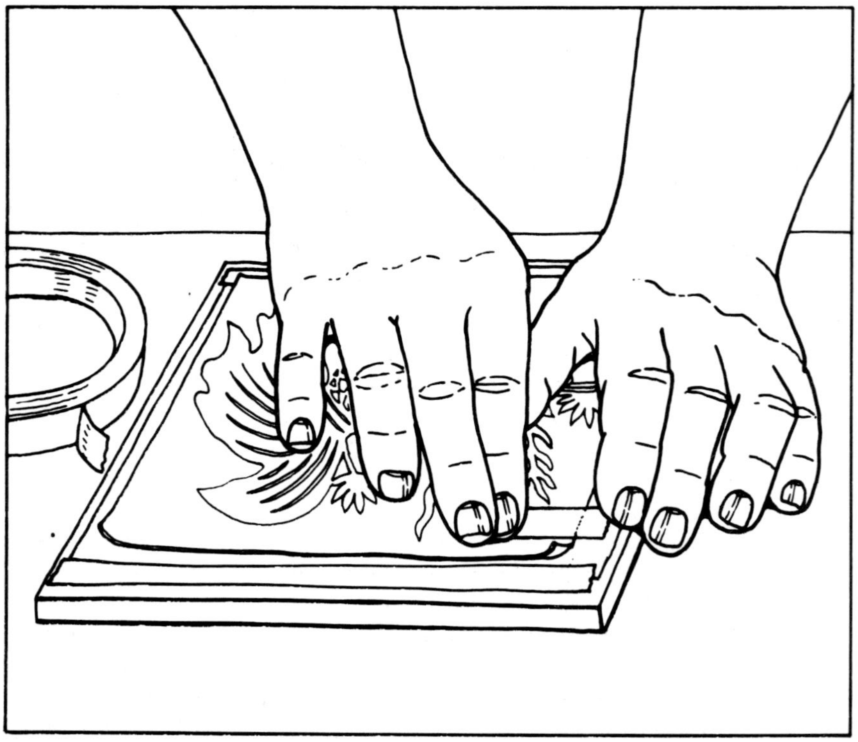

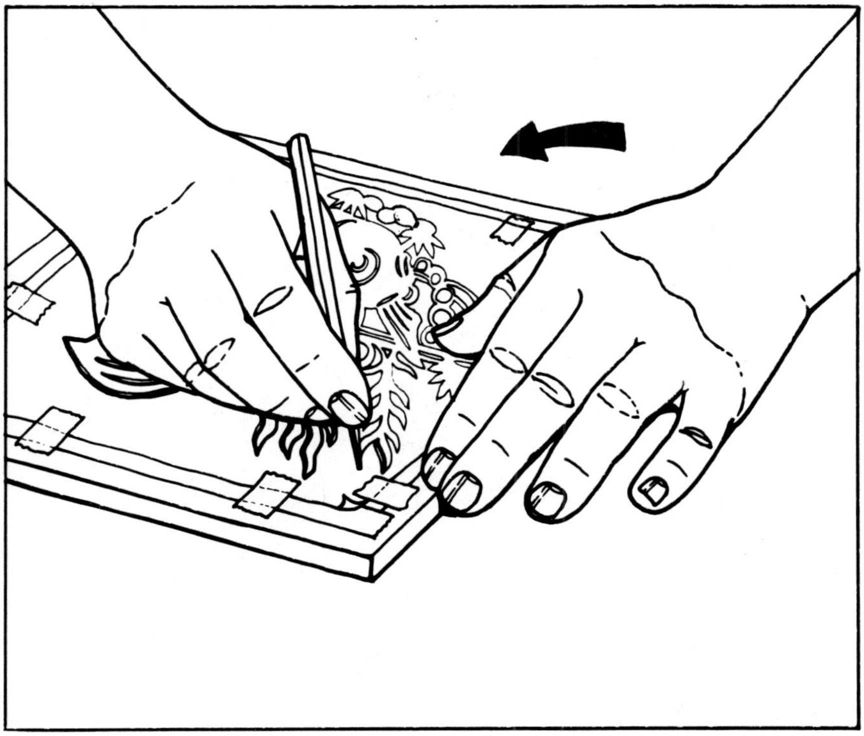

Once you have secured the tissue, use a fine-point scalpel to cut out the various profiles and 'windows'. To achieve a perfect smooth-line finish, turn and guide the board so that the knife is always presented with the line of next cut.

of long fibred tissue paper, tracing paper, a couple of small long haired water colour brushes, a box of watercolours, a backing card, pencils and a ruler, cow gum, masking tape, and of course you need all the usual items, like a clean worksurface, the use of water, and newspaper.

SETTING OUT THE DESIGN

Once you have either traced off and scaled to size our working drawing, or worked what you consider to be a good alternative motif, then take a tracing from your master design. This done secure your tissue paper to the drawing board with a few tabs of masking tape, then, with great care, pencil press transfer the traced lines. Now take a soft pencil and delicately shade in the 'windows' of the design, that is to say the parts that need to be cut away and wasted.

CUTTING

When you have transferred the design, take the tissue paper, support it with a couple of sheets of backing paper, then secure it to the cutting board with the four tabs of masking tape.

Now, before you start cutting, have a look at the working drawings and the inspirational illustrations and see how, in all instances, the cuts have been worked so that the edges are crisp and the forms well defined. This being so, it is most important that you use a razor sharp,

Make sure that the tissues are colour fast, then use a fine brush and paints to tint the cuts – scrap paper under the cuts will soak up the excess colour.

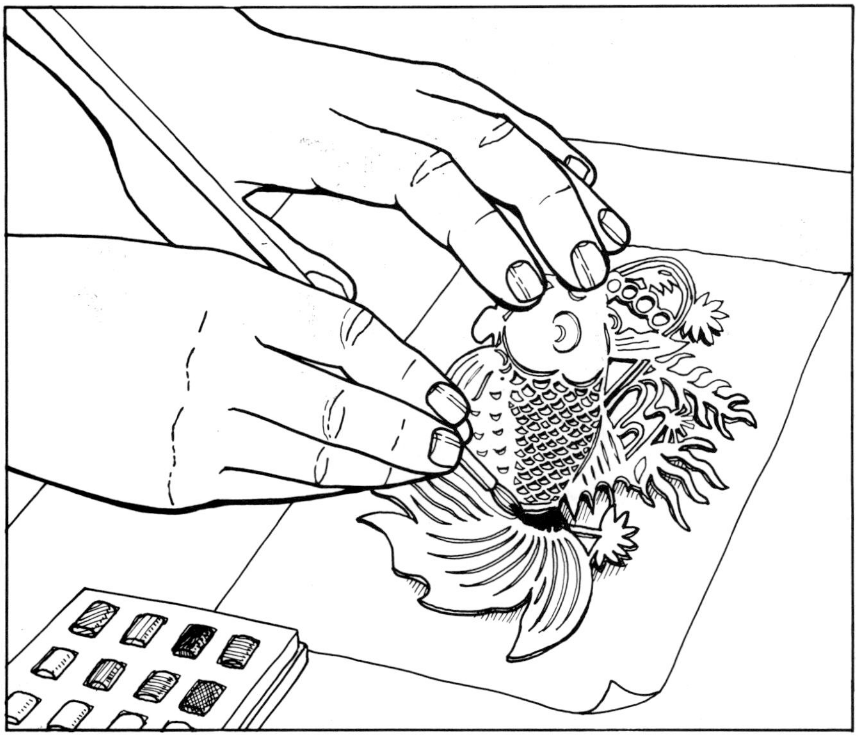

When you have achieved a nicely cut and tinted motif, let it dry and then put it in a book-and-glass press.

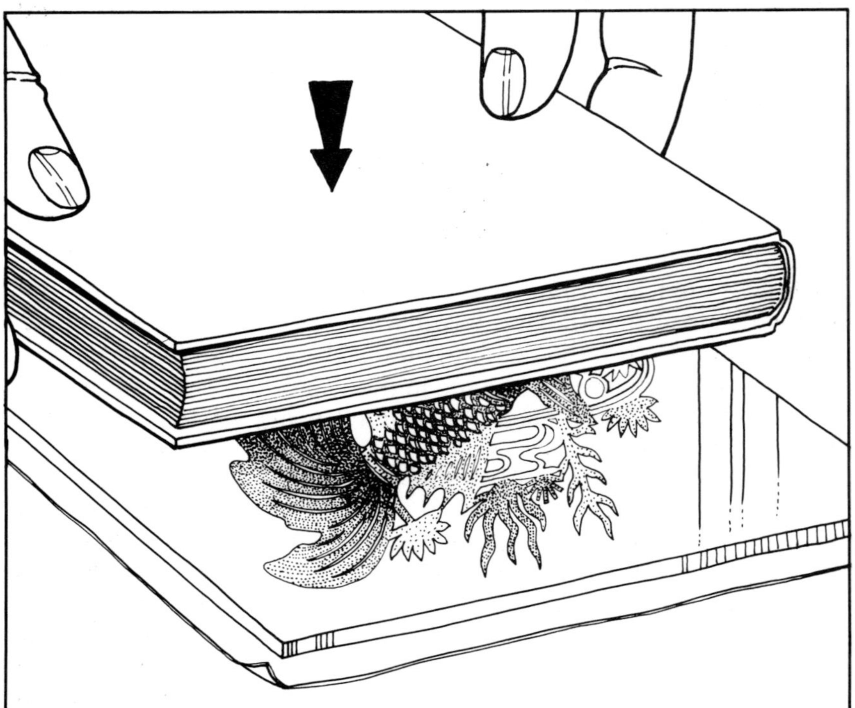

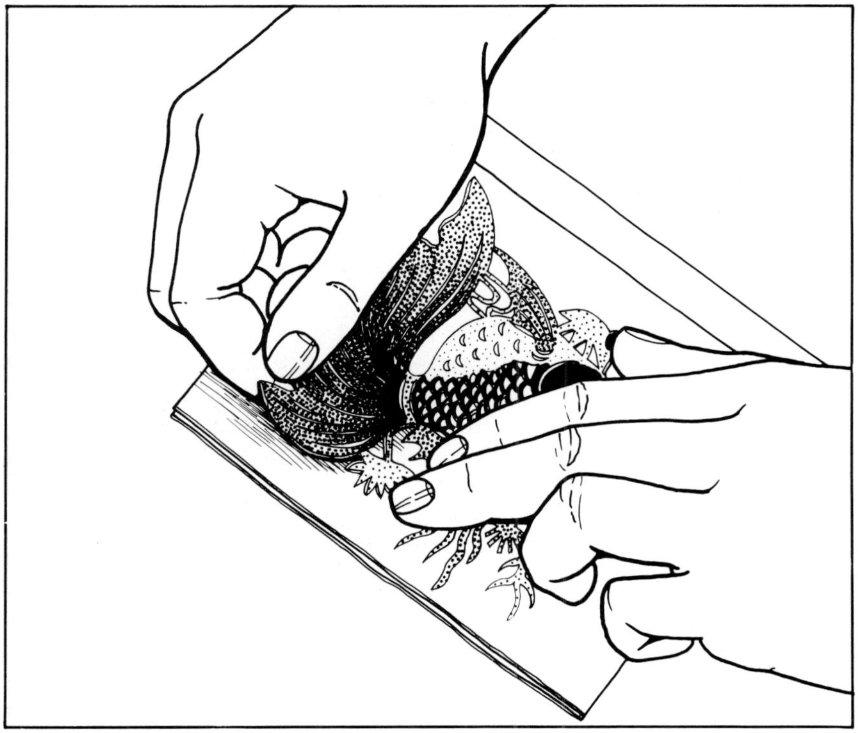

Use a gum or a special paper-to-paper adhesive to mount the paper cut on the card. Note – do not use a water based adhesive/paste.

fine-point knife and work with a steady hand. As you work, support the paper and the small board with one hand, while you draw the blade along the lines of the design with the other. Try, as you hold and guide the board, to manoeuvre the paper so that the knife is always presented with the line of next cut.

PAINTING

When you have worked what you consider to be a crisp well cut motif, then clear the worksurface of all clutter, and set out your tools and materials, the paper cut, the drawing board, the brushes and the colours. Now have a look at the project design, and see how although it has been worked with relatively bright and bold colour washes, the colours have never-the-less been applied with considerable delicacy.

Start by choosing your colour range, then if you have any doubts, have a trial run on some scrap paper. Lay on the various washes, start with the lightest most subtle colours and working through the colour range to the darker areas and outlines. Work the main colour blocks, pick out the details with a fine point brush, and then put the finished piece to one side to dry. Finally when the paint is dry, put the paper cut in a press and leave it be for about twenty four hours.

MOUNTING

When the cut has been pressed, select your mounting or backing card, and have a trial placing. See how by having two identical mirror-image cuts, or by playing around with the placing, it is possible to achieve a uniquely beautiful motif composition. When you have decided how you want your card to be, have a last minute check just to make sure that all is correct, then using a few touches of cow gum, or one of the other special paper-to-paper adhesives, carefully adjust the placing, and the job is done.

AFTERTHOUGHTS

You might adjust and modify the working order, and apply the colour washes before you do the cutting – there are points in favour of both ways of working. Have a trial run on some scrap paper, and go for the working order that suits the size and character of your project.

You might use coloured inks rather than water colours – go for the medium that suits your style.

If you want to make several identical paper cuts, then you can tape together a stack of tissue sheets and then cut through the whole sandwich. If you do decide to work in this manner, then you must make sure that the scalpel blade is very sharp.

PROJECT THREE

SILHOUETTE PICTURE

PROJECT PICTURE
A paper cut in the Swiss folk tradition – note the characteristic animals, trees and natural forms.

INTRODUCTION

THOUGHTS ON THE PROJECT

The craft of paper cuts, that is to say cutting fine paper so as to make silhouettes, patterns and stencil pictures, is a craft that has its roots in the folk way of life. Villagers in isolated communities in China, Vietnam, Japan, Russia, Turkey, Mexico, Poland, and Europe, all seem to have a strong paper cuts tradition. Within these communities, it was the ordinary people who cut paper, the peasants and farm workers, and naturally enough, they drew their inspiration from their everyday lives, ploughing, harvest celebrations, dancing, animals, flowers and such like. However, as with most folk crafts, paper cutting was such an every-day activity, rather like say thatching or spinning, that it was taken very much for granted. And so it was, that paper

INSPIRATIONAL
TOP *Part of a design by Johann Hauswirth.*
MIDDLE *A traditional heart design with figures and flowers by Louis Saugy.*
BOTTOM *Traditional cockerels, horses and cows by Johann Hauswirth.*

cuts were made, used for a few days or weeks to decorate such and such room or window, and then they were discarded.

Paper cuts have been variously described as being, of the people, transitory, ephemeral, and anonymous. That said, there is a community in Switzerland, that seems to have a distinctive paper cutting tradition; a community where known and named individuals have made, and still continue to make, cuts of amazing virtuosity. One such individual was a certain John Jakob Hauswirth, who was born in Saarnen in 1809. Not much is known about the man, except that he was an itinerant who lived rough, hired himself out as a woodcutter, and died in great poverty. As to how Hauswirth actually worked his craft, examples indicate that he halved or quartered fine black papers, and then, without the need for preliminary sketches or

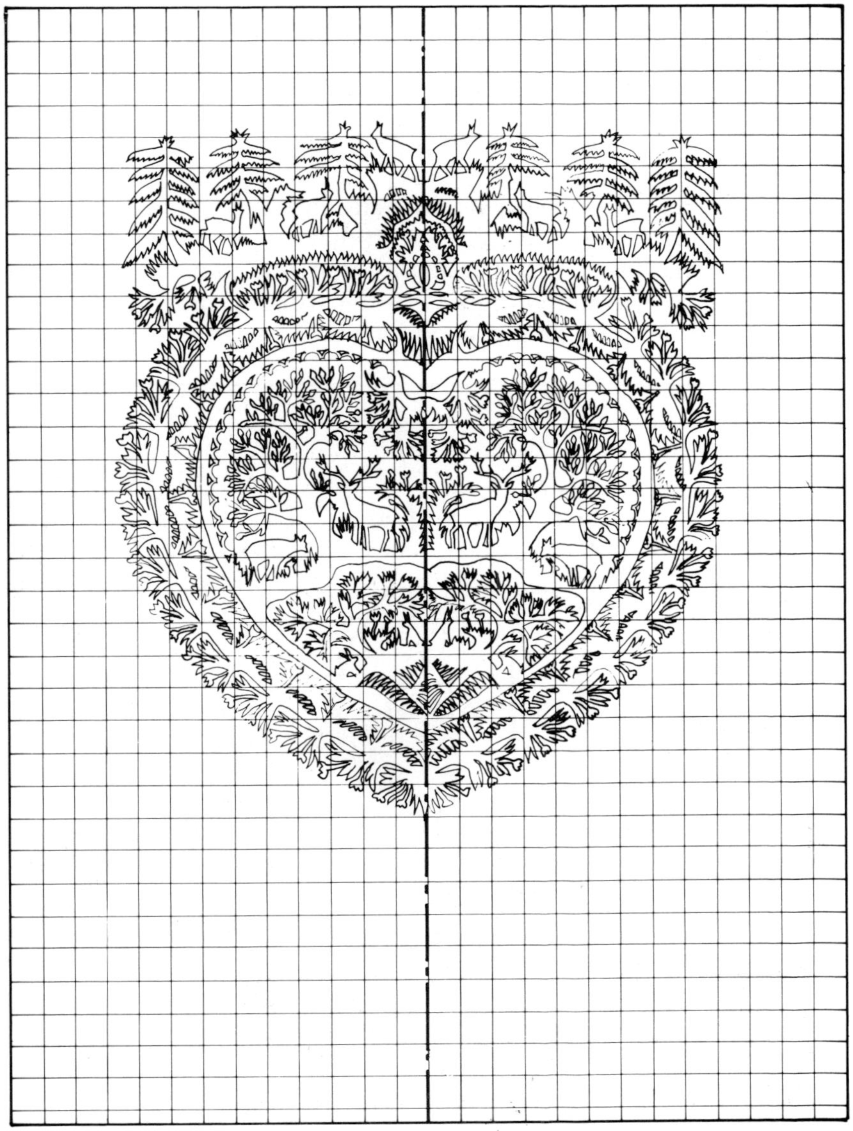

WORKING GRID
Scale to suit – a good scale for beginners would be about two grid squares to 1 inch.

designs, he systematically worked the paper backward and forward until he had achieved a lace-like tracery – a tracery made up of what we now take to be characteristic Swiss designs and motifs.

Hauswirth took his inspiration from everything he saw – horses, cows with bells, stags, rabbits, love-hearts, trees, coats of arms, birds, and bushes; his cuts illustrate just about every aspect of life in rural, nineteenth century Switzerland. Fortunately he left behind him a huge collection of papercuts and these are now housed in a museum in the village of Chateau d'Oex. Note – If by chance you get to see the collection, see also the work of Louis Saugy and Christian Schwizgebel.

As to why the craft grew and developed, and how it came to be concentrated in one small corner of Switzerland, maybe Hauswirth had a pupil, or perhaps there was some sort of tourist market for the cuts, who can say. Enough to know that in the area in and around Chateau d'Oex the craft of working paper cuts and silhouettes lives on.

CONSIDERING THE PROJECT

Although making a paper cut silhouette in the Swiss tradition is in essence a simple, low-tech craft, a craft that can be managed with the minimum of expense, it's fair to say that this particular project is difficult. Take a magnifying glass to the working drawings and the inspirational designs, have a good long look, and see how, turn-by-

Take your chosen sheet of tissue paper and fold it carefully in half.

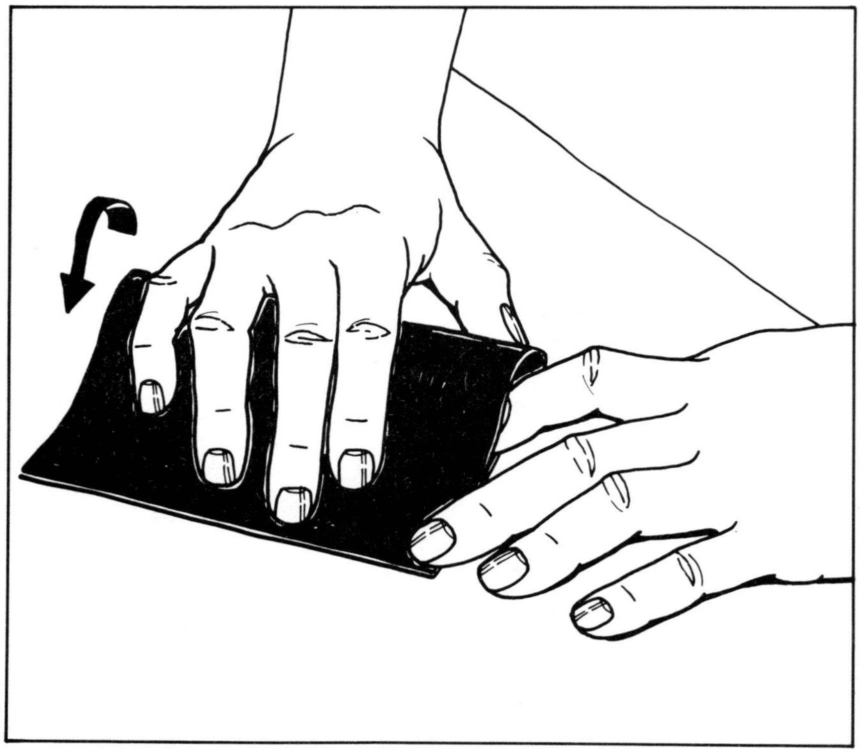

turn, the motifs are delicate, convoluted, minute and altogether tricky. However, that said, why don't you take up the challenge, and have a go. With a bit a care and a deal of practice, there's no reason at all why you shouldn't adapt and modify the Swiss techniques and make them your own.

Before you start, study the designs in detail, then with a pair of fine-point scissors, have a trial run with a scrap of black tissue. Don't, in the first instance, try to work one of the more complex details, but rather go for a cut that contains basic and stylized forms, say one of the flower groups, or one of the pine trees. See how although the whole design looks to be unbelievably complex, when it is broken down into its parts, it can be seen to be made up of a great number of relatively simple and repetitive cuts. When you have had a number of trial cuts, and when you have achieved a good standard, then sit down with a sketch pad and a scrap of tracing paper, and modify the project to suit.

TOOLS AND MATERIALS

For this project you need, a fine-point scalpel, a small pair of fine-point nail scissors, a pencil and ruler, tracing paper, a sketch pad, card, glass and sticky tape for the frame, a sheet of handmade black long fibred tissue paper, masking tape, and all the usual workshop items.

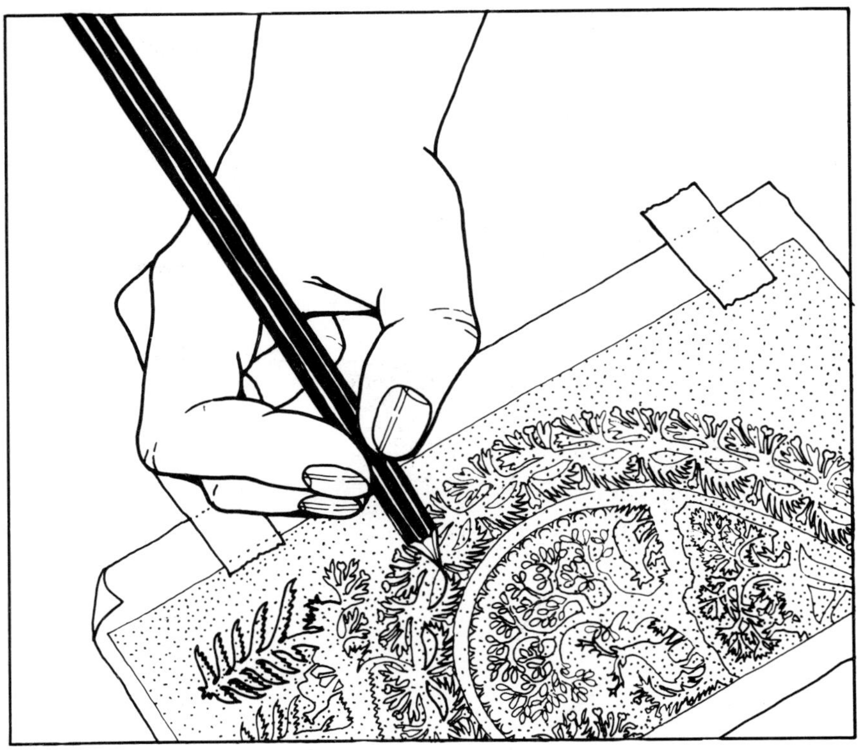

Trace the master design with a soft pencil and then use a hard pencil to press the traced lines through to the tissue.

Use a small pair of fine-point scissors to cut and work the design, see how we use a card 'sleeve' to protect the delicate tissue.

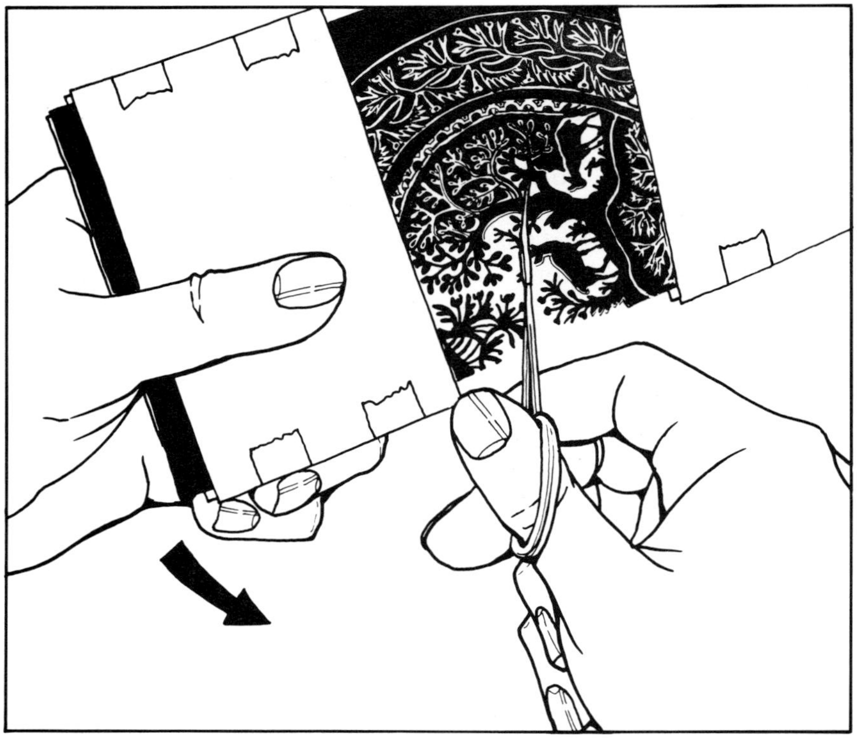

Once you have fretted out the centre of the design, use a large pair of scissors to clear away some of the edge waste.

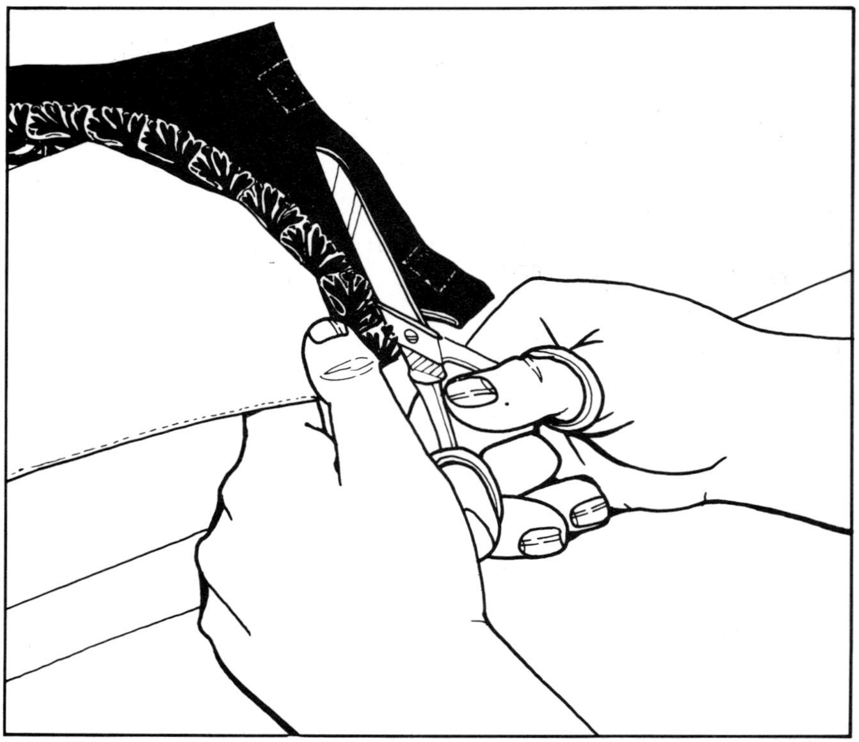

SETTING OUT THE DESIGN

Have another look at the working drawings, and make final decisions as to whether or not you are going to simplify the motifs. When you have noted all the design and technique implications of any such modifications, then take a sheet of good quality tracing paper, establish a centre line, and set about tracing the master design. Using an HB pencil, and working from the centre line, carefully trace off one half of the total design. Aim to keep the traced lines crisp and fine, and to that end work on a smooth grain-free surface, and spend time keeping your pencil sharp.

When you have traced off the master design, then carefully fold your sheet of black tissue in half, and pin/tape it out on the drawing board. Note how the traced image is to be pencil press transferred, see how the design is reversed, then tape the tracing down on the workboard. This done, check that both the black tissue and the tracing paper are aligned and secure, then take an H pencil, and work over the traced lines.

FIRST CUTTING

When you have pencilled in all the lines of the design, peel up one corner of the tracing, just to make sure that all the lines have been transferred. If all is correct, carefully remove the black tissue and clear away any unnecessary clutter. Now check that the folded centre line

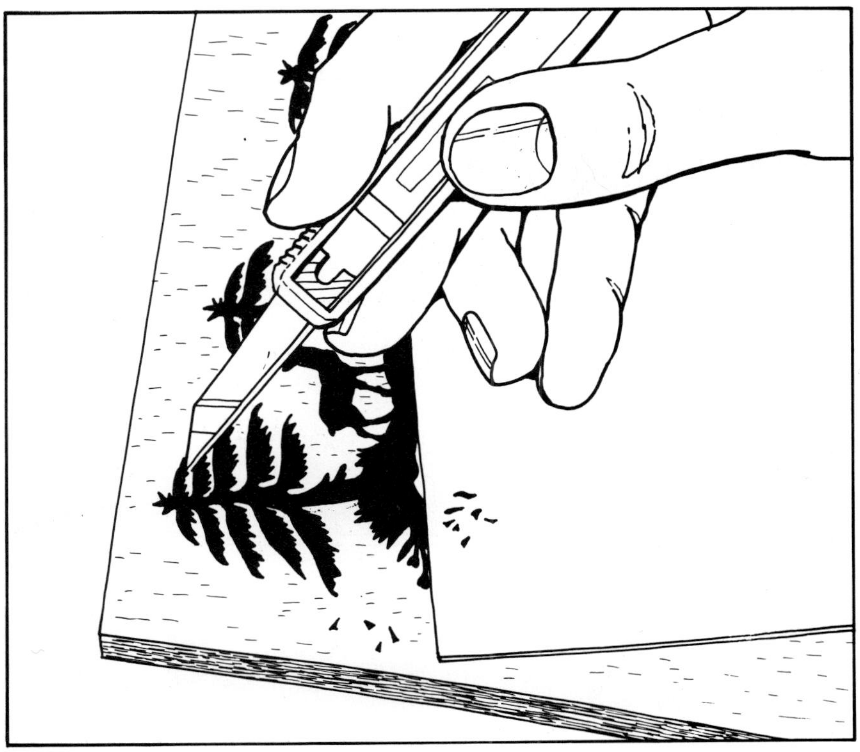

When you have fretted the centre, trimmed off the edge waste and scissor worked the delicate edge motifs, then use a fine-point scalpel to clean up the details.

is well placed, then take a few strips of masking tape and secure the tissue so that the three outer edges of both halves are linked. This done, have a look at the transferred design, and establish the areas that need to be cut away.

Now take the paper in one hand and the small fine-point scissors in the other, and gradually start cutting outwards from the centre fold. As you work, aim to keep the paper moving so that the scissors are always presented with the line of next cut. Having said that, of course there is no single correct ways of working, you must simply manoeuvre the paper and the scissors as you think fit.

KNIFE WORK

When you have completed most of the scissor work, that is to say the relatively open part of the motif that is contained within the upper and lower part of the heart, then start to work some of the smaller totally enclosed cuts. Have a look at the working drawing, study the band of flower motifs that frame the heart, and see how the little flower-and-foliage repeats are tightly worked, enclosed on all sides, and made up mainly of little triangular and lozenge shape 'windows'. This being so, these small areas are best cut with a razor sharp fine-point scalpel.

Work the motifs systematically and piece at a time, removing three-cut triangles, and two-cut lozenges. And so you continue, gradually, with scissors or scalpel, working out from the centre-line fold.

Finally, mount the finished cut in a simple card, glass and tape passepartout frame.

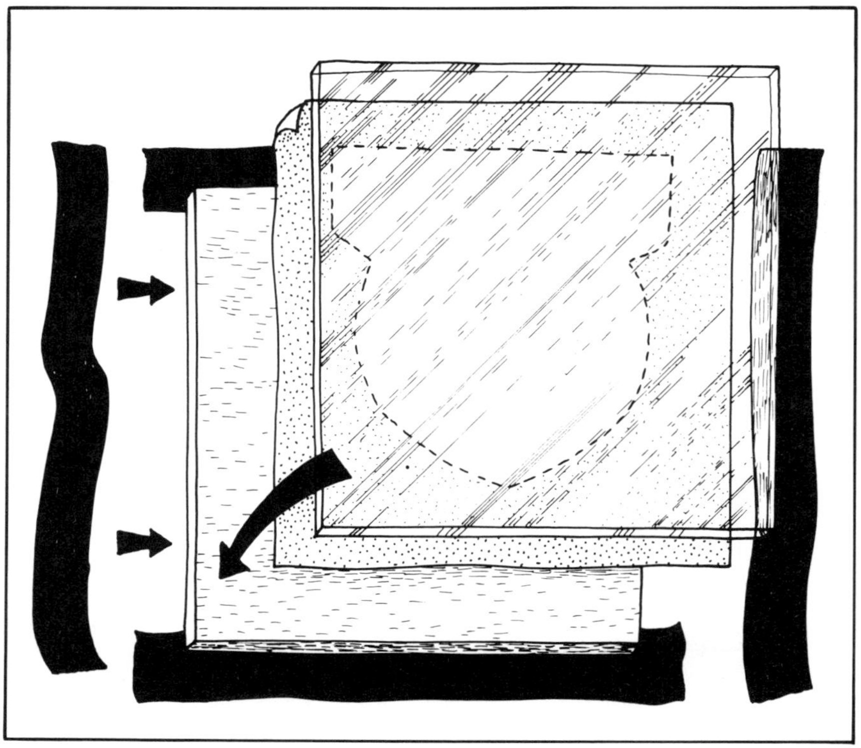

When you have worked all the open areas, and the first band of outer-heart motifs, then cut away the bulk of the unwanted tissue, and start working the outer band of flowers, and the crowning belt of deer and trees. Finally, when you have achieved what you consider to be a good silhouette, then take the scalpel, and go over the whole design cutting in the fine details and making good.

MOUNTING

Once the cut is finished, stop awhile and consider just how you want it to be protected and displayed. Now see how we have chosen to mount it in a simple passepartout frame; that is to say a frame made up of a backing board, a sheet of mounting paper, the paper cut, and a sheet of glass, with the whole sandwich being edged and held together with gummed paper or sticky tape binding.

When you come to the framing, choose your backing paper with care, start by establishing a centre line, then place and position the paper cut with a few small dabs of special paper-to-paper gum, and build the frame, as illustrated.

AFTERTHOUGHTS

We have chosen to work the cut in handmade black tissue paper, but that is not to say that you can't use a natural textured Japanese paper, a coloured tissue, or whatever. The only point to bear in mind when you are choosing a paper, is that cuts of this character are best worked with strong, matt, thin, firm, tissues – avoid bulky slippery loose fibred or brittle papers.

This project needs to be worked with a pair of fine-point curve-bladed nail scissors, so go for a pair that have very short blades and long handles – check, when the scissors are being used, that they cut at the point.

When you are cutting with the knife, protect the areas that have already been worked with a sheet of paper.

When you are opening up the finish paper cut, be careful that the two sides of the tissue don't catch and tear – open the paper with a gentle easing action.

PROJECT FOUR

VICTORIAN SILHOUETTE PORTRAIT

PROJECT PICTURE
A simple but rather charming costume silhouette. Note the period-setting shape of the dress, the ribbons and the mop cap.

INSPIRATIONAL
A selection of costume ideas from the 'Girls Own' paper dated 1880–1890.

INTRODUCTION

THOUGHTS ON THE PROJECT

Although the word silhouette is now generally taken to mean a profile or portrait cut out of black paper, there was a time when it referred to any painted, sculptured or ink drawn outline of an object in sharp shadow or profile. In seventeenth and eighteenth century Europe, before the coming of photography, it was fashionable to have one's portrait or shade 'taken', by one of the many professional silhouettists. A candle or lamp was set up in a studio, the sitter was positioned so that his or her shadow was thrown onto a screen, the professional practitioner drew around the image, and finally, via various complicated mechanical devices, the drawn image was reduced in size and worked in ink or paint onto glass or vellum, or, as with a cameo brooch, onto wax or plaster. At a later date, when paper was generally available, it became more fashionable to have one's portrait cut and worked directly from life. That is to say, the artist would study his subject and then, without the need for pencil or pen, he would scissor-work an instant slightly caricature portrait.

The term 'á la silhouette' originally meant, to be done cheaply or on the cheap. However when in the eighteenth century a French minister of finance, a certain Etienne de Silhouette, whose hobby it was to cut paper portraits, became involved in a series of complicated penny pinching tax reforms, so his rivals linked his name with a fashion for wearing pocketless coats that were simple in outline; the inference being that de Silhouette wanted to cut financial resources to the minimum. Silhouette cutting was very popular in the nineteenth

century, so much so, that the craft is now characterized by the use of Victorian imagery, meaning rather elaborate and fussy romantic period costume portraits.

CONSIDERING THE PROJECT

Have a look at our working drawings and see how we have placed the design emphasis not so much on a head and shoulders profile portrait, but rather on a full figure costume image. However, there is no reason why you shouldn't modify the project and make say a silhouette study of your daughter, your grandson, your pet dog or whatever.

When you have considered all the implications of the project, as

WORKING GRID
The scale is about four grid squares to 1 inch. See how by cutting, reversing and pairing the figures you might work a symmetrical design.

Work up a design on a sketch pad and modify the details to suit.

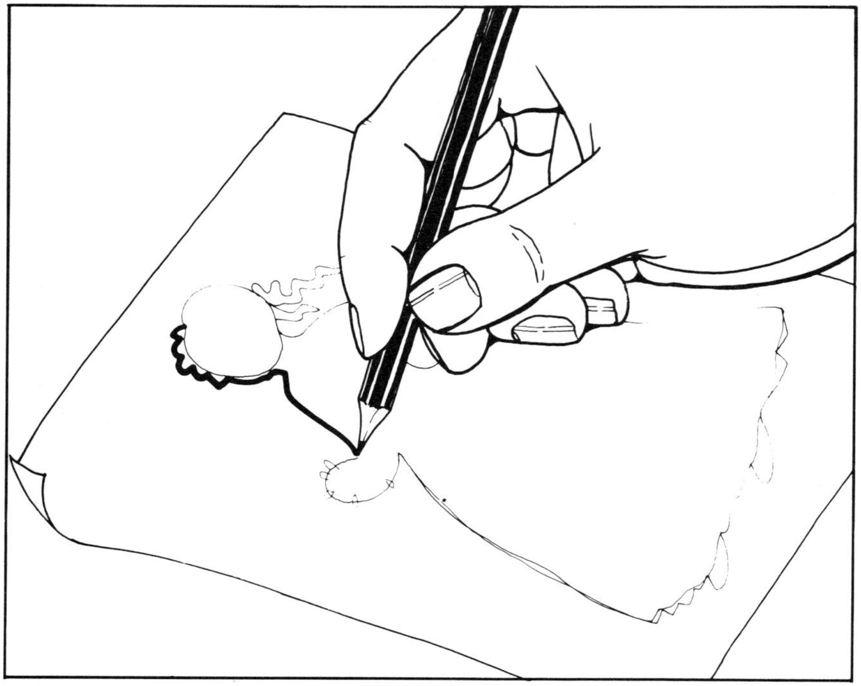

described and illustrated, then visit the Victoria and Albert museum, or another museum of your choice, and have a look at English, American and European silhouettes as worked between 1780 and 1880 – search out works by Johann von Goethe, Luise Duttenhofer and John Miers. When you get to see examples of work from this period, note how the eighteenth and nineteenth century silhouettists managed so beautifully to capture the spirit of their age. A slender neck, hair piled up, a bustle, a parasol, a high collar – all these beautifully considered and meticulously worked images have been crafted and cut with a fine attention to crisp spare-line detail. Before you put pencil to paper have a look at a friends profile, use a lamp to cast a sharp shadow, and note how for a successful silhouette it is necessary to seize upon some distinctive characteristic. An angular nose, a droop of the shoulders, a paunch, a beard, a particular costume detail, a beautiful figure – one or all of these features might be used in your silhouette study. When you have considered all the technique and design problems, then take your sketch book and make a series of pen and ink studies.

TOOLS AND MATERIALS

For this project you need, a sheet of good quality matt black paper, a sketch pad, an overlay pad or tracing paper, black ink, pencils and brushes, a pair of fine-point scissors, a fine-point craft knife, a cutting board, a sheet a white or cream card, paper-to-paper adhesive, a suitable picture frame, preferably one with a black oval mount, and finally of course you need illustrations of historical costumes and such like.

FIRST STEPS

Once you have decided how to approach this project, then take your pencil and sketch pad and make a few trial workouts. Pay particular attention to such things as the shape of the nose, the overall pose, the hair, the period of the costume, the shoe details and the trim. Note how, with our rather basic silhouette we have avoided drawing complicated face details, but rather we have concentrated our efforts on the custome. The emphasis is on the ribbons, the posy, the mop cap and the full skirt. However, if you do want to adapt this project and relate it to say your own daughter, then you must modify the design so that it includes some detail or other that is instantly recognizable. This detail need not be related to the face profile, because anyway children tend to have very rounded faces – it might be her favourite doll, her pet rabbit, or some other feature, item or possession that is uniquely hers.

THE MASTER DESIGN

Take your overlay pad or tracing paper then with a soft pencil, a brush and black ink, work up your design. Don't rush straight in with the brush and ink, much better to draw out a trial profile with a pencil. When you have what you consider to be a good starting pose, ink it in, let the ink dry and then, if necessary, retrace and rework your initial design. And so you continue, drawing out the profile, inking

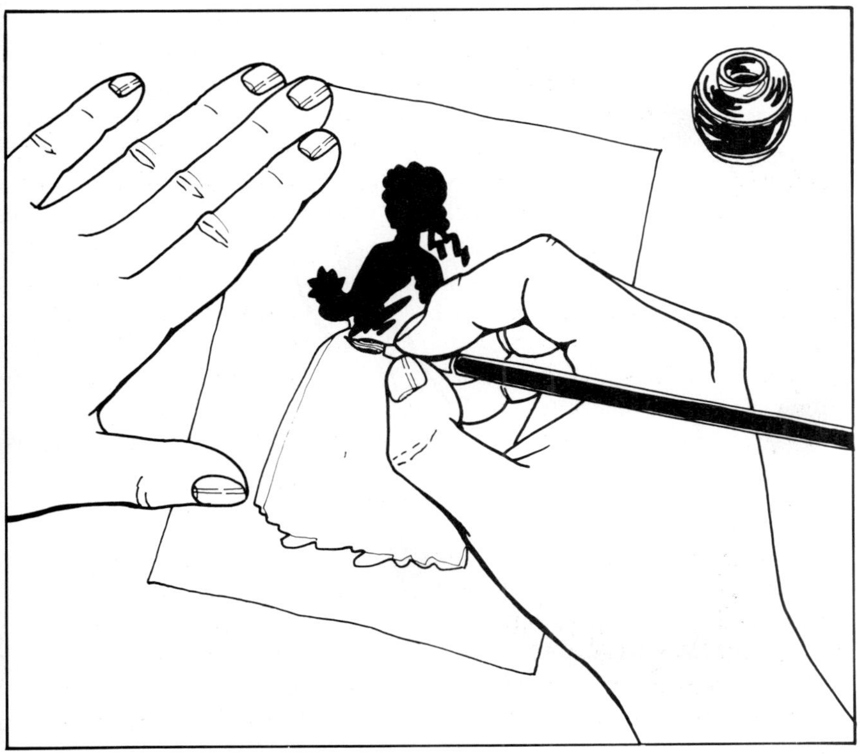

Once you have drawn up what you consider to be a reasonable profile, block it in with a brush and indian ink.

Continue tracing and inking in until you achieve a fair design.

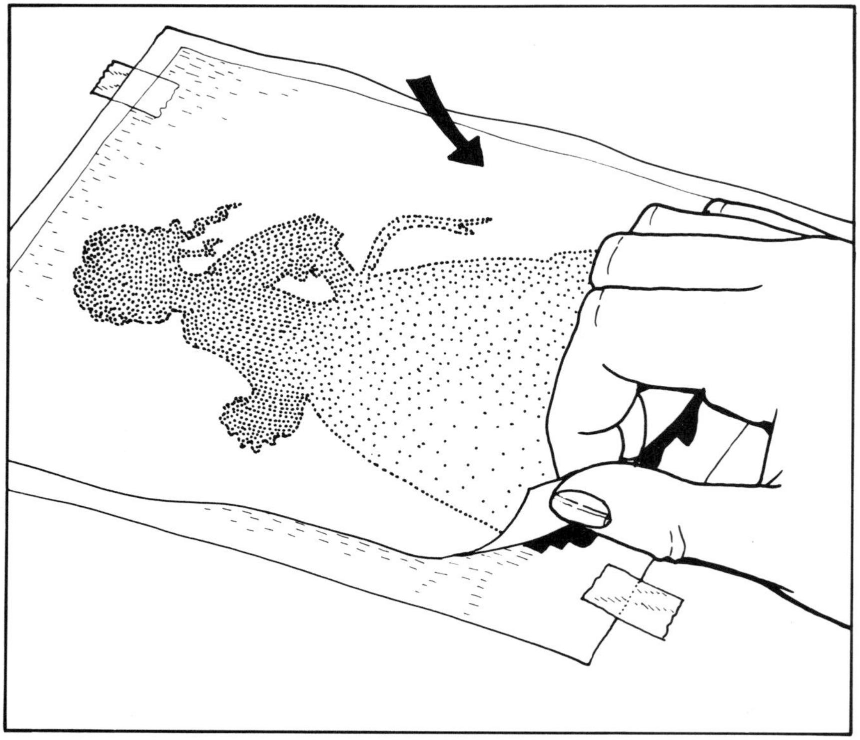

When you have worked a good design, then take a tracing and pencil press transfer the traced lines through to the working face of the black paper.

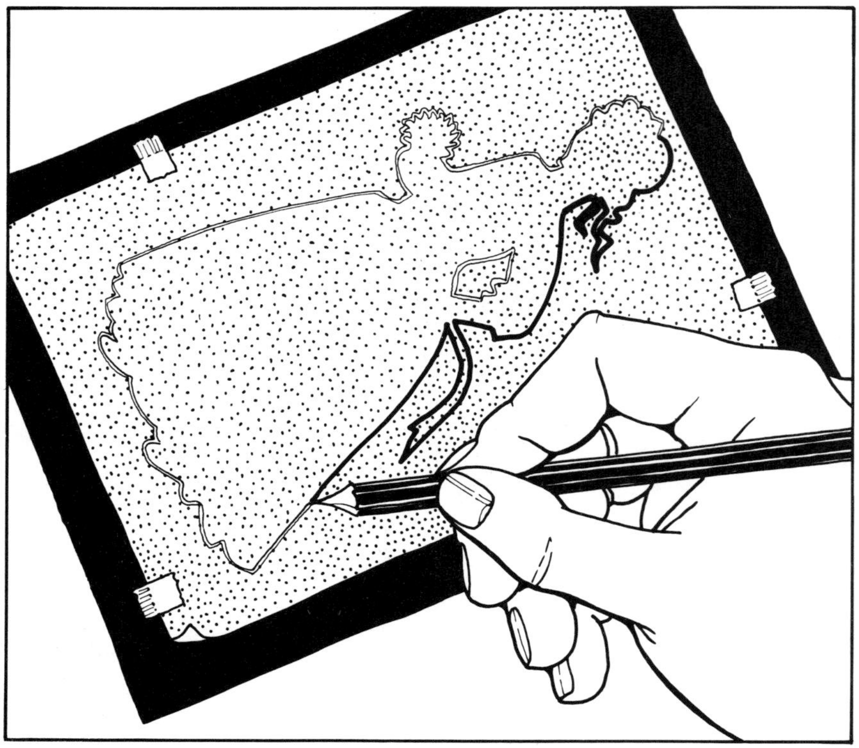

in, and then re-tracing and re-inking until little by little you work up a good, crisp nicely detailed image.

When you have a fair design, then take a fine brush or a pen, and draw in the details – little flicks of hair here, a slight roundness to the cheeks there, and so on. Finally, take a sheet of tracing paper and trace off the completed design.

TRANSFERRING THE DESIGN AND FIRST CUTS

When you have achieved a fully worked and traced master design, then pencil press transfer the traced lines through to the working face of your sheet of black paper. This done, remove the bulk of the waste with a large pair of scissors and then take the small pair of scissors and start cutting out the fine details. There is no single best or easy way of cutting – I usually cut out the large forms first and then finish off with the intricate and delicate details.

When you are working, make sure that your scissors cut right to their points, then hold and manoeuvre the paper in one hand, and work the scissors with the other. Don't try to follow the lines of the design with the scissors, but rather, keep turning the paper so that the scissors are always presented with the line of next cut. Finally take the sharp-point craft knife and cut into all the little nooks and crannies of the profile – aim to leave the cut lines smooth, crisp and free from fuzzy edges.

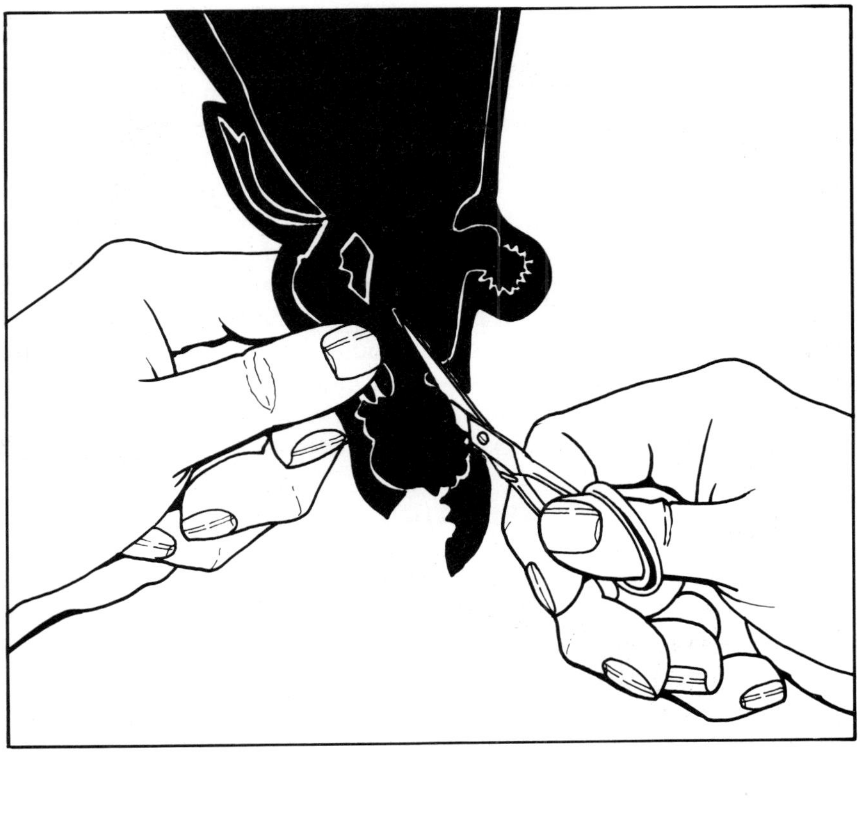

Clear away the bulk of the waste with a knife or a large pair of scissors, then set-to with a small pair of fine-point scissors.

Finally, take the silhouette and mount it in an enhancing period frame.

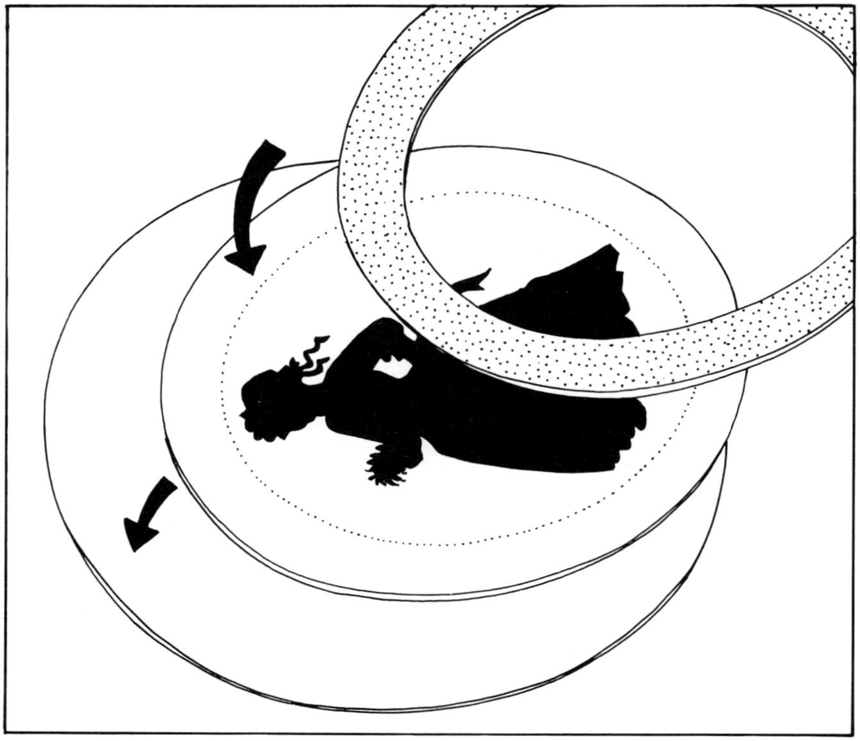

MOUNTING

When you have achieved a good crisp silhouette image, then place it in the frame and decide just how you want it to be mounted, meaning do you want it set in a square frame, does it need to be trimmed with lace, does the mount need to be bevelled and gold edged and so on. See how we have settled for a very simple oval frame with an oval mount. Once you have settled on the frame and the mount, then clean the glass, brush out the frame and generally make sure that the whole project is free from bits and pieces of waste. Now, position the black silhouette on the cream or white ground paper, secure it with the smallest dab of special paper-to-paper glue, arrange the oval mount, trim and cut both the mount and the backing paper to size and then finally pin and tape the backing board into position.

AFTERTHOUGHTS

When you are pencil press transferring the traced lines through to the matt black paper, aim to work it so that the pencil lines occur on the back of the silhouette.

Use indian ink to block in the trial designs.

When you are choosing your silhouette paper, go for a paper that is thin and hard – avoid full bodied fat papers.

PROJECT FIVE

MODERN EUROPEAN MOBILE

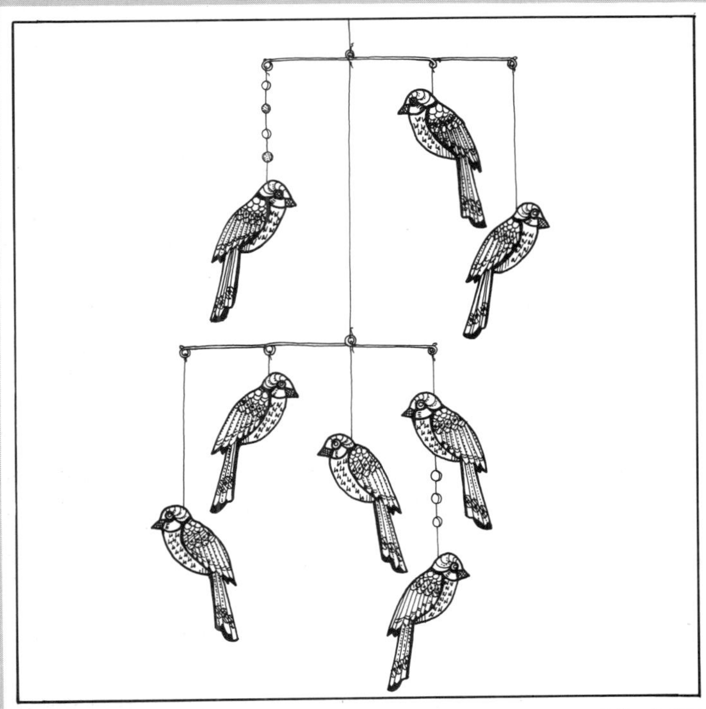

PROJECT PICTURE
Eight identical bird inspired paper sculptures mounted so as to make an Alexander Calder type mobile. Note how the birds are offset and see also the little balance adjusting beads, these might be actual beads or made of say plastercine or wood.

INSPIRATIONAL
Various bird sculptures and mobile structures.

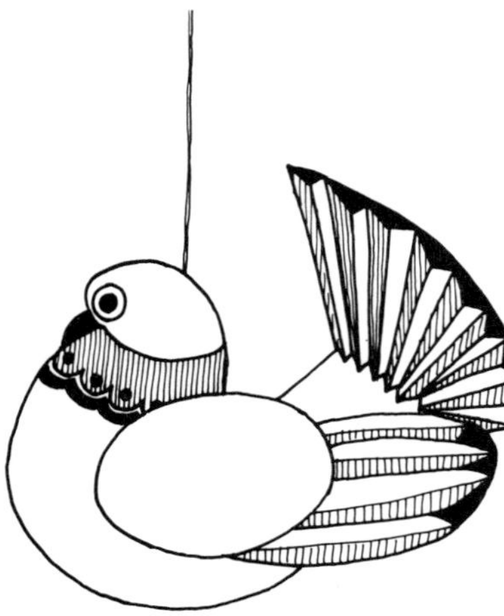

INTRODUCTION

THOUGHTS ON THE PROJECT

European Paper Sculpture, meaning the paper sculptures that were made in England and Europe between the wars, say between 1920 and 1940, are characterized by their sophisticated clean cut imagery; stark white architectural displays, hard edged Cubist figures, and reliefs that we now describe as being Modern and Art Deco. Of course generally speaking artists and craftsmen can do no more than reflect the feelings and notions of their times, but that said, the paper craftsmen of the thirties and fourties period weren't just swept up in the backwash of Art deco, Industrial art or whatever; in many instances they were the prime movers and the inspiration for other art and craft disciplines.

With the paper sculptures that were made in England, Germany and France, there was a strong positive and considered move away from traditional decorative naive intuitive folk ways of working, and a swing towards what might be called applied Functional Paper Art. In fact so seriously did some countries view the industrial and functional potential of paper modelling, that they taught it in their art schools and academies. So where, you might ask, are these paper modellers now? – the answer is simple enough, they became the initiators of post war art and design, the packagers, the car designers, the television and motion picture stage-set designers, and the architectural model makers.

CONSIDERING THE PROJECT

Have a look at the working drawings and inspirational illustrations,

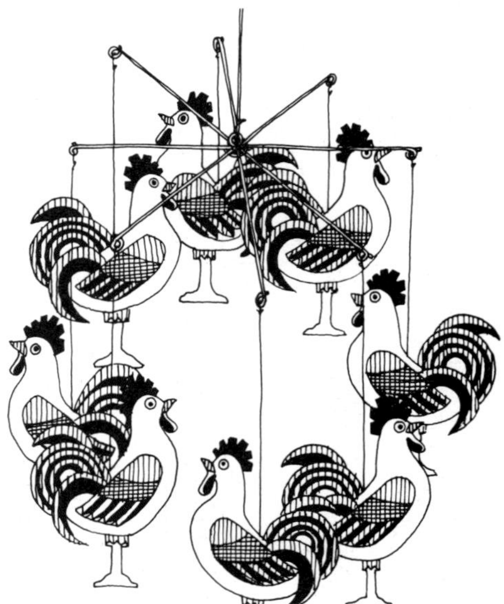

and see how this project uses the little paper sculpture bird forms in a mobile context. That is to say the birds are hung from slender wires and counterbalanced so as to make characteristic mobile forms. Note how identical mirror-image bird forms are designed and mounted back-to-back so that they look to be rounded and three dimensional. Of course there is no reason why you shouldn't modify the project and use the sculptured forms in another setting, say under glass, as a three dimensional model or whatever. See also how we chose to stylise the bird form and make it from white, colour-tinted and textured papers – you can use white papers, silver foils, decorative printed papers and so on – work the project to suit your own needs.

When you have taken into account all these design, context and material considerations, then take a trip to the nearest art school,

WORKING GRID
The scale is about four grid squares to 1 inch. See how the sculpture is built up from two identical mirror image profiles, that is to say all the little cut-outs are mounted on the two identical but reversed bird profiles, and then they are mounted back-to-back so as to make a three dimensional form.

architectural college or gallery, and get to see as many examples of paper sculpture as possible. Back up your researches by having a look through magazines, newspapers and journals – note how currently paper sculpture techniques are being used to good effect in advertising and on television. Finally, when you have made decisions as to the style and context of your sculpture, then take a sketch book, some scrap paper and a pair of scissors, and have a few trial workouts.

TOOLS AND MATERIALS

For this project you need, a sheet of smooth-faced white or coloured card, several sheets of single-faced coloured paper, meaning white papers that have a coloured face, several sheets of paper that have colour all the way through, a work board, a sheet of tracing paper, a cutting board, a measure, a pencil, a packet of coloured pencil crayons, a metal straight edge, a fine-point scalpel, a small pair of fine-point scissors, a pair of long nosed pliers, a quantity of stiff, slightly sprung wire, a packet of ball-headed dress makers pins, a quantity of micro poly plastic fishing line, plastiscine, a quick-dry paper adhesive, and finally, you also need a packet of paper clips.

DESIGNING AND FIRST STEPS

When you have made your preliminary sketches, then work your design up to size and colour; that is to say, work out your chosen form, decide how the elements are to be cut, stuck, coloured and mounted, then draw up a carefully coloured detailed master design. This done, carefully analize your design and break it down into its component parts. There will be a card foundation or base, this can be

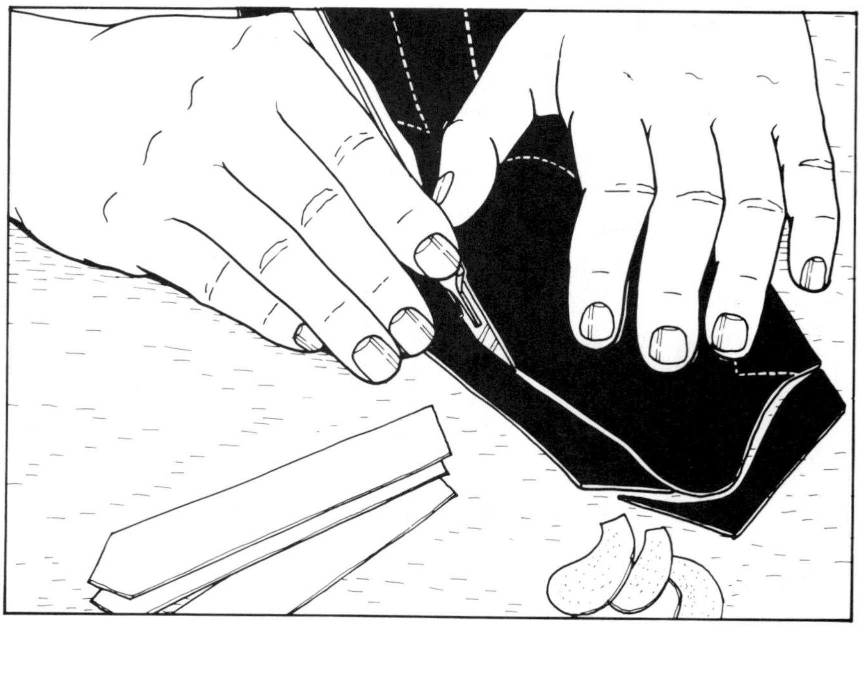

Once you have drawn up a master design and pencil press transferred the lines of the design through to the correct colour faces of the various sheets of card, then cut out two identical but reversed bird images.

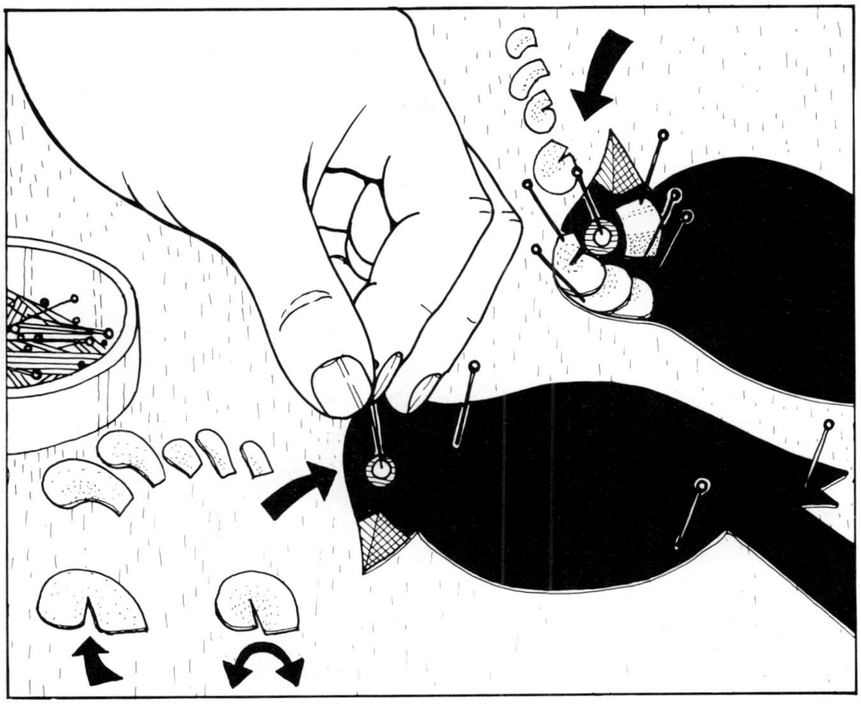

Pin the two bird images out on the workboard, make sure they are reversed, then with pins and adhesive, start layering and placing the little paper shapes that go to make up the design.

white or coloured on one side, and then there will be individual units, eyes, feathers, a breast plate, a beak, and so on. Note – if you are making a mobile, or an in-the-round sculpture, you will need two mirror-image forms for each motif.

When you have drawn up, as it were, a cutting plan, then take tracings of all the individual elements. This done, take a hard pencil and press transfer the traced lines through to the working face of your chosen papers. Finally, label all the transferred images so that they can be matched up with your master design. Note – if you are using coloured single-sided papers, then reverse the transferred image so that it occurs on the correct side of the paper.

CUTTING

Clear the worksurface of as much clutter as possible, then pin up your working drawings and master designs so that they are at hand and within view. Now take the cutting board, the scissors and the scalpel, and set about cutting out all the pieces. Aim to work shapes that are clean and crisp edged. As you cut out each shape, put it to one side – its a good idea to have a number of little trays or boxes, then you can organize the cut-outs into pieces of the same colour, feather units and such like.

SCULPTING AND MOUNTING

When all the paper shapes have been cut, then clear away the scrap and set out the working board, the pins, the clips and all the other

Each feather needs to be individually decorated with its little applique cut-out and then creased, glued, positioned and pinned in place.

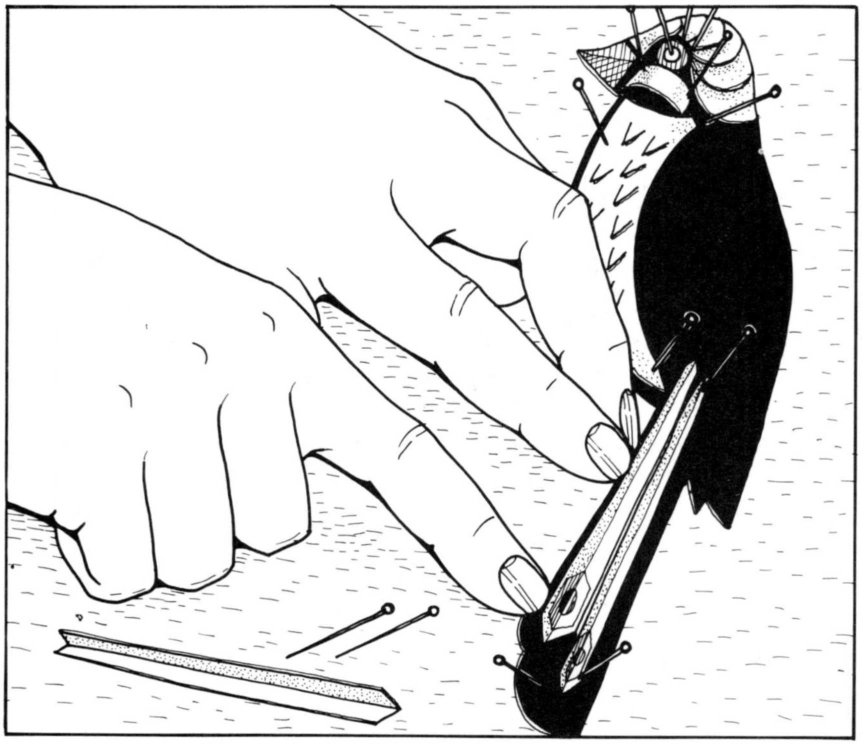

Use a small knitting needle type tool to curl and shape the feathers.

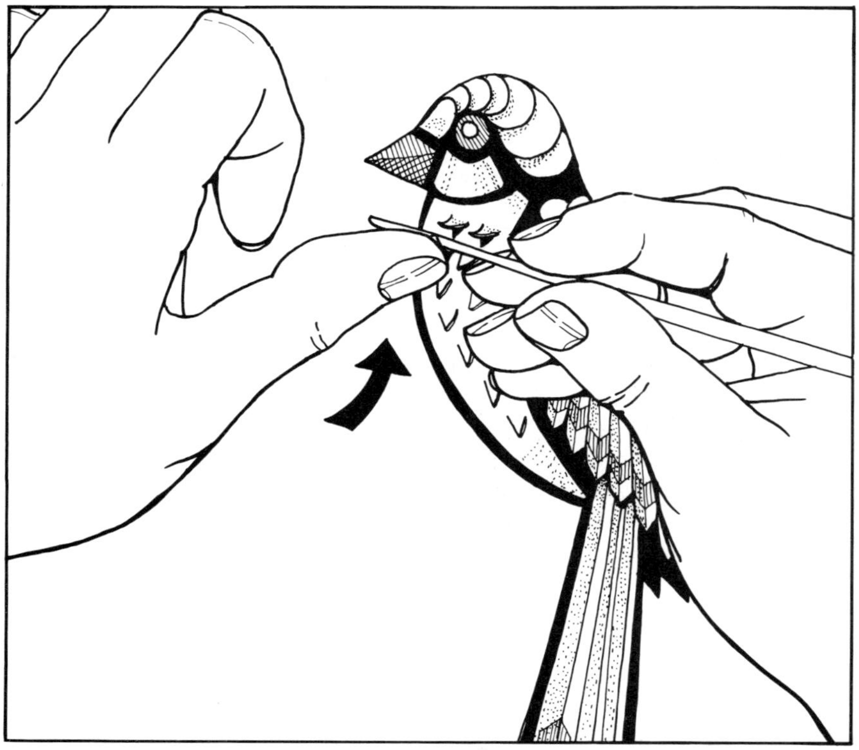

tools and materials. Start by pinning both card bases to the work board. Now, working from the base up, proceed to layer, glue, set and pin the various elements. So, for example, the main breast form can be 'V' cut, slightly arched and then glued on the base plate, the eye and beak can be worked and positioned, and so on. When you come to the main tail and wing feathers, these need to be worked and folded prior to placing – glue the coloured flashes onto the wings, let the glue dry, trim, then fold and place as illustrated.

As to the actual layering of all the feathers, work the tail feathers first, and then gradually work upwards towards the head, layering and overlapping as you go. And so you continue, using pins and clips to hold the various shapes in place. When you have made both sides of the identical mirror-image forms, then take a round section pencil or the handle of a brush and set about curling the ends of the feathers.

Finally, when you have achieved pairs of well worked bird forms, carefully smear their backs with adhesive, loosely knot and place the end of the micro yarn on one or other of the backs, and then bring both forms carefully together, as illustrated. And so you proceed until you have made four or more birds.

PUTTING TOGETHER

When you have made all the birds forms, put them carefully to one side, and set out the wire, the micro yarn, the plastiscine and the pliers. This done, have a look at our project details and see how the

Take a pair of matched bird forms, smear their backs with adhesive, place and position the knotted micro yarn, and then bring the two halves together.

Bend the wire frame with the long nose pliers, tie on the various bird sculptures, and finally add the counterbalance weights.

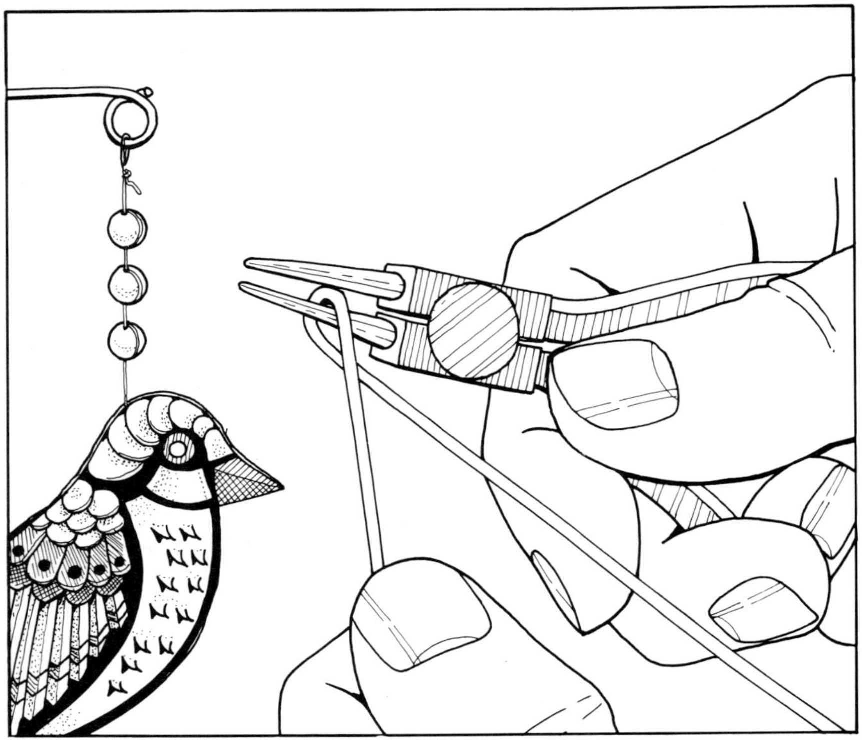

wires are variously shaped and balanced so as to make an interesting whole. Now take the pieces of plastiscine, check that they are identical in weight to the paper sculptures, and then make a balanced mock-up. Meaning decide roughly where on the wire you want to suspend the paper sculptures, decide how many forms you want, and then experiment and shape your prototype accordingly.

When you have achieved what you consider to be an exciting mobile structure, then start bending and shaping the main wires. Have a look at our working details and note how we have used the long-nosed pliers to make the looped link-up points. See also how on each of our wires there are four link-up points, one for the main suspension thread, and three for the secondary wire and the sculptures. Note the placing and direction of the link-up loops.

Finally when you have shaped your wires, hang the primary wire from the ceiling and then, by trial, error and fine adjustment, set about building the total mobile form.

AFTERTHOUGHTS

When you are building the two identical mirror-image birds, use the pins to hold the paper shapes while the glue is drying.

Some glues and adhesives leave stains, so work with care, and if possible check the adhesive on a scrap of your chosen coloured paper.

When you are folding the main wing and tail feathers, establish the position of the fold with a delicate score-line.

PROJECT SIX

PAPIER-MACHE TRAY

PROJECT PICTURE
A small papier mâché tea tray decorated with traditional flower inspired canal boat motifs.

INTRODUCTION

THOUGHTS ON THE PROJECT

Japanned papier-mâché wares, as produced in England in the middle of the eighteenth century, were made of paper-pulp, chalk and sand, all mixed with glue; the mixture was pressed into moulds, baked and painted. The process was used for making small domestic items like boxes, ornaments, mirror frames and tea trays. As to the style, decoration and naming of these wares, there was in England and Europe in the 1750's a fashion for finishes and designs that looked to be oriental, and so it was that the papier-mâché items, painted with colours, designs and lacquers in the Japanese style, came to be called

INSPIRATIONAL
A selection of traditional canal art flower motifs. Note how the flowers and leaves are made up from a number of very simple, direct, carefully ordered brush strokes.

'japanned' wares. At first the patterns and motifs used on these wares were stroke-by-stroke copies of Japanese lacquered items, but gradually over a hundred or so years the designs became simpler, swifter and more removed.

No doubt this swiftness of style was initially inspired by the manufacturers commercial need to cut labour costs, speed up production and such like; but no matter, once the designs and motifs had ceased to be slavish copies, so there evolved a strong, true, independent style that we now call generically English folk primitive. This naive style of painting is characterized by the use of brilliant primary colours and big bold abstracted brushstrokes. When we now see naive and primitive English folk decoration of this character, it is usually in a narrow boat

DESIGN GRID
Note how the circle is quartered and see how the small motifs are placed symmetrically around the border.

or canal boat context; decoration on the actual boats, patterns and motifs on the small pieces of boat furniture, and pictures and designs on items used within the boat; cans, plates, trays, barrels, buckets, handbowls and the like. As to why and when this direct way of painting came to be taken up by the canal boat artists, who can say, all we really know, is that in the middle of the nineteenth century and well into the twentieth century, when general commercial art and style trends had moved on, and papier-mâché wares were no longer being produced, the canal artists had made the primitive, naive, style their own.

CONSIDERING THE PROJECT

Have a look at the working drawings and the inspirational designs and motifs, and see how we have chosen to make a straight forward papier-mâché tea tray, that is to say a round curve-lipped tray that we have decorated in the canal boat tradition. Before you start this project, it would be as well to take a trip to a canal boat museum, a museum of Victoriana and maybe even a fairground museum, search out examples of naive folk art in general, and canal boat art and papier-mâché wares in particular. Have a close up look at the wares and see how variously they are strong, delicate, and vigorously decorated with flower inspired motifs. Of course some papier-mâché items are less direct than others, and some canal boat decorations are more over-worked than others, but no matter, try, as it were, to take note of the characteristic middle-ground works.

Now go back to our working drawings and see how we have tried to achieve a making and decorating balance. Of course there's no reason why you shouldn't modify our project, and say concentrate your efforts on the papier-mâché techniques rather than decorative, or vise-versa. When you have made as many museum and gallery research visits as possible, take your various notes, photographs, working drawings and sketches back to your workshop, and make firm decisions as to size, form, style, function and design.

Note – if you want to research English papier-mâché, see inlaid and painted furniture C. 1845, especially works by Benjamin Cook, and Jennings and Bettridge.

TOOLS AND MATERIALS

For this project you need – a quantity of old newspapers, a quantity of starch/wheat paste, a paste with a fungicide, a cellulose plaster filler, as used by painters and decorators, a small quantity of petroleum jelly, (Vaseline), a small round, smooth contoured tin tray, to use as a mould, a plastic bucket, a collection of plastic mixing bowls/jugs, a wooden spoon, a large jam-making pancheon/saucepan, a fine-mesh sieve or a jam makers straining bag, a pack of graded glasspapers, a knife, a metal cooking spatula or a potters rubbey kidney tool, a workboard, a tin of wood primer, a tin of black gloss japan enamel,

Bring the torn paper and water to the boil, simmer until the mass has broken down into a grey porridge-like pulp, keep the mixture on the move with a wooden spoon.

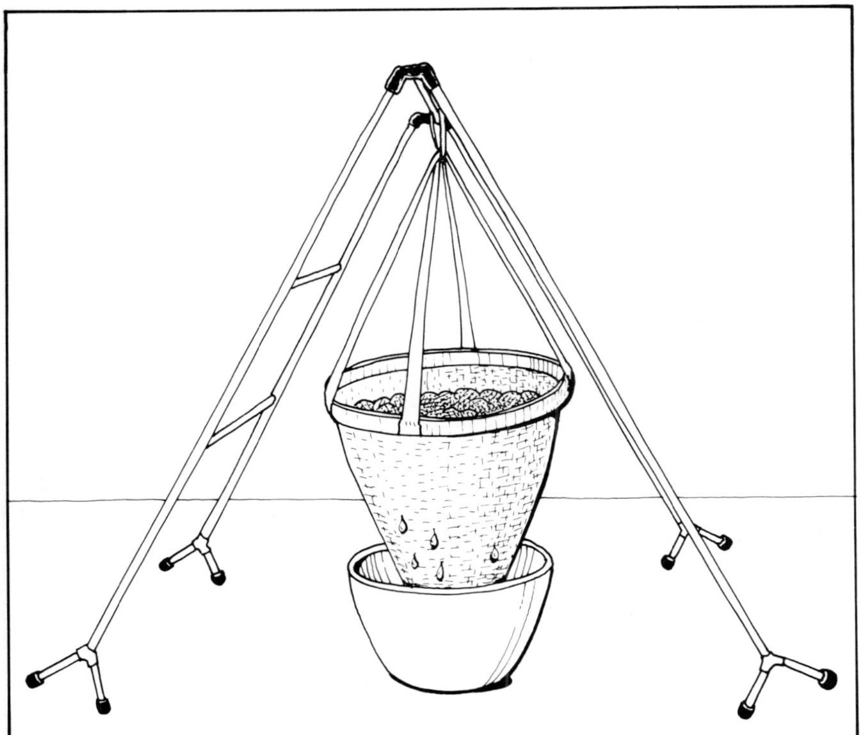

Pour the paper pulp into a straining bag and leave it to drain off overnight.

a suitable undercoat for the enamel, several tins of model makers enamel, colours to suit, a tin of yacht varnish, several brushes, sizes to suit, and paper and pencils.
Note – you also need the use of a sink, running water and a cooker/cooking ring.

MAKING THE PULPED PAPER

With a plastic bucket close at hand, take about fifty large sheets of newspaper, meaning double page sheets from a common or garden daily paper, and tear them into thumbnail size pieces. Don't try for time saving shortcuts, tear the paper as small as possible. When you have a bucket full of newspaper confetti, and this operation might well take an hour or so, top the bucket up with hot water and leave it overnight to soak. This done, transfer the wet mass to the pancheon/large saucepan, top it up with water, and then, just as you might do with jam making, bring it to the boil, let it simmer, all the while keeping it moving with the wooden spoon. And so you continue until the mass of newspaper has broken down into a grey porridge-like pulp.

Now pour the pulp into your sieve or straining bag and leave it overnight to drip and drain off. When most of the surplus water has run off, decant the cold grey pulp back into the plastic bucket, and add the starch paste and a quantity of cellulose filler. As to just how much filler and paste you need, reckon on about 4 oz of starch paste

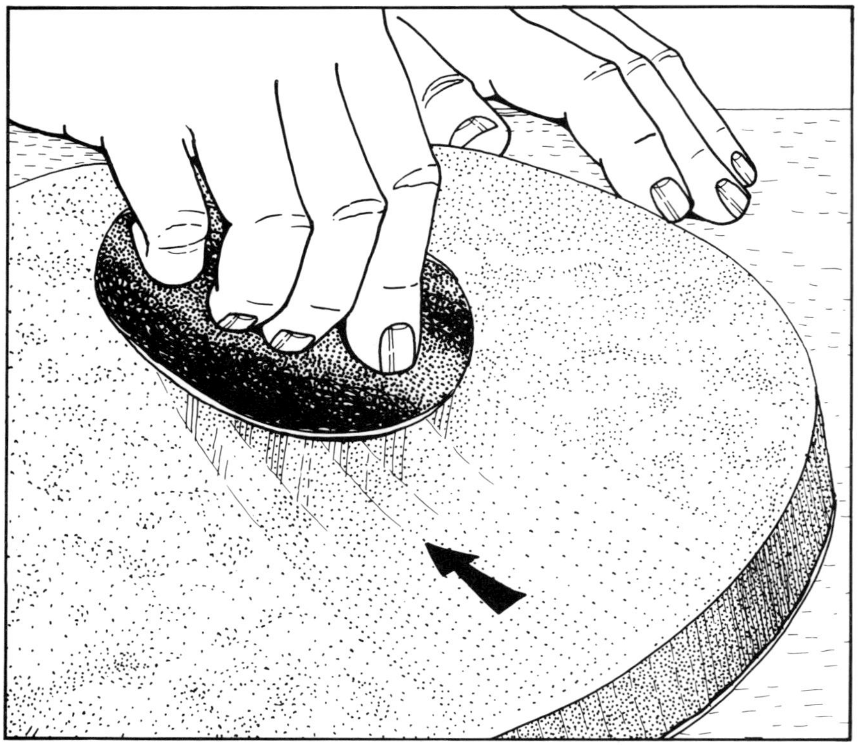

Vaseline the upturned tray, spread the pulp over what is now the mould, and then work the 3/4 inch layer until it is smooth and the filler begins to come to the surface.

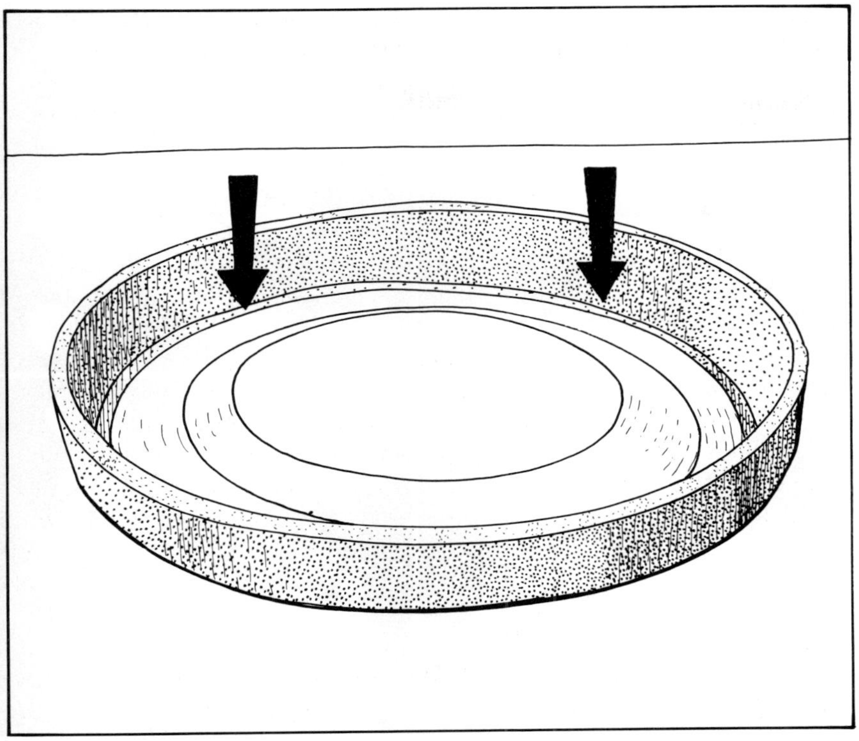

Ease the papier mâché form away from the tray, set it right side up on the worksurface and weight it down at its centre with a heavy dinner plate.

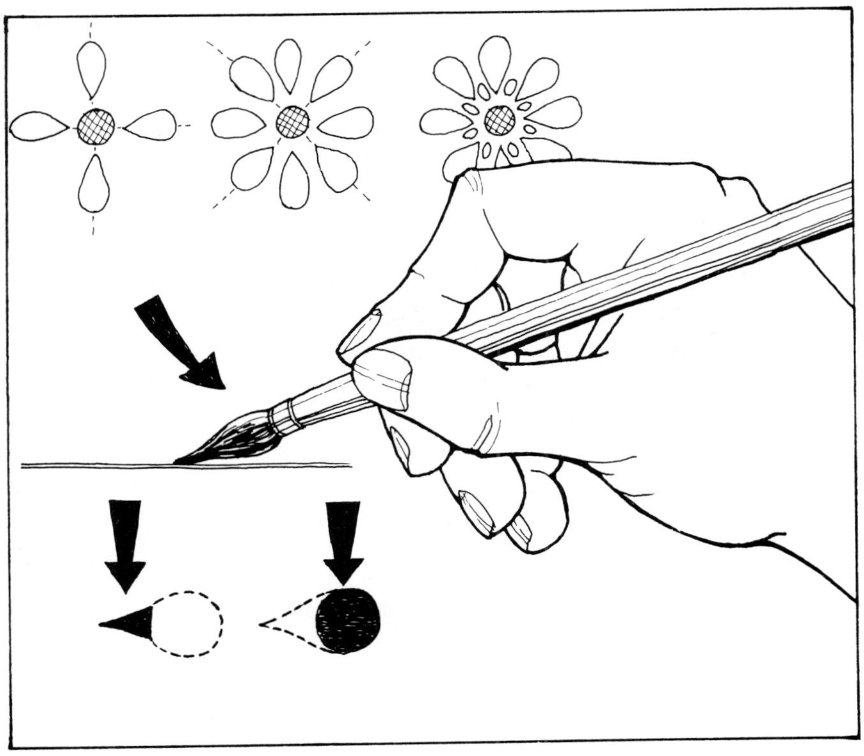

While the papier mâché tray is drying out, have a workout with the brush and the paints – try for uncomplicated and naive flower forms – see how, small petal forms can be achieved by using the natural shape of the brush.

Finally when the tray has been filled, rubbed down and given its various coats of ground paint, then lay on the different coloured areas of the motif in a carefully ordered and yet swift manner. That is to say, work out from the centre, paint the main design blocks, fill out with the secondary blocks of dark colour, work the petals and flower centres, and finally dot and dash in all the little details.

and 4 oz of filler to every 20 oz of dry torn newspaper. Finally, add the dry ingredients little by little, and keep stirring and handworking the pulp until you have a smooth uniformly consistent grey/white clay-like mixture.

PREPARING AND FILLING THE MOULD

When you have made the paper pulp, then clear your worksurface of as much clutter as possible and set out the round tin tray, the workboard and your various tools and materials. Set the tray down bottom side up on your newspaper covered workboard and give it a liberal coating of Vaseline. Now, add a little more filler to the pulp, work it well in, and then start covering the mould. Of course just how thick the pulp layer needs to be, will depend on the size and complexity of your chosen mould and the water and filler content of the pulp – aim for a coating of no less than ¾ inch thick. When you have set down an evenly thick layer of pulp, as illustrated, take the cooking spatula or better still the potters rubber kidney tool, and work the pulp until the filler comes to the surface as a smooth slick sheen. Now clear away the mess and put the whole works to one side to slowly dry out.

Finally, when the paper pulp is almost dry and has started to shrink away from the tray, ease it off both the tin tray former and the workboard, set it down right side up on the worksurface and weight it down at its centre with a large plate.

RUBBING DOWN AND PREPARING THE GROUND

When the paper pulp is at the leather hard stage, take the rubber kidney tool and small amount of filler and work the inside surface until all the small cavities have been stopped. Now wait awhile for the tray to become completely dry and chalky, than take the graded glass papers and rub down all surfaces. When you have achieved a well worked form and all the surfaces look to be smooth, sound and dust free, then, drying and rubbing down between coats, lay on a couple of coats of white primer, a couple of undercoats, and finally a single smooth coat of black japan enamel.

DECORATING AND FINISHING

Have a good look at the working drawings and the inspirational illustrations and see how the traditional canal boat 'rose' design is made up from a series of stylised brushstrokes. That is to say the flower forms are not realistiic interpretations of roses but rather they are simple motifs that suggest flowers. Now before you start working the tray, take some scrap paper and a medium, long haired, fine-point brush and have several trial runs. Aim at a loose wristed and swift 'on-and-off' style, and see how it is possible with half a dozen or so brushstrokes to build up quite a complex flower design. Bearing in mind that you are after basic, bold, naive flower imagery, don't attempt to mix subtle blends of secondary colours, or try for fussy details, but rather use raw primary colours and work the motifs with direct paint-loaded brush daubs. When you have achieved a number of confident workouts, decorate the tray with the 'rose' motifs, as described and illustrated. Finally, when the paint is dry, give the tray a couple of coats of clear varnish, drying and rubbing down between coats, and the job is done.

AFTERTHOUGHTS

If you decide to use a traditional flour and water paste, be sure to add a proprietry fungicide.

Before you apply the primer and various paint and varnish finishes, make sure that the papier-mâché form is absolutely crisp dry.

At the painting stage, the task will be that much easier if the tray is placed and worked on a cake decorators or a potters turn-table.

If you are a bit unsure of your painting skills, it might be as well to use water based acrylic colours, then, if you have problems, the designs can be quickly dried and repainted. Note – Acrylic paints dry within minutes and hours rather than days.

We chose to set the design out by eye – if you prefer a more formal approach you might use tracing paper and a compass.

For a tray with an extra hard wearing and dense surface, make sure the painted decoration is dry, then lay on a two-part catalyst/resin finish.

PROJECT SEVEN

POP-UP GREETINGS CARD

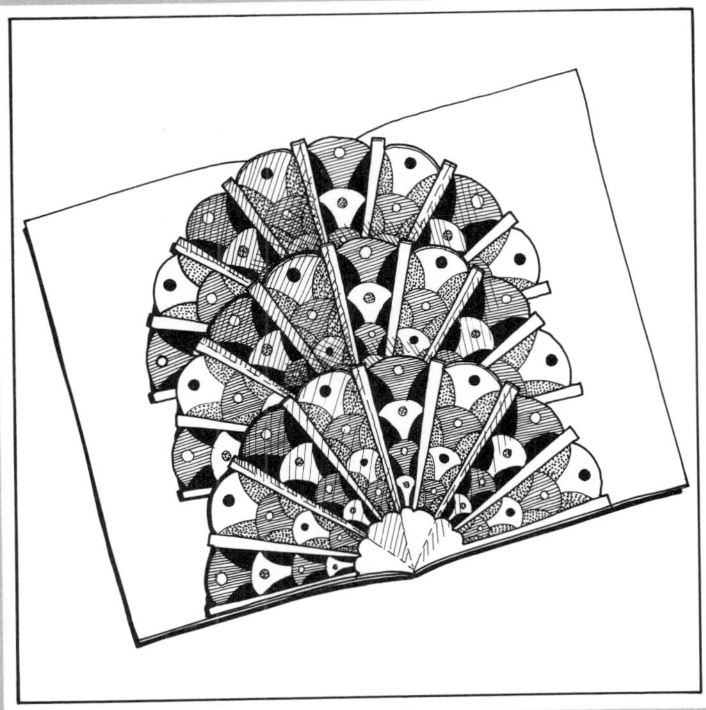

PROJECT PICTURE
The opened out card. See how the total design draws its inspiration from Art Deco imagery.

INTRODUCTION

THOUGHTS ON THE PROJECT

Paper pop-ups are beautiful! Cunningly coloured, cut and folded characters that spring out from childrens story books, scenes in splendid perspective that rise up as the pages are being opened, and strange figures in books and cards that can be operated with discs and levers; in all their many and varied forms, pop-ups are great fun. Historically they have been described as . . . the parent of the peep-show, the grandparent of cut-out theatres, and the great grandparent of the magic lantern. Looked at in this light, perhaps it could even be said, that paper pop-ups are in some way related to the greatest pop-up of them all, television! However, all that apart, pop-up paper

INSPIRATIONAL
Note how the Art Deco imagery is characterized by strong geometrical lines and curves.

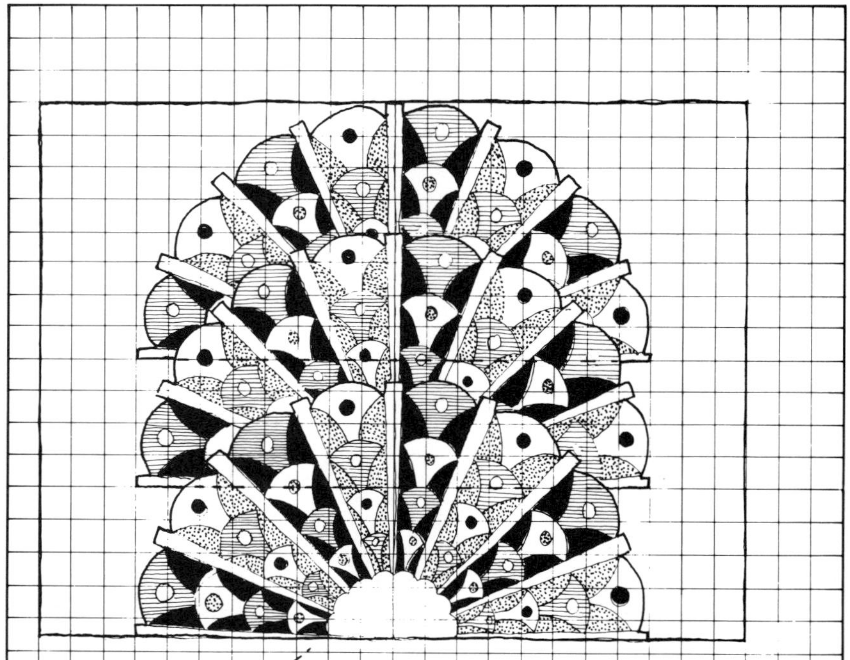

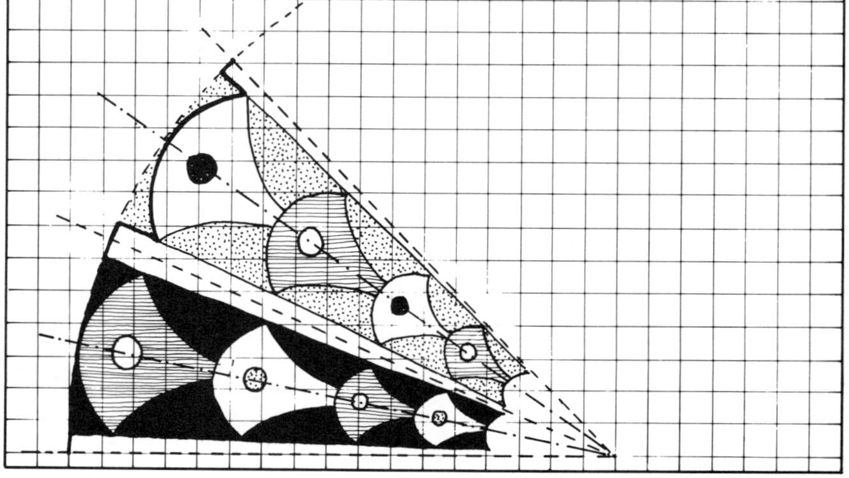

WORKING GRID
TOP *The scale is two grid squares to 1 inch.*
BOTTOM *The scale is about four squares to 1 inch. Have a good look at the fan design structure and see how it relates to a circle that has been broken down into sixteen 22.5 degree wedges.*

sculptures have been around for at least two hundred years. In the middle of the eighteenth century there were pop-up books that featured such colourful characters as, Harlequin, Robinson Crusoe and Puss in Boots; and then a hundred or so years later the Victorians had a craze for book pop-ups that contained all manner of weird paper 'spring' operated scenes and figures.

Since the sixties there has been a revival of interest in the whole subject, with a great many firms world wide producing nothing but childrens pop-up story books, pop-up novelty items, and best of all, pop-up greetings cards. That said, in our opinion there is only one thing better than receiving a pop-up greetings card, and that's making one.

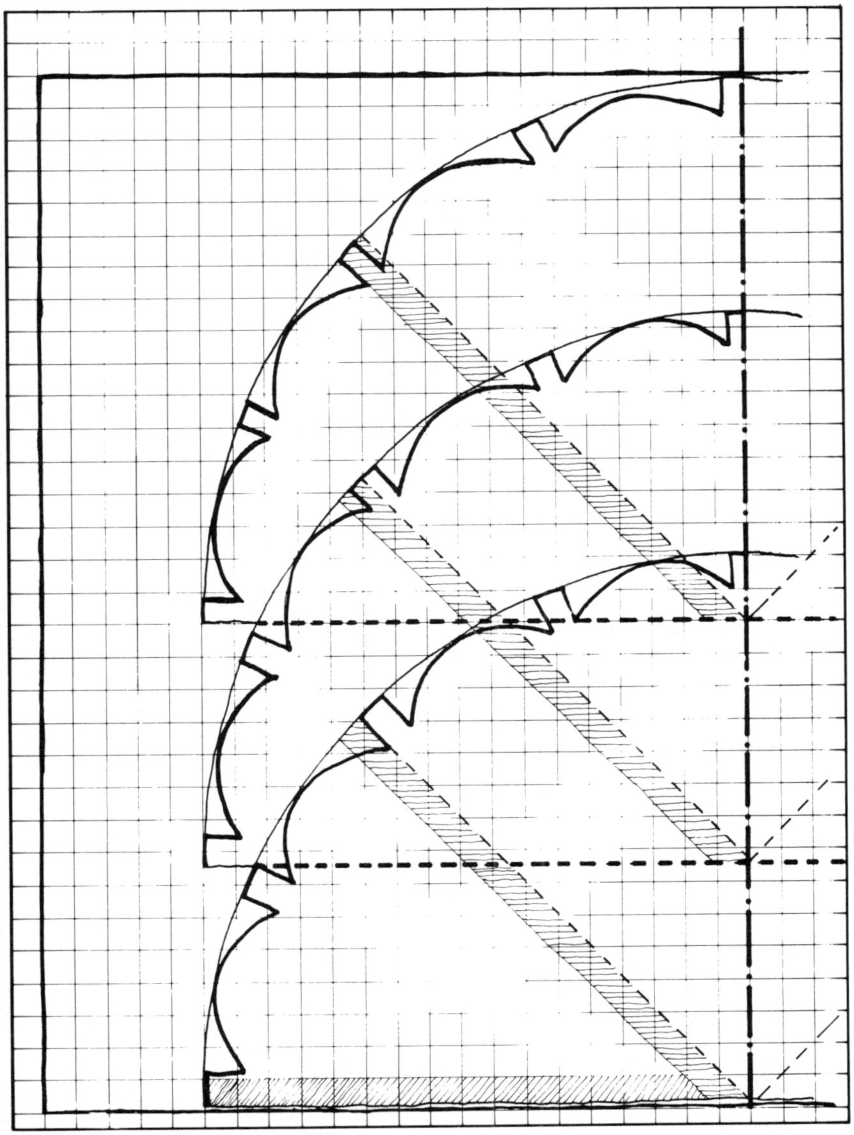

WORKING GRID
The scale is about four grid squares to 1 inch. Note the centre line, the layered structure of the three fans and the shading that indicates the glue points. As the card is opened and closed, so the unglued fan sections pop in and out.

CONSIDERING THE PROJECT

Start by having a look at the various working drawings, and see how we have chosen to work a pop-up design that relates to characteristic Art Deco imagery. That is to say, the half circles or fans have been intentionally worked so that in design terms they are Art Deco look-a-likes. At first sight this project may look a little tricky, but not a bit of it. If you study the details you will see how all the making stages relate to very simple and straight forward paper craft techniques. Have a look at the cutting and folding details and see how the three half circles have been folded and quartered so that there are four identical 45 degree wedges. Note how the half circles are placed and glued so that when the card is folded or opened, the pop-up is operated by the card hinge.

It's worth noting that when we initially considered this project, we wanted the card to be designed so that when it is opened, the recipient, is, as it were, presented with a naturalistic bunch of flowers. However, see how, in the design process, we reworked our preconceived notions, and decided to have stylized flower imagery. Take a ruler to the working drawing and see how the card has been designed so that it relates to a popular size – 9.½ × 6.½ inch envelope. Finally, before you make firm decisions as to your design, visit a museum and see if you can have a close up look at Victorian paper cut theatres, go to a good modern bookshop and see what current pop-up books and cards are like, and take a trip to the nearest specialist paper shop and see what's on offer.

Note – if you like the idea of this project, but want to go for a quick and instant card, consider using motifs cut from printed wrapping papers.

TOOLS AND MATERIALS

For this project you need, a piece of good quality white or coloured card, we have chosen to work with a piece 11 × 8 inches, you also need, four pieces of good quality coloured paper at 9 × 5 inches, coloured pencils, tracing paper, pencil and ruler, a compass, a special metal card-cutting straight edge, a set square, scissors, a craft knife, a special quick-dry paper-to-paper adhesive, a cutting board, and a deal of scrap workout paper.

DESIGNING

When you have gathered together all your tools and materials, then take a sketch pad and your workout paper and make a series of experimental try-outs. Taking into account such pointers as – the size of the card in relationship to the envelope, the bulk of paper within the folded card, the complexity of the folds, and such like, see if you can improve on or maybe completely modify our design. Consider having naturalistic flower imagery, or perhaps several pop-ups.

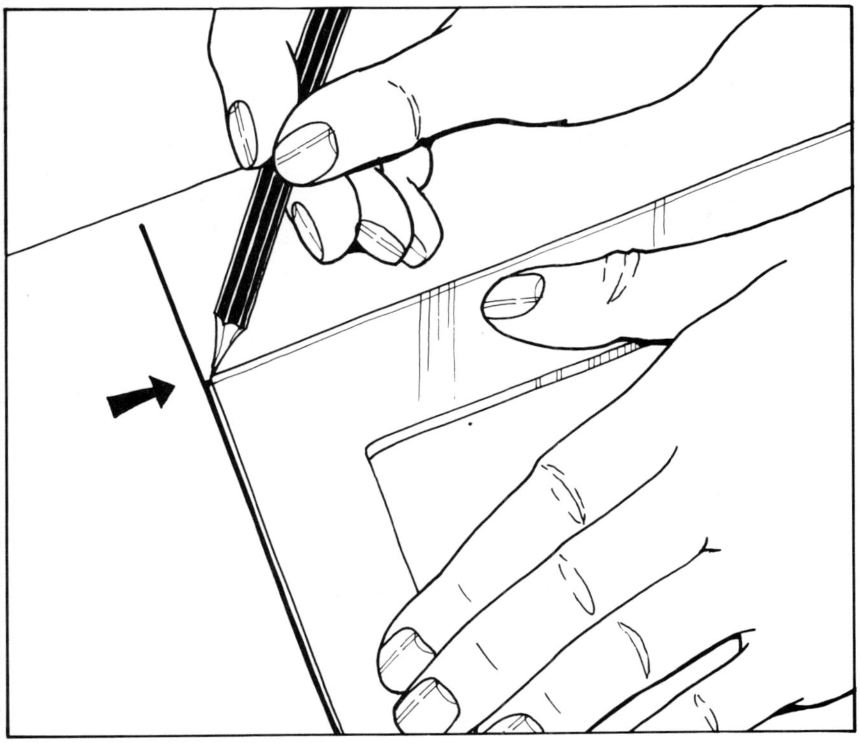

Use a pencil, set-square and a straight edge to achieve a card that, when open, measures about 11 × 8 inches. The measurements and angles are critical, so be sure to check.

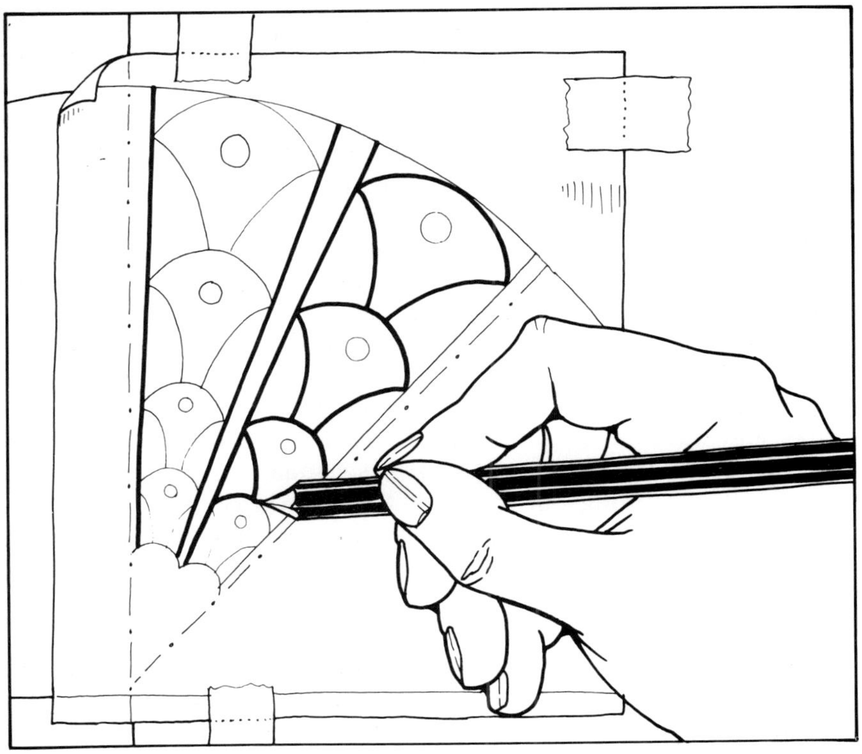

When you have drawn up a good design, pencil press transfer the traced lines through to the working face of your card.

TOP LEFT *Place the cut and coloured fan face down on the worksurface and fold it in half.*
TOP RIGHT AND BOTTOM LEFT *Fold the card back on itself so that you have a four-thickness wedge.*
BOTTOM RIGHT *Apply a little glue to the shaded area.*

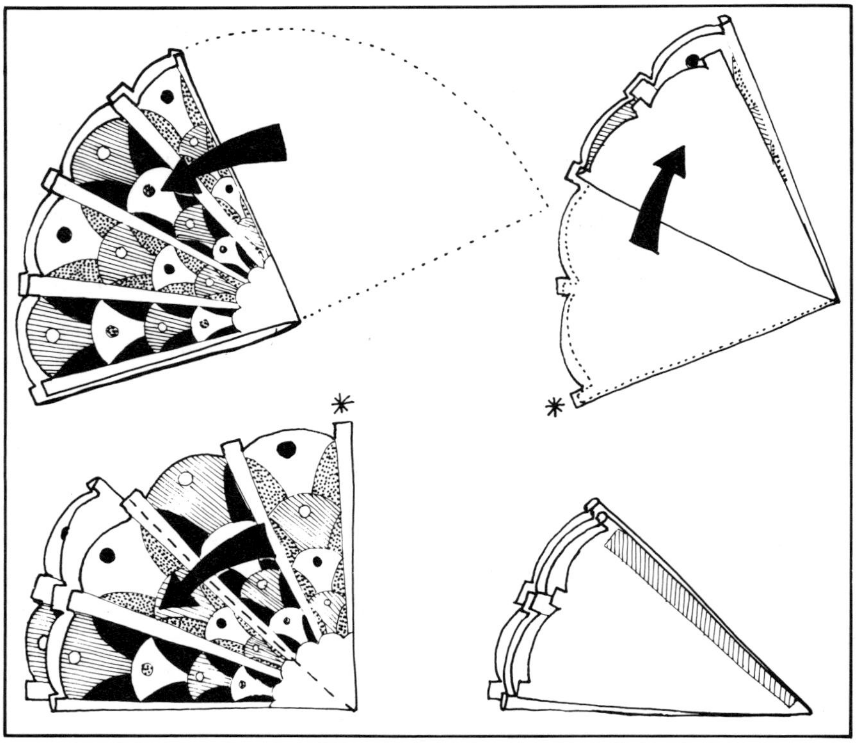

When you have considered all the design and technique details, then sit back with your sketch pad and workout paper, and make a full size prototype. Don't at this stage cut and colour the pop-up, but rather finalise the overall size of the card, the size and number of the inter-card half circles, the complexity and the position of the inter-card folds, and the size and placing of the cover motif. Note – with this particular greetings card, the cover motif is of secondary importance, in fact it need to do no more than set the scene for the inside pop-up. This being so, you might have a flat motif on the cover, or perhaps just a personalized name or title.

CUTTING THE CARD

When you have made a full-size prototype, then take a sheet of tracing paper and trace off the lines of your master design. Now take your card, cutting board, measure, pencil, set-square and straight edge, and set about cutting out the 11 × 8 inch card cover. Use the set-square to achieve will set out right-angle corners. This done, measure, crease and fold the card, so that you have a folded cover that measures 5.½ × 8 inches.

Note – make sure that your hands and the tools are completely clean, and if necessary, when you are folding the card, shield it with a sheet of clean paper.

MAKING THE COVER AND POP-UP MOTIFS

Take your four sheets of coloured paper, fix the compass to a radius of 4 inches, then strike off four 8 inch diameter half circles. This done, take the traced motif and pencil press transfer the lines of the design to the working face of the half circles. Now with your coloured pencils, line-in the design and block in the areas of colour. Have a look at the working drawings and see how our design fills out and further emphasises the classic Art Deco fan motif. When you have achieved four colour-worked fans, then take the scissors and fret the curved edges. That is to say, scissor work the edges so as to give the motif a more exciting visual impact.

Now take all four of the coloured and cut half circles and, piece at a time, place them face down on a clean working surface and start the folding. First fold the fan in half, then fold the resultant quarter circle back on itself so that you have a four-thickness wedge. If you have any doubts as to the working order, have a practice run with some scrap paper. Finally when you are sure that all is correct, then run your thumb or a tool along the folded edges of the paper and establish clean, crisp and accurate creases. You should now have four, coloured, cut and creased fans.

PUTTING TOGETHER

Clear your worksurface of all clutter, and set out the card cover, the four fans and your various tools and materials. Place the open cover on the worksurface. Now take one of the folded fans and smear a little adhesive on the edges, open the fan out making sure that the centre-lines of both the cover and the fan are well aligned, check that the top edge of the fan is just touching the card at top-centre, and

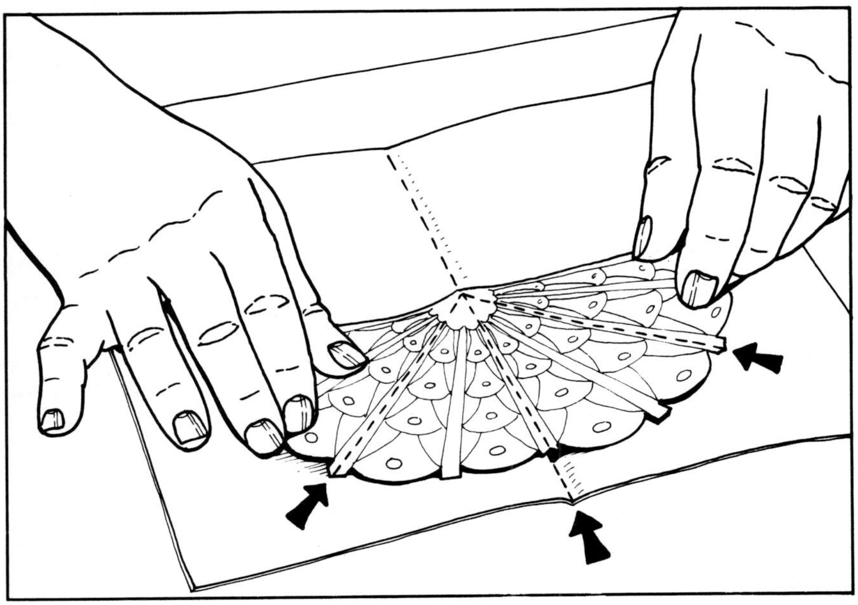

Working from the top of the card, align the fan with the card's centre line and press into position – do this with all three fans. Note the bottom fan will need a little glue along its bottom edge.

The cover motif needs to relate to the pop-up, see how the fourth fan can be used to make various interesting applique designs.

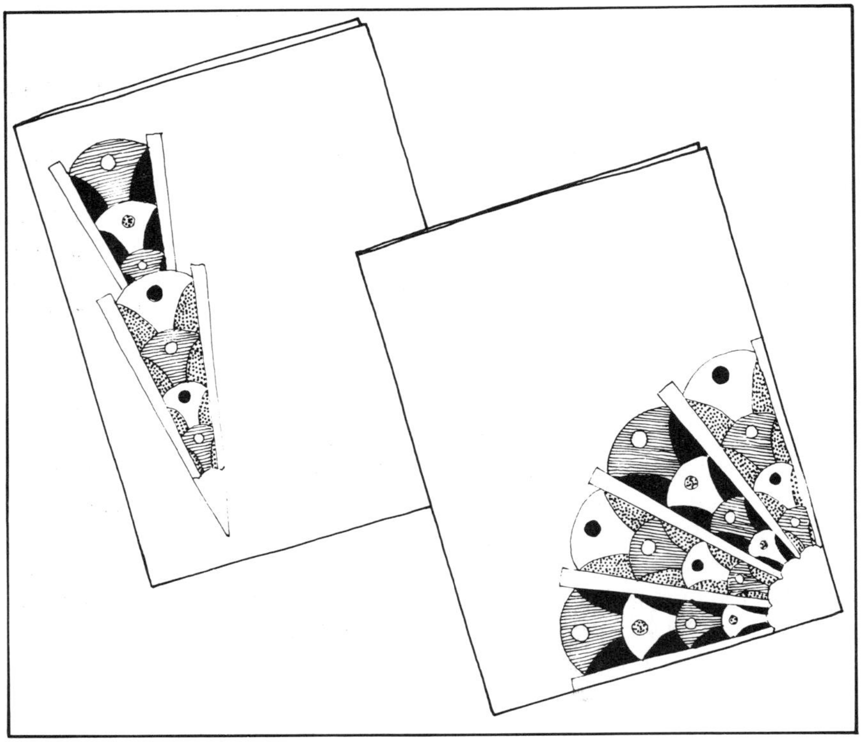

then finally place and press the fan into position.

Now have a look at the working drawings, check the position of the other two fans, then glue them down in like manner. Note – the last fan to be placed, that is the fan at the bottom of the card, also needs to be glue-fixed along its bottom edge. When the inside pop-up fans are in place, close the card then take the last fan and use it to decorate the cover.

The cover decoration can be as simple or as complex as you wish – the fan can be halved and reversed, the fan can be quartered and then the quarters overlapped, and so on, no matter, as long as the cover motif in some way adds to the total visual impact.

AFTERTHOUGHTS

When you are at the design stage, consider using a greater number of fans, say seven or eight – experiment with a prototype and maybe pierce and cut the layered fans so as to create a delicate lacy effect.

When you are placing and gluing the fans, make sure that all the centre lines are aligned, also be careful that you don't get glue on the pop-out part of the motif.

With a card of this character, the written message is best placed on the front cover.

Do not use water based pastes, go for one of the special paper-to-paper gums or adhesives – we favour an adhesive that is packaged in an easy-to-use 'lipstick' type container.

PROJECT EIGHT

'UNDER GLASS' DOOR PLATE

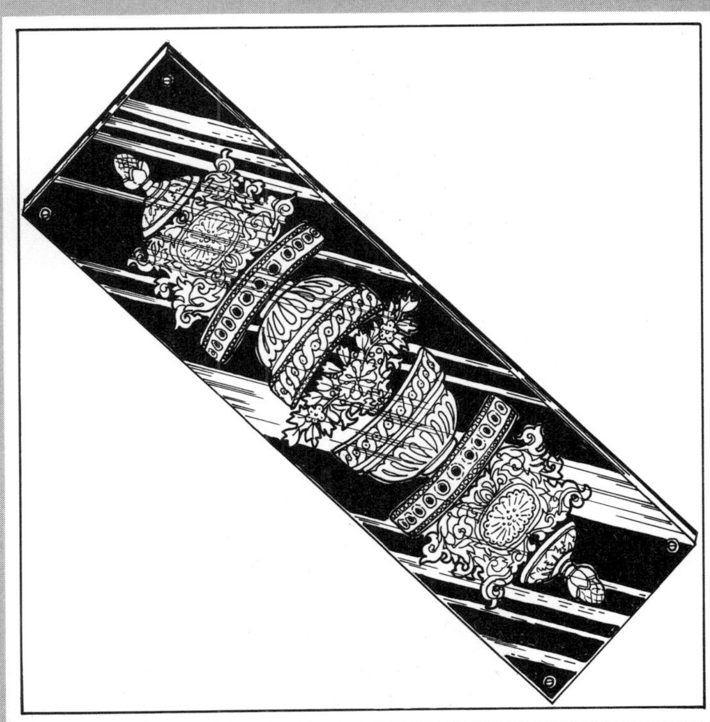

PROJECT PICTURE
The finished door plate.

INTRODUCTION

THOUGHTS ON THE PROJECT

Découpage is the art and craft of cutting, decorating and arranging paper prints, in such a way that they appear to take on another dimension. The craft has many faces; shadow découpages, where the cut-outs look to be three-dimensional, découpages under varnish, that is where découpages are used to decorate furniture and are worked in such a way that the embellishments look as if they have been inlaid or painted, and there are découpages under glass.

Of all these techniques, under glass Découpage is perhaps, at one and the same time, the easiest to work, the best starting point for beginners, and the most illusory. Découpage under glass simply

INSPIRATIONAL
Two door plate découpages – see how the coloured cut-outs have been put together so as to make a believable naturalistic scene.

means that instead of the prints being painstakingly glued, arranged and then repeatedly varnished, they are either stuck directly to the underside/inside of a clear glass object, or they are sandwiched between a sheet of glass and say a sheet of wood or card. This being so, an under glass découpage might take the form of a glass vase, where the whole vase interior is lined out with découpaged cut-outs, or it might be designed as a picture, that is with the découpage worked on the underside of a sheet of glass then the whole, backed, framed and mounted.

CONSIDERING THE PROJECT

Before you rush out and start buying your materials, stop awhile and

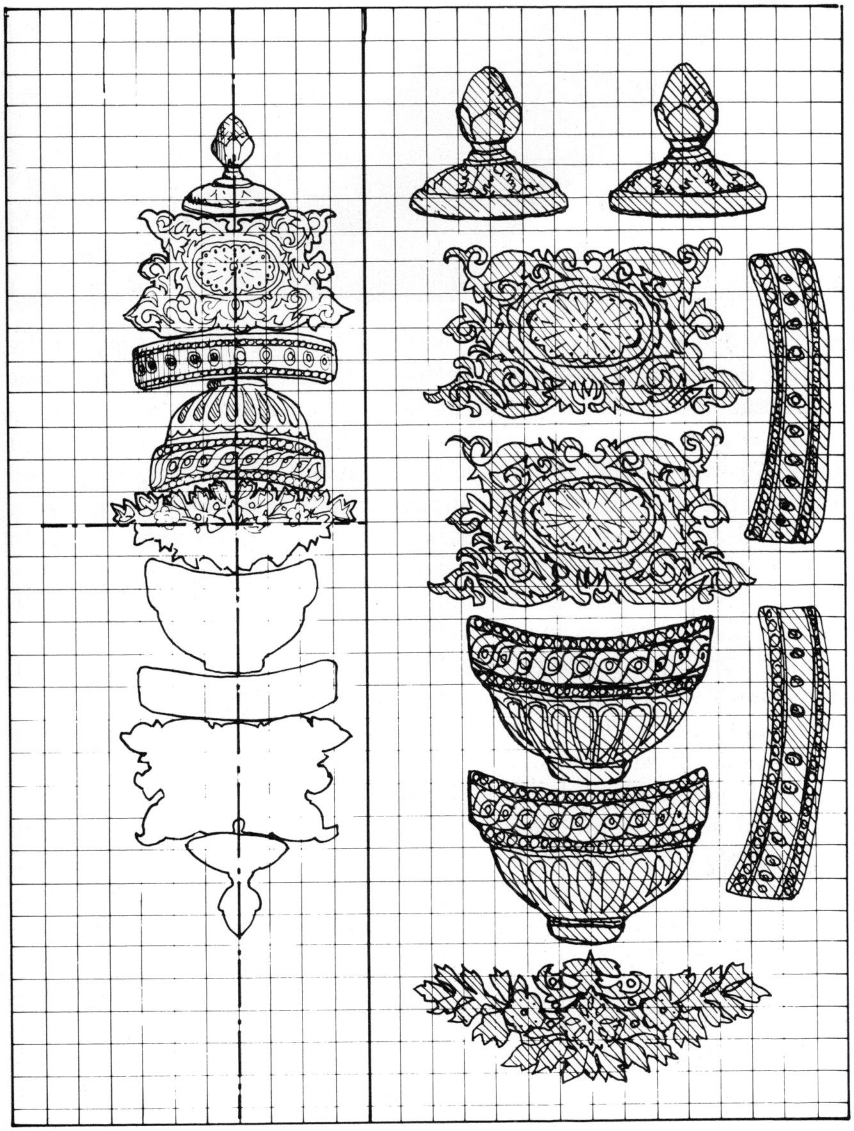

WORKING GRID
The scale is about four grid squares to 1 inch. When you start collecting your illustrations go for objects/images that are linked by a common scale, theme and colour quality – our gold and silver details were taken from an antiques magazine. You of course might prefer birds, flowers or whatever. Note – specialist craft shop sell special découpage quality prints that you can colour and tint.

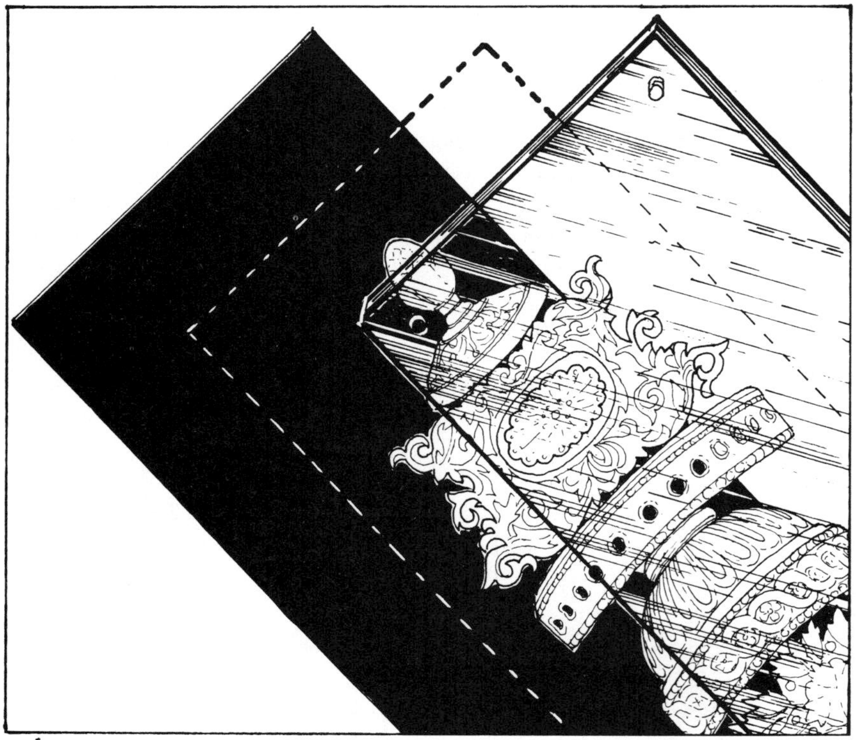

See how in effect the door plate is a sandwich that is made up of a sheet of ground paper – the découpage cut-outs, and a sheet of glass.

consider just what it is that you want to decorate. Have a look at the project details, and see how we have chosen to make a very basic traditional, decorative and functional piece of door furniture, that is to say, a glass plate, a plate that is fixed onto the edge of the door nearest to the handle. Also have a look at the working drawings and see how the design of our découpage relates to a simple rectangular form and a collection of very basic magazine photographs. It might be as well at this stage, to research the project by visiting say a museum or perhaps a grand house of the eighteenth or nineteenth century. Get to see as many door plates as possible, and note how variously they are made of brass, silver, glass, or ceramic, and in all shapes and sizes. Take measurements and note how, depending on the period and the type of house, doors have one or two plates, plates on both sides of all doors, and so on.

Now have a look at the project details, and the inspirational drawings, and see how the designs need to be worked around a strong theme; they might relate to your own illustrations of birds, actual embroidery, magazine cut-outs, antique porcelain door plates and so on. Consider the design theme, as illustrated, then adjust and modify the project so that it relates to your own needs. When you have settled on a theme, then make a series of exploratory design sketches, and start collecting suitable magazine clips. Note – it might be a good idea, at this early stage, to consider making door plates for the whole house – you can perhaps relate all the plates to a single grand design, and you can save money by buying the materials in bulk.

TOOLS AND MATERIALS

For this project you need, a well considered collection of magazine pictures, a bevel edged and drilled sheet of plate glass, see the working drawings, a sheet of good quality backing paper, a small pair of fine-point nail scissors, a special gum based paper-to-paper adhesive, a ruler, a metal straight edge, a scalpel, a cutting board, indian ink or water colours, brushes and such small items as newspaper and cloths. Note – you can use clear Perspex sheet, rather than glass, but better still, you might search around for a set of Victorian glass door plates.

CUTTING

When you have made a collection of magazine clips, and this could well involve all your friends and relations, then you can start the very relaxing business of sorting and cutting. Let's say then, that you have followed this project pretty closely and that you have collected together magazine photographs of anything and everything that relates to the gold, silver and brass metalware theme. You have pictures of antique cups, pictures of the crown jewels and so on. First sort through the material, and group it according to type, style, colour, and size. As for the actual cutting, best to use a small pair of nail scissors, ones that have fine points and slightly curved blades – it's simple enough, as long as the scissors are sharp. Hold, manoeuvre and guide the paper to be cut with one hand, and work the scissors

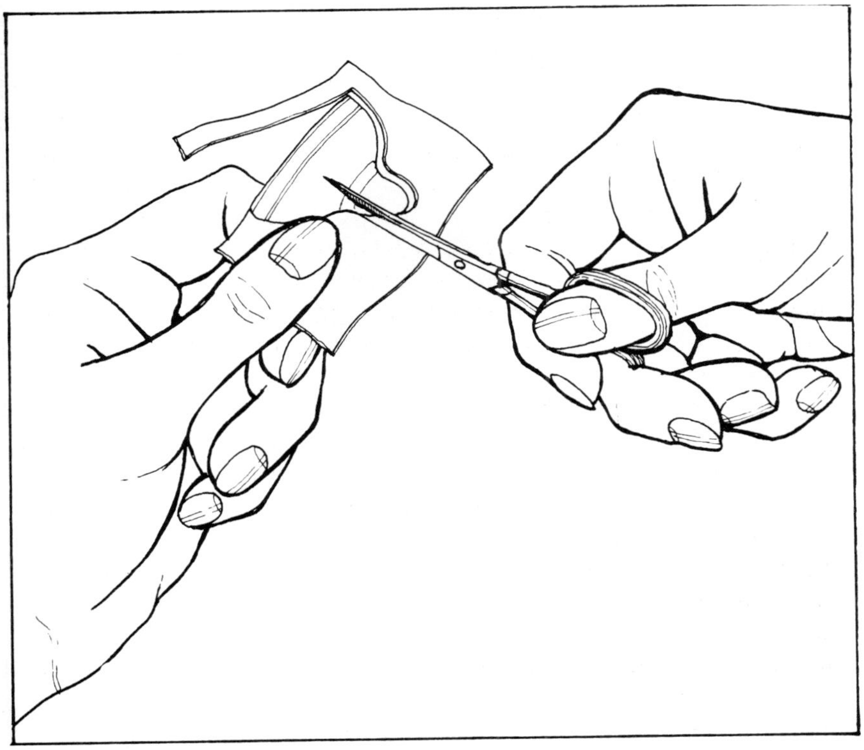

Cut out your chosen prints or photographs with a small pair of fine-point scissors – make sure that each and every piece is perfectly worked.

When you have a good design layout, take the cut-outs, a piece at time, and very carefully smear their backs with glue, work from centre to edges.

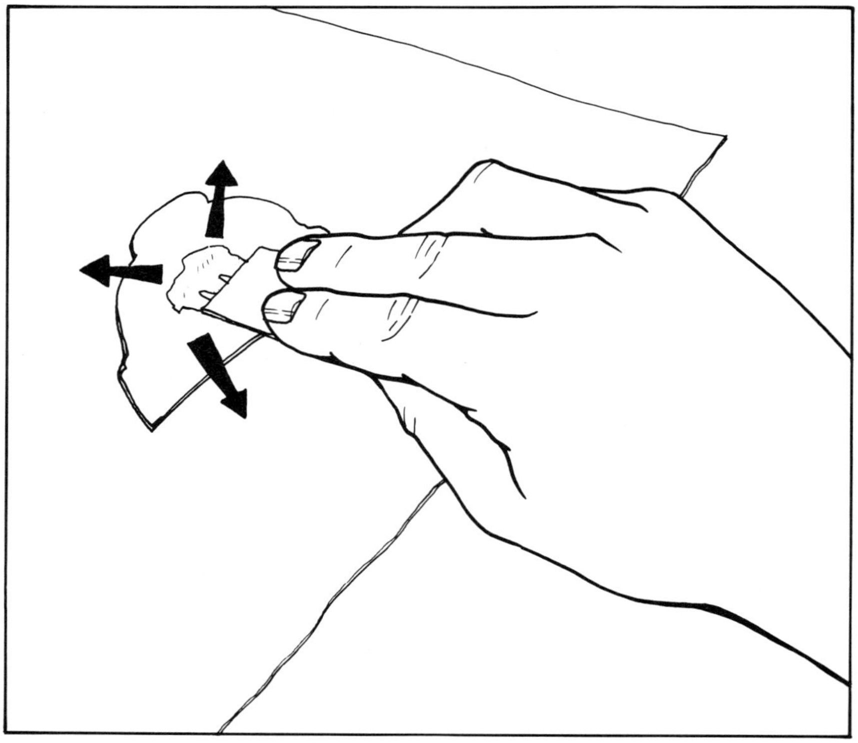

Place, position and press the glued cut-outs on your chosen ground.

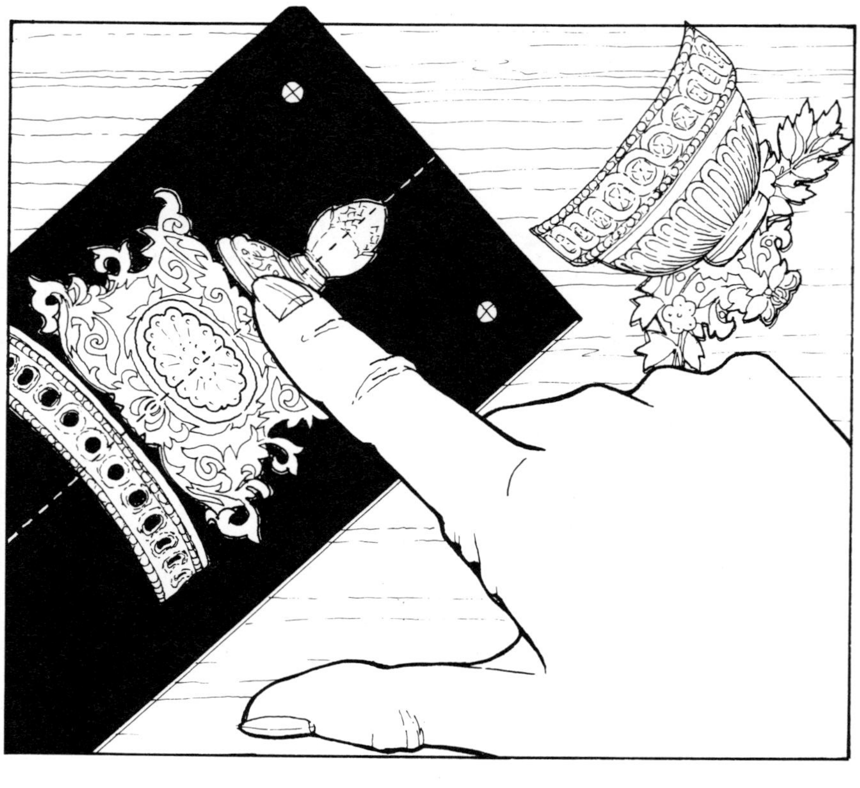

with the other. Piece at a time, decide which part of the photograph you want to keep, then cut away the bulk of unwanted paper.

This done, start cutting out the small profiles, trying all the while to keep the cutting action smooth, and aim for a cut edge that is sharp, and clean. Trim away all fuzzy and ragged areas. As each small unit is cut out, put carefully to one side and then go on to the next.

PREPARING THE GROUND

When you have cut out all the elements that are to make up the design, sit back with a measure, pencil and sketch book and decide on the size and colour of the ground. That is to say, try to link the cut-outs by mounting them on a carefully considered, contrasting or colour co-ordinated background. See how we have linked our cut-outs together by mounting them on a piece of slightly textured black card. You might choose a complete print, a sheet of gold foil, a piece of lace, or whatever.

When you have achieved what you consider to be a good arrangement, then measure the glass and cut the ground so that it is just slightly smaller than the glass. So for example, if your glass is 3 × 10 inches, then aim to cut the ground so that it measures about 2.7/8 × 9.7/8 inches.

MOUNTING THE CUT-OUTS

When you have chosen the ground and cut it to size, take your

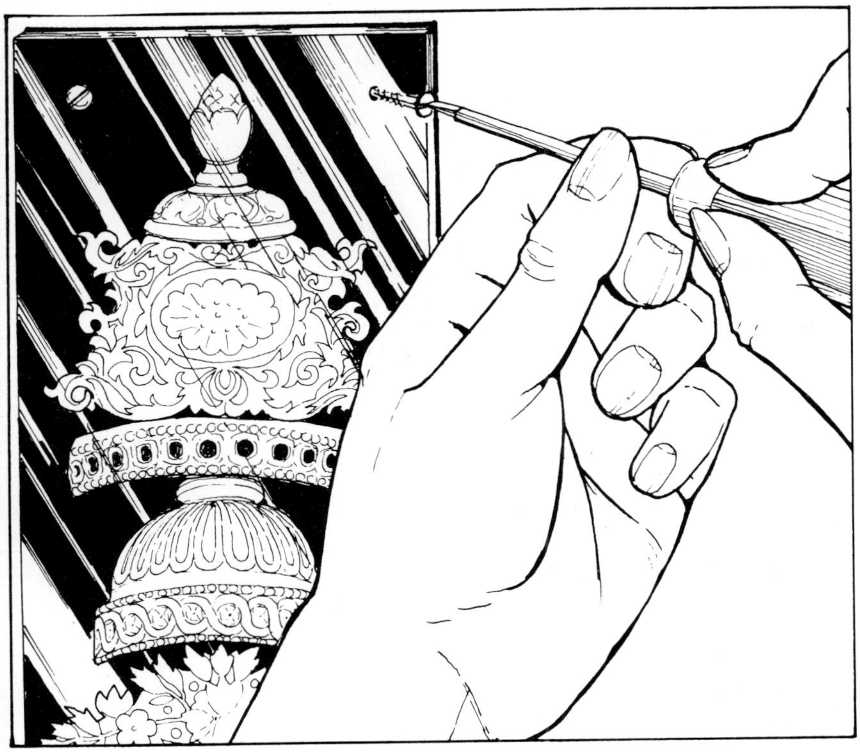

Finally screw the plate on the door.

découpage cut-outs, and make several trial arrangements – experiment with alternative placings. Now with the greatest of care, and only working one element at a time, smear a little gum on its back, and set it on the ground. Do this with all the cut-outs, then, while the gum is still flexible, fiddle around until the design is as you have planned. When all the cut-outs have been well placed, then decide whether or not the ground needs to be adjusted or modified. For example when we set out our clips on the black background, they looked, in design terms, not only to be slightly at odds with the ground, but also with each other. This being so, we took a fine point brush and indian ink, and actually lined in the photograph so that visually and texturally, the design looked to be a total, unified whole.

Finally when you have what you consider to be a successful découpage, polish the glass, sandwich the découpage between the door and the glass, drive home the screws, and the job is done.

AFTERTHOUGHTS

When you are choosing your magazine clips, be they pictures of ornamental metalwork, birds, butterflies or whatever, try, if possible, not only to link them in terms of colour, but also to go for photographs that are of a similar scale.

Make sure that you use the correct paper-to-paper, or fabric-to-paper, adhesive.

If, when you are cutting out the clips with the scissors, you come across a passage that is difficult to work, try using a fine-point scalpel – long curves, straight edges and small 'windows', are all best worked with a knife.

PROJECT NINE

DECORATING A BOX

PROJECT PICTURE
A box with an overlapped, layered and varnished découpage decoration – découpages of this character need to be given at least ten coats of varnish. Note – some modern découpage workers favour a single thick coat of resin.

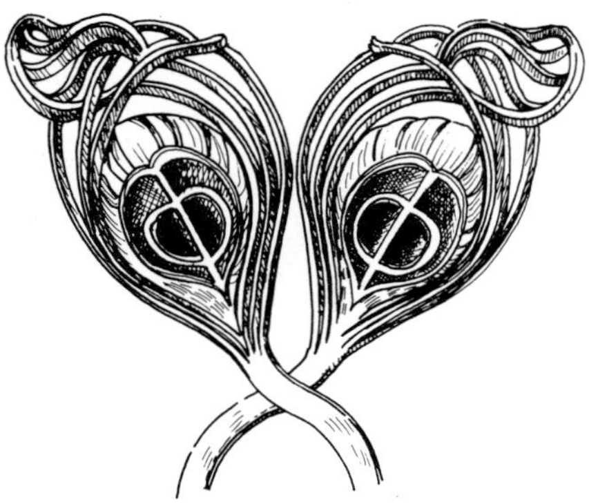

INSPIRATIONAL
A silver and enamel hairpin dated 1900, you could well choose to use such a picture/print. Our chosen design relates to Art Nouveau imagery, decide on your theme and then search around for suitable material.

INTRODUCTION

THOUGHTS ON THE PROJECT

Découpage under varnish is the art, craft or process, of decorating a surface with small shapes or illustrations cut from paper. That is to say, illustrations are worked, or prints are chosen, the material is then coloured and cut out, the cut-outs are glued onto an item, and finally, the découpage is covered with twenty or so coats of varnish. The end result of all this cutting colouring, gluing and varnishing, is a decorative feature that looks as if it has been painstakingly painted, inlaid, or lacquered. Indeed it is more than likely that you have seen or even handled a piece of under varnish découpage and taken it to be painted or lacquered. It's fair to say, that the technique is generally so misunderstood, or just not appreciated, that many museum items that are described as being hand painted, are in fact examples of antique découpage. And of course eighteenth century découpeurs, worked their craft with the very express intention of imitating the more expensive wares.

About that time, it was fashionable to have Chinese lacquered furniture, or furniture decorated with hand painted motifs, but then, as now, not everyone could afford the real thing, so canny furniture makers developed a technique of printing sheets of motifs, colouring them, cutting them out, sticking the cut-outs to the furniture and then varnishing them over. In fact the craft of Art Povero, as it came to be called, or poor mans lacquer, was so successful, that it soon became

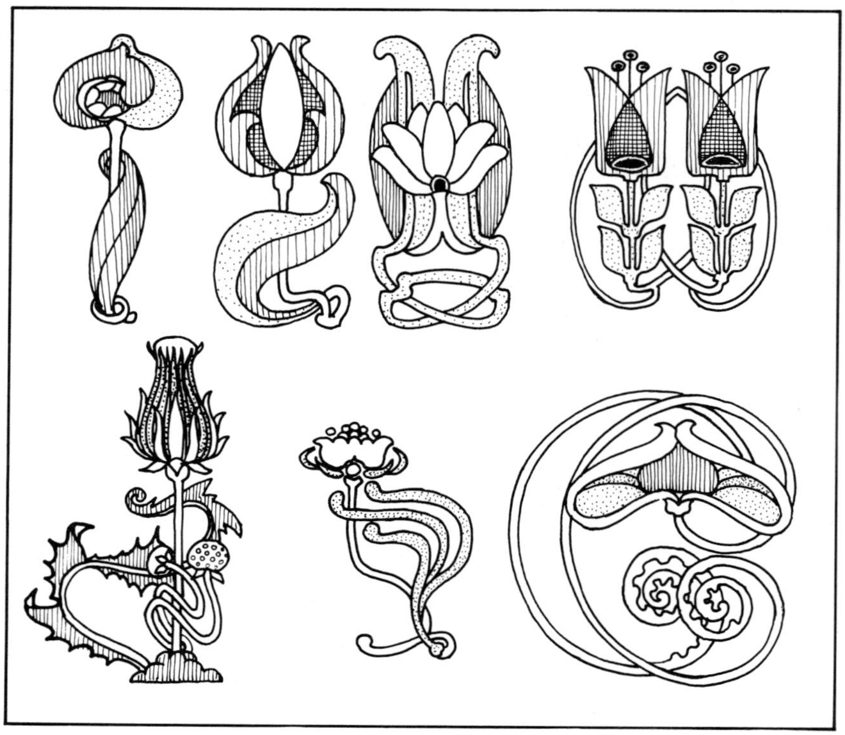

more popular than the hand painted work it imitated.

CONSIDERING THE PROJECT

Découpage under varnish is a beautifully flexible technique, and with a minimum of expense, and a little care, it is possible to totally transform the most ordinary item. An old box, a chair, a mirror surround, a tea tray, and such like, can all be successfully découpaged. And as for what cut-outs should be used for the choice is of course unlimited. Eighteenth century découpeurs favoured classical designs, architectural backdrops, garlands, swags and cherubs, whereas Victorian craftsman, tended to use everything and anything from magazine clips, through to stamps, letters, pieces of sheet music and photo-

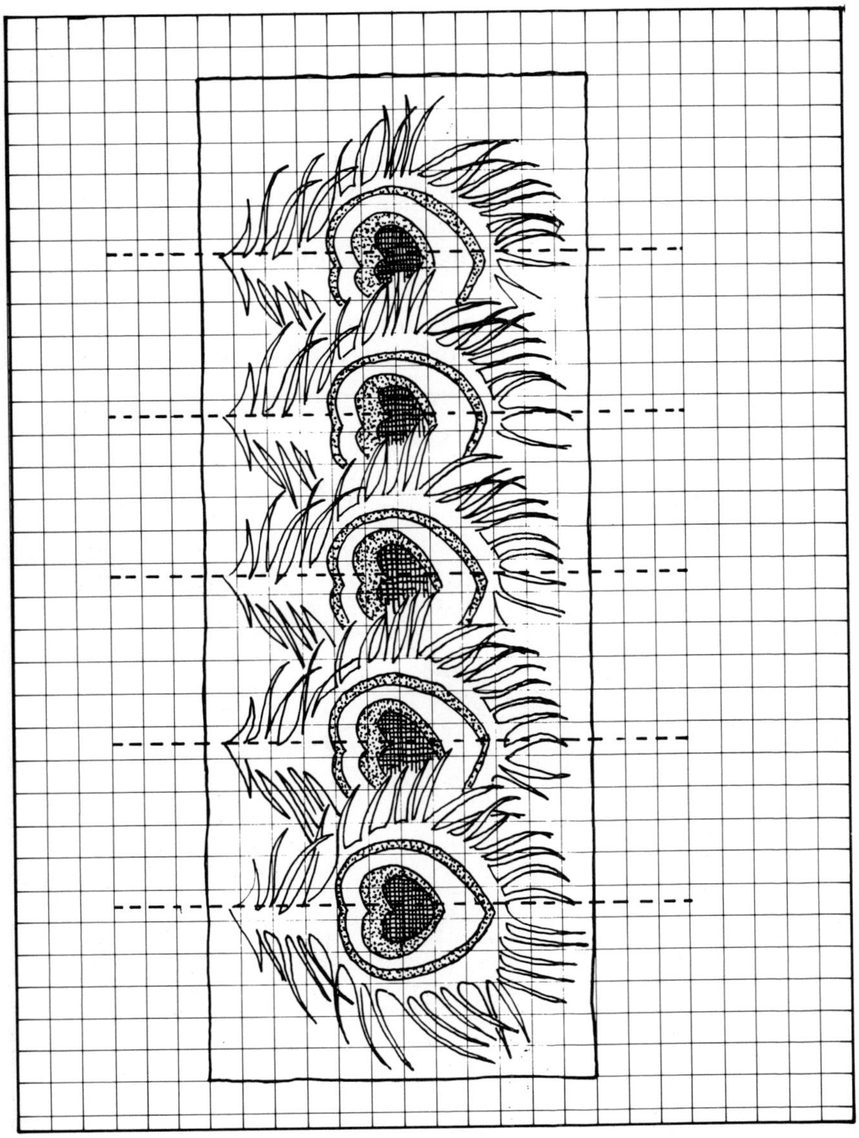

WORKING GRID
The scale is about four grid squares to 1 inch. Once you have chosen your cut-outs and the object to be découpaged, then mark out the area to be decorated. See how we have chosen to overlap the cut-outs.

graphs. If it's printed on paper, then it has découpage potential.

Now have a look at the working drawings and the various inspirational illustrations, and see how we have chosen to decorate a very ordinary white wood pencil box with motifs cut from wrapping paper. If you are looking for inspiration, take a trip to a museum and get to see either pieces of eighteenth century découpage decorated furniture, or perhaps better still search out examples of Victorian scrapwork découpage. Finally start a collection of prints and illustrations – prints from old books, modern and period wrapping paper, greetings cards, packaging labels, magazine clips, photographs, theatre programmes and so on – these all have découpage potential.

TOOLS AND MATERIALS

For this project you need, the item to be découpaged, a selection of suitable prints, a sketch pad, a pencil and ruler, coloured pencils, a pair of small curved-bladed nail scissors, or a pair of fine-point surgical scissors, white PVA glue, (note that PVA looks milky but dries clear), a can of traditional yacht varnish, brushes, turps, fine grade glass paper, newspaper, and throw-away containers.

COLOURING THE PRINT

Start by searching out an item to be decorated. This might be a wooden box, a tray, a table, a cupboard, or whatever. When you have decided

Shade in one side of the motif with a soft pencil.

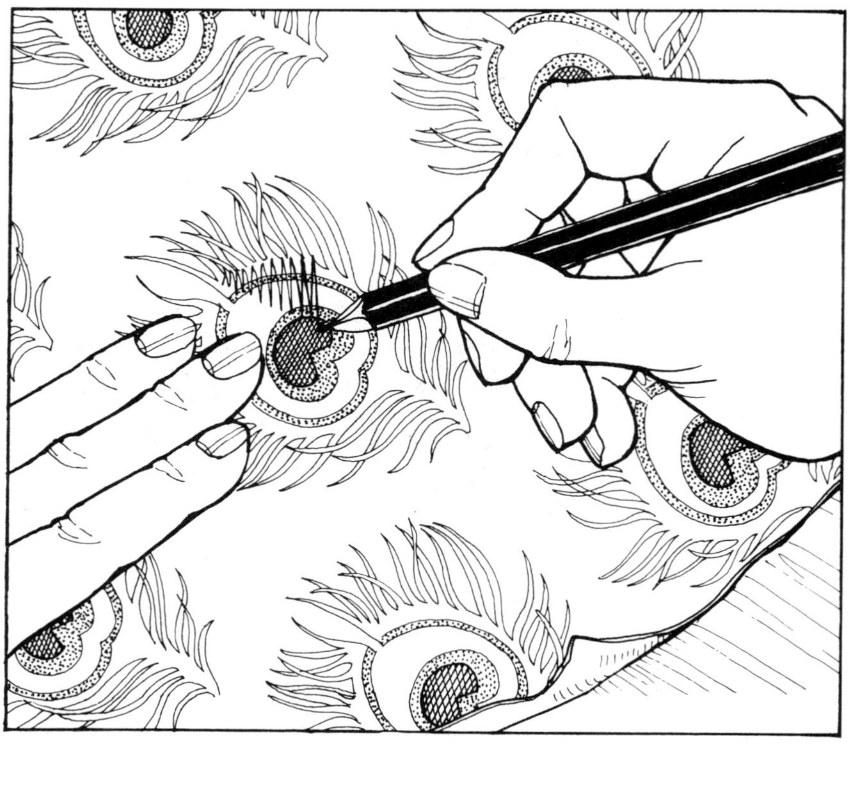

what it is that you want to decorate, then go through your print collection and select what you consider to be a suitable print/s. Now have another look at working drawings and see how we have chosen to decorate a pencil box with a modern wrapping paper motif, a feather motif printed in green and gold. When you have chosen your print or prints, then make decisions as to whether or not they need to be fully coloured or just toned.

This done, support your print on a firm soft grained surface, something like a sheet of card will do just fine, then set about working the motifs with the coloured pencils. Don't try to work dense colours and tones, but rather go for soft and subtle shades and delicate tints. Finally, use slightly denser colours and soft lead pencils to line in hard edges, shadows and points of emphasis. Aim to colour and tone your chosen print/s so that the motifs look to be rounded, to have three dimensional depth, and to be in partial shadow. See how we have delicately pencil shaded the feather designs so as to create the illusion, when they are overlapped, that there is real depth and space.

CUTTING THE PRINT

When you have coloured and toned your print, then comes the very soothing and relaxing business of cutting – no noise or fuss, just you, the print, and the scissors. If you are a beginner, then it's a good idea to have a trial run with a page cut from a magazine. Hold the paper to be cut in one hand and the small fine-point scissors in the other.

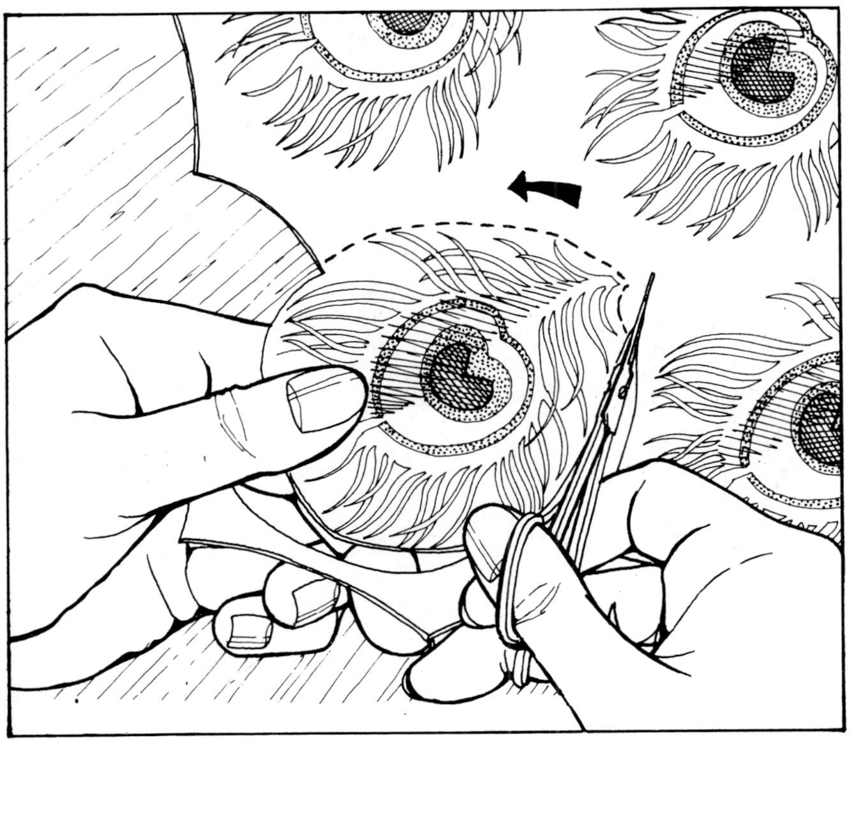

Cut out the motif and remove the bulk of the waste.

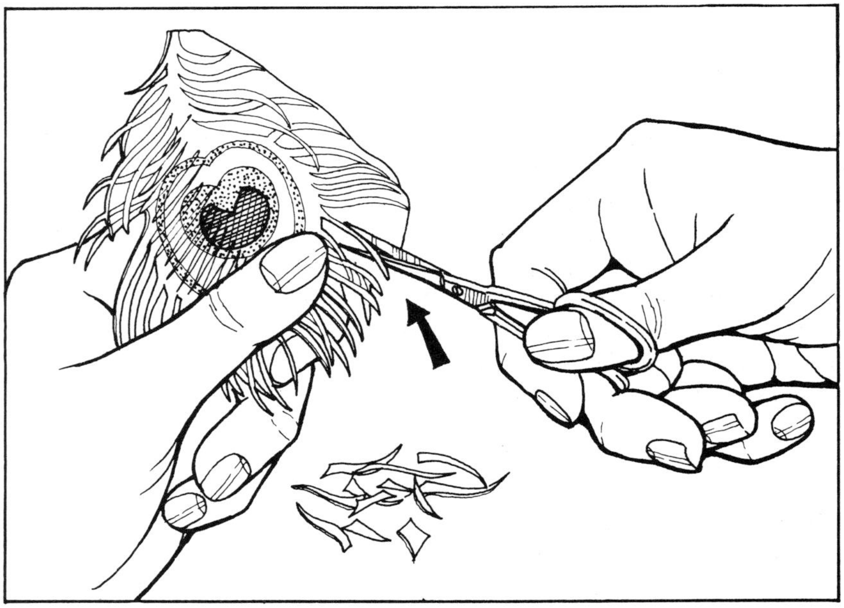

Use a pair of sharp fine-point scissors to cut out all the details.

Go at it slowly, all the time gently feeding the paper into the scissors. Don't move the scissor hand, apart that is from moving the blades up and down, bur rather keep manoeuvering the paper so that the scissors are always presented with the line of next cut. Once you can snip away with a steady relaxed smooth action, then start on your print. Tackle the inside 'windows' first, meaning little islands of paper that occur within a motif, and gradually work outwards from the centre. Be extra careful with large designs and linked patterns, because sometimes the weight of the paper drags and tears areas that are still to be

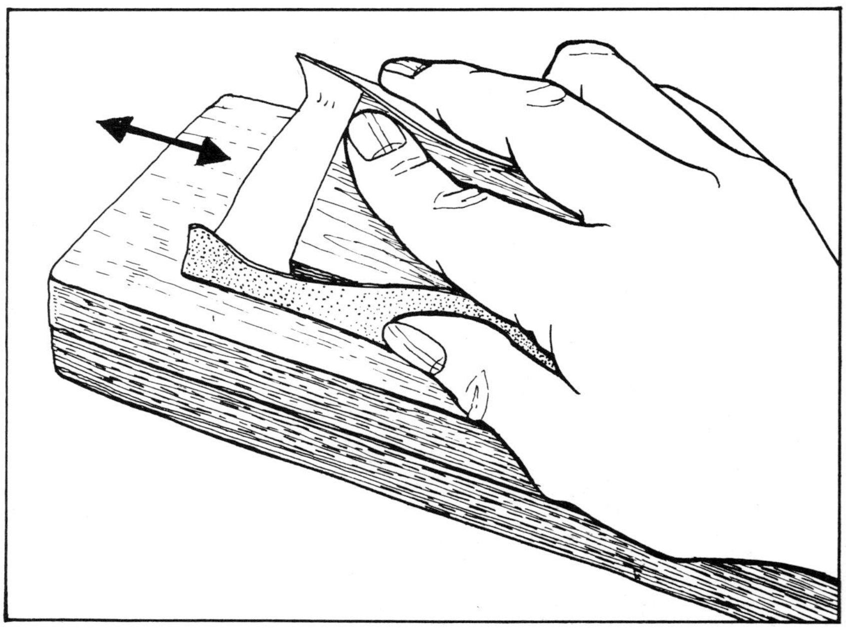

Rub down the box with a fine glass paper and lay on a single thin coat of varnish.

cut, so work on a tray or at a table.

PREPARING THE SURFACE TO BE DECORATED

When you have coloured and cut all your prints, put them out of harm's way. Now take your chosen item, and check it over making sure that it is structurally sound. Repair loose hinges, glue and clamp split areas, punch in proud nail heads, use a resin filler to make good dead knots or holes, and generally bring the item to a good condition.

This done, take the graded glass papers and rub down the surface of the wood until it is smooth and free from paint, stains, old varnish and such like. Finally wipe the wood over with a spirit soaked cloth, then lay on a single thin coat of varnish.

GLUING THE PRINTS

When the varnish is dry, set out all your tools and materials, establish where on the box the cut-outs are to be placed and arrange them in order of working. Now take up the first cut-out, dribble a little PVA glue onto the box, add a few drops of water, smear and work the mixture into the surface, and then place and position the cut-out. And so you continue, gradually gluing and placing, until you have built up the design. Finally when you are happy with the whole arrangement, put the box to one side to dry out.

VARNISHING

When the PVA glue is completely dry, and this might take anything from twenty four to fourty eight hours, make sure the cut-outs are

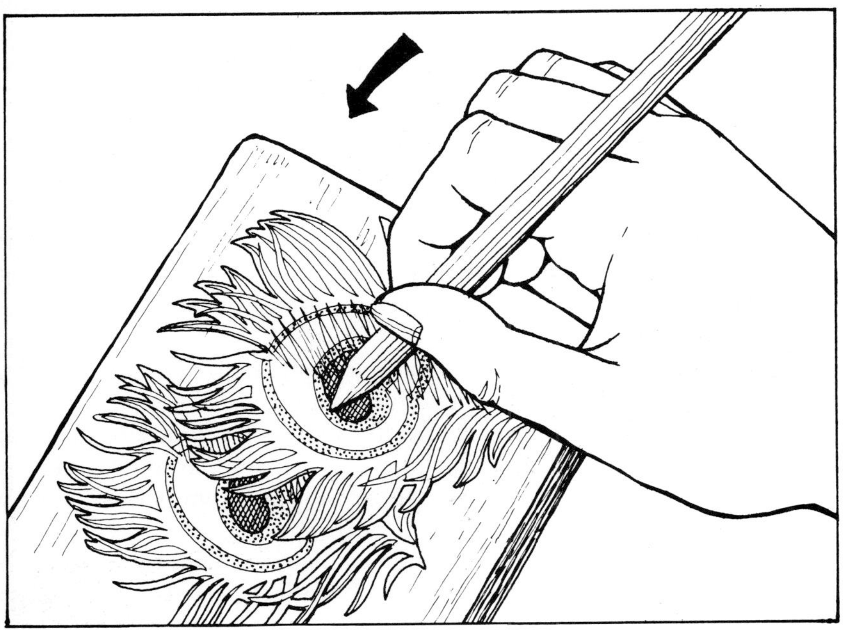

Once the varnish is dry, dribble a little PVA glue on the box and the use a pointed stick to slide the cut-outs into position.

Finally, when the cut-outs are all in place and the glue is dry, lay on at least ten coats of varnish. Note, for a perfect finish, use a fine glass paper to rub down between coats.

well and truely glued down, then take a soft haired brush and lay on another coat of varnish. And so you proceed, making sure that one coat of varnish is touch dry, laying on another coat, waiting until that is dry, and so on, until you have brushed on between ten to twenty coats.

When the penultimate coat of varnish is hard and dry, take the finest glass paper and cut the varnish back so that the whole item feels to be smooth and unstepped. Finally, wipe the box over with a spirit soaked cloth, and lay on another coat of varnish.

AFTERTHOUGHTS

If you want your découpaged box to be coloured rather than left natural, just prepare the box as described, but then instead of laying on a thin varnish prior to gluing, lay on your chosen base colour – use a matt paint.

If one or other of the varnish coats looks to be wrinkled, don't panic, just continue varnishing and they will disappear.

If the varnish goes bloomy, that is to say it looks cloudy or opaque, then you are working in an atmosphere that is too damp or cold.

Between coats of varnish, make sure that your item is dust free by wiping it over with the spirit soaked cloth.

Some découpage workers lay on ten coats of varnish, others reckon to put on at least twenty – aim to varnish until the print-to-wood step disappears.

PROJECT TEN

JAPANESE ORIGAMI BASKET

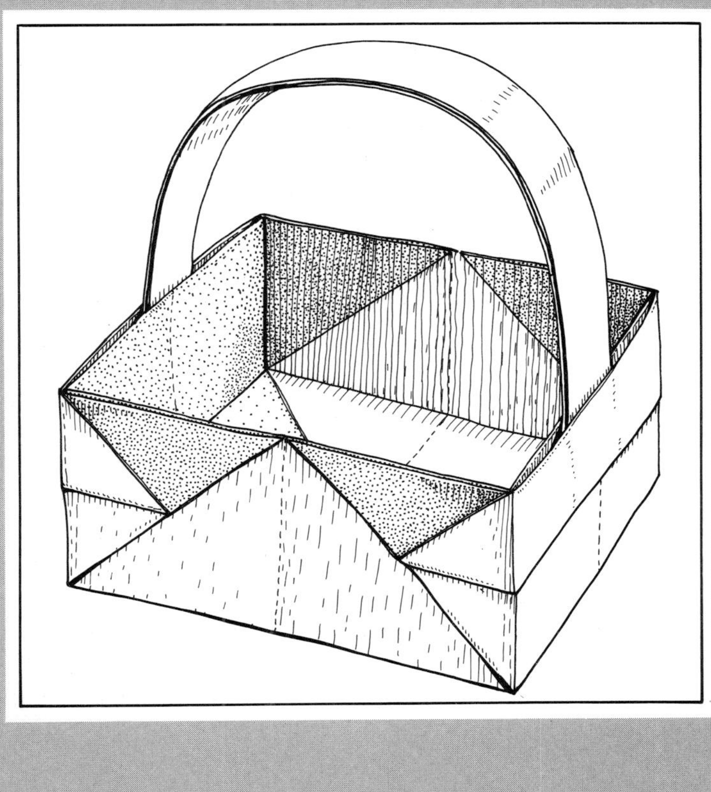

PROJECT PICTURE
A traditional Japanese Origami basket – note the characteristic carefully ordered and folded structure.

INSPIRATIONAL
Origami basket and box forms are many and varied.

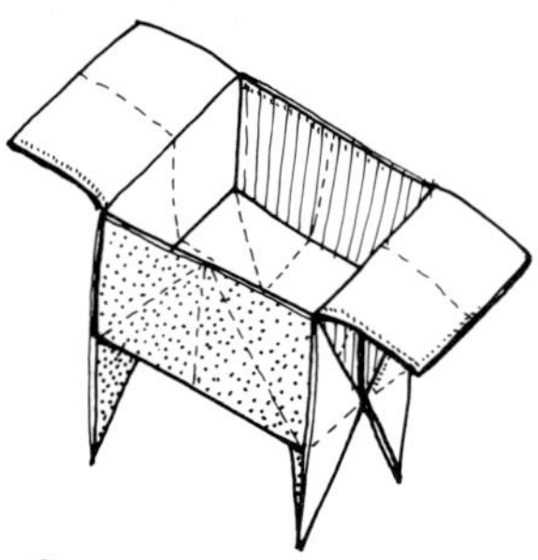

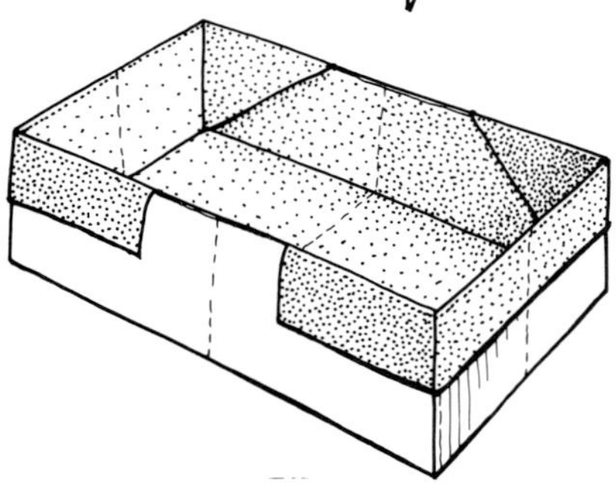

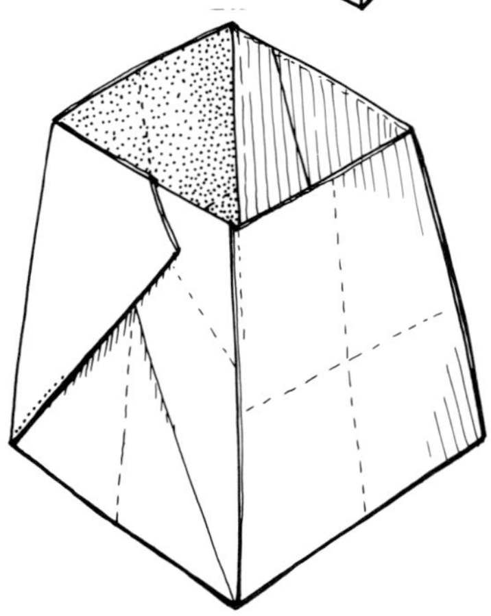

INTRODUCTION

THOUGHTS ON THE PROJECT

Origami is the art and craft of folding paper. The term comes from two Japanese words, 'ori' meaning folding, and 'kami' meaning paper. Very little is known about the roots of the craft, other than that there is written and illustrated manuscript evidence that suggests that it was practised about 900 hundred years ago at the Japanese imperial court. Originally the Japanese considered origami to be not an applied art, or even a functional craft, but rather they thought of it as being an intellectual exercise, an exercise akin to say making raku pottery tea ceremony bowls, or poetry. As to how and when the craft became generally popular, who knows? Perhaps it was when the more ordinary Japanese courtiers found it to be an amusing and elegant way of passing the time.

However, history and origins apart, origami is now practised by young and old the world over. Of course for a few paper foldering orientalists, it is still an intellectual mind cleansing meditational activity, but for the majority it is now no more or less than a pleasuresome, interesting, decorative, even functional craft. Certainly origami requires a deal of concentration, imagination and a light delicate touch, but that said, it is also a low-tec activity that can be worked with a minimum of tools and materials.

If you are searching for a mind soothing craft that can be worked on buses, on trains or in your lunch break, then Origami is for you. A square of clean firm crisp paper, and you are off!

CONSIDERING THE PROJECT

Before you start this project visit a specialist paper shop and get to see their stock of genuine Japanese Origami papers. See how the papers are variously coloured, patterned, grained, textured and of different weights and strengths. Don't settle for a quick glance at the papers, but rather take them up in your hands and feel out their character, that is to say, note how some papers are smooth hard and shiny, while others are soft, puffy, long fibred and altogether flaccid.

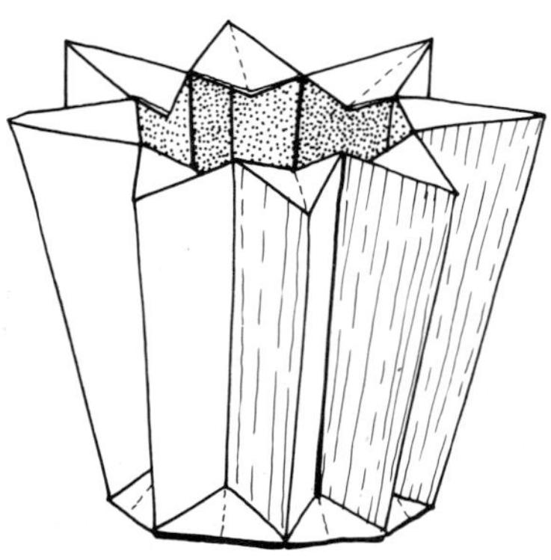

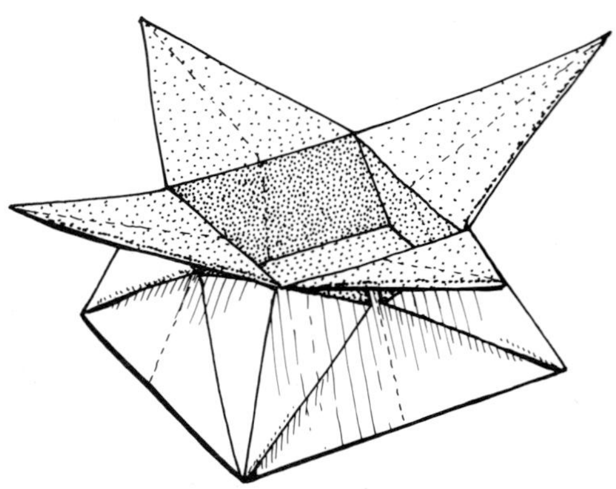

An ideal origami paper should be firm, it shouldn't stretch or flop over when it is being folded, and perhaps most important of all it shouldn't tear easily.

Now have a look at the working drawings and the various details and see how in this project accurate creasing is the essence. This being so, when you want to fold the paper, start by aligning the edges, check that all is correct and then firmly establish the fold with the back of your thumb nail, or a bone tool. As you are working, so there will be occasions when you will need to fold several thicknesses of paper. To do this, make an alignment, open the paper out and then pre-crease. The paper should hinge at the creases so that everything, as it were, falls into place. Finally, if you have any doubts as to your skills, or the suitability of your chosen paper, then have several trial

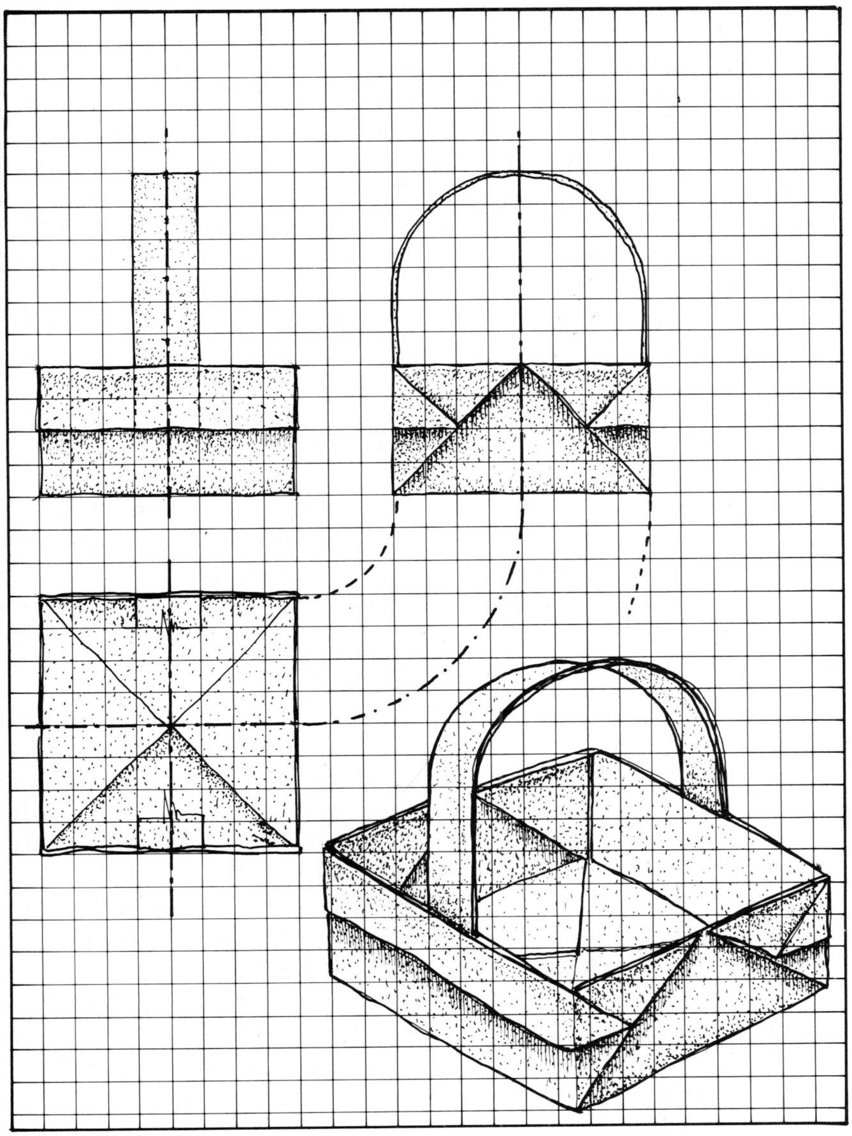

WORKING GRID
Scale to suit
It is critical that each and every fold and crease be well considered and accurate.

Take your perfectly square sheet of paper and fold diagonally.

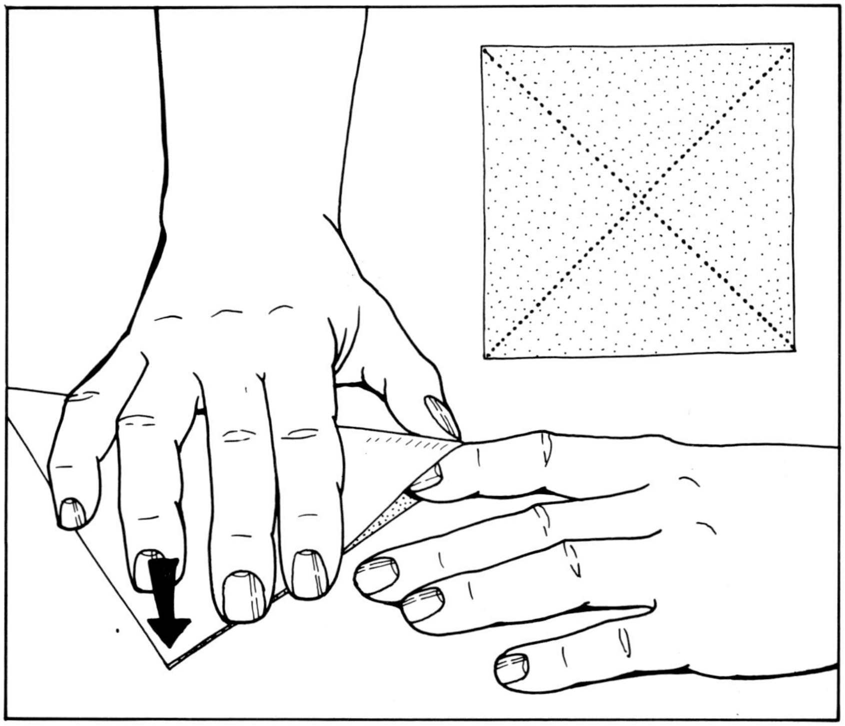

runs with off-cuts, experiment and doodle until you have some understanding of how paper behaves.

TOOLS AND MATERIALS

For this project you need, a clean worksurface, a cutting board, a steel rule, a spatula, a fine point scalpel, and two sheets of good quality Origami paper – one piece at 8 × 8 inches, and the other at 3 × 12 inches.

INITIAL CREASES AND FOLDS

Take your straight edged, right angled 8 × 8 inch piece of origami paper, and if it is coloured on one side decide which is to be the right side, and then place it face up and square on the worksurface. Now bring the top right corner towards you, and take it over towards the left side. Check that the top-left folded angle is halved, make sure the edges that meet are aligned, and then fold and crease the diagonal with the tool. Now open the paper out, and repeat this action, but this time take the top left corner of the paper down to the right side.

You should now have a square sheet of paper that has two beautifully creased diagonals. If this is so, open the paper out, and flip it over. Now halve, fold and crease the paper, first from top to bottom and then side to side, and again establish the creases with the tool. As you now look at the paper, once again opened out, so the diag-

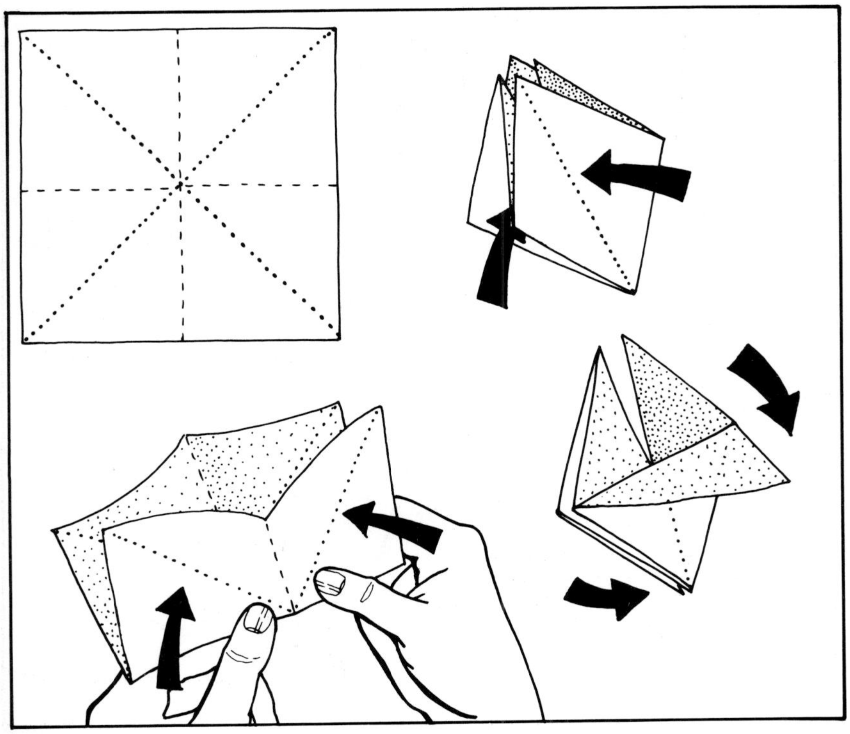

Now turn the sheet of paper over, fold and crease it from side to side, and then push it into a 'tulip' shape. Fold down the two top flaps.

nonals should look to be 'mountains' and the quarter creases to be 'valleys'.

THE QUARTER FOLDS

Take up the sheet of creased paper, hold it in both hands, then with a careful finger and thumb pinching action, push and fold it into the classic on-corner square. Stop a moment and see how the original piece of paper has been quartered so as to make a four-thickness square. Now hold the quartered form so that the open edges of the paper are uppermost, take the top corner, pull it down to meet the bottom corner, check that all is correct and well aligned, then fold and crease.

Repeat this action by turning the project over and folding the other side in the same way.

MAKING AND FIXING THE HANDLE

Take up the 3 × 12 inch strip, place it flat down on the worksurface and halve and crease it along its length. Now open the strip of paper out, tuck and fold the sides into the centre, and then fold and crease so as to make a four-thickness 12 inch long strip.

This next step is rather tricky, so be warned – place the main form on the worksurface so that the centre-to-corner opening is at the top, and position the strip handle so that it is aligned with the centre line.

Fold the 3 × 12 inch strip first side to centre and then fold to centre, align the folded strip with the 'tulip' flap and then roll up both the strip and the flap. Do this on both sides.

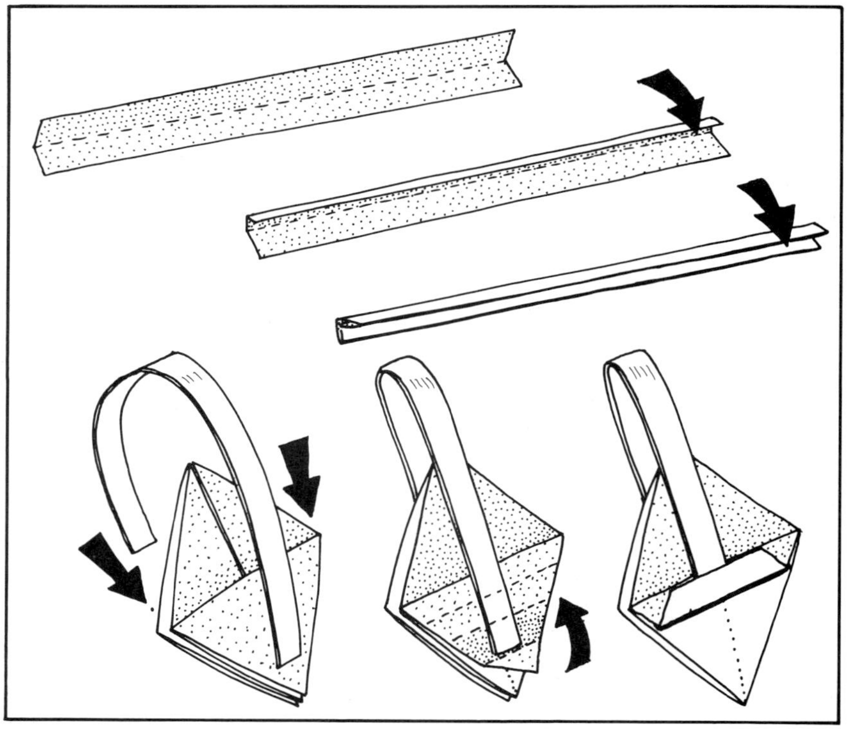

Tuck the sides of the 'tulip' inwards.

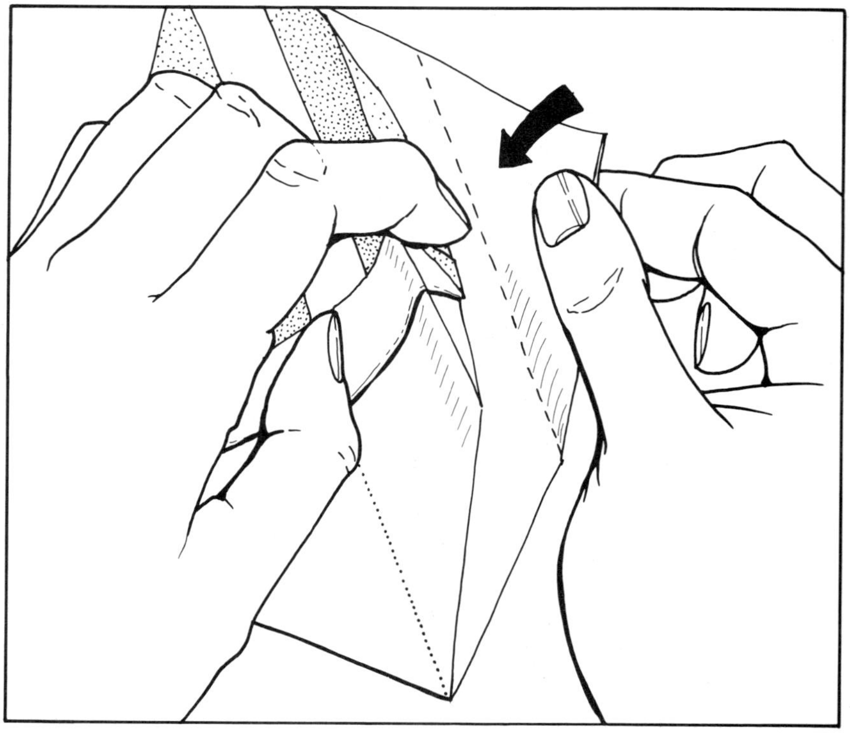

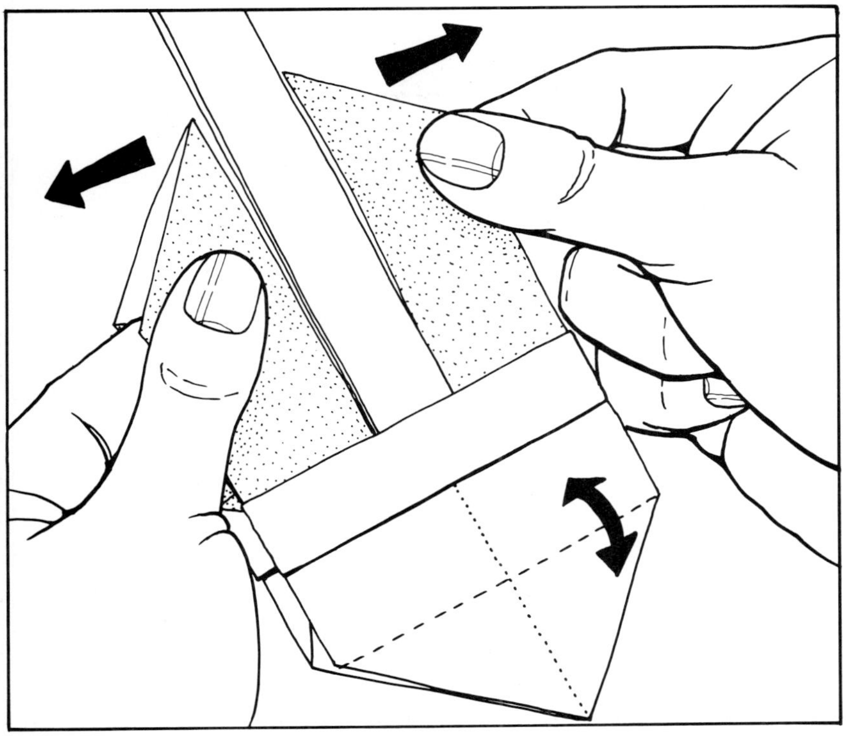

Crease the bottom 'point', do this both ways, then gently ease out the sides so as to make the box form.

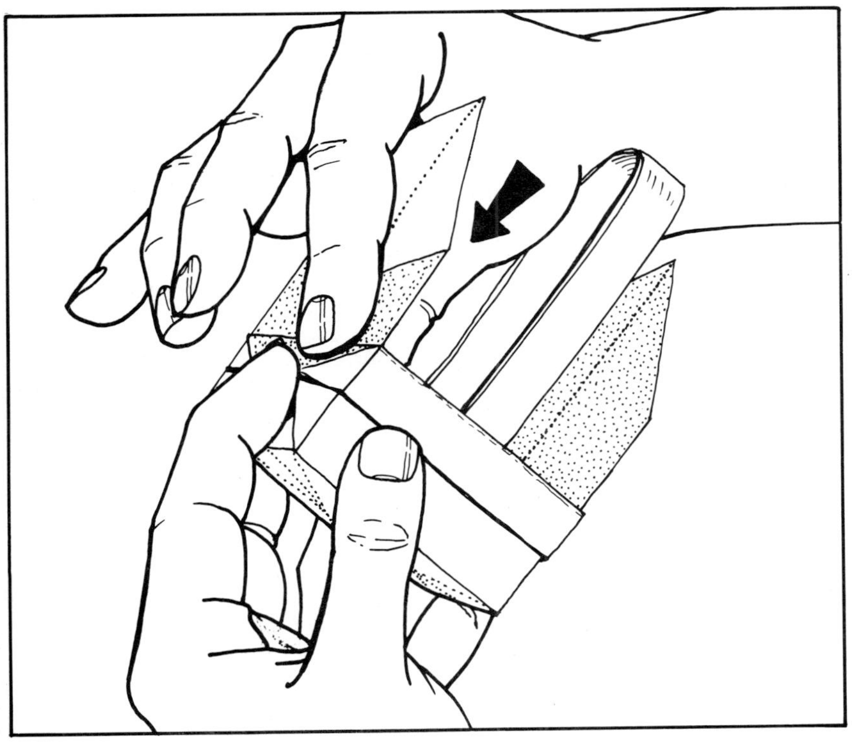

Support the basket sides and carefully shape the bottom.

Finally turn the flaps over the sides of the basket, and establish all the creases and corners.

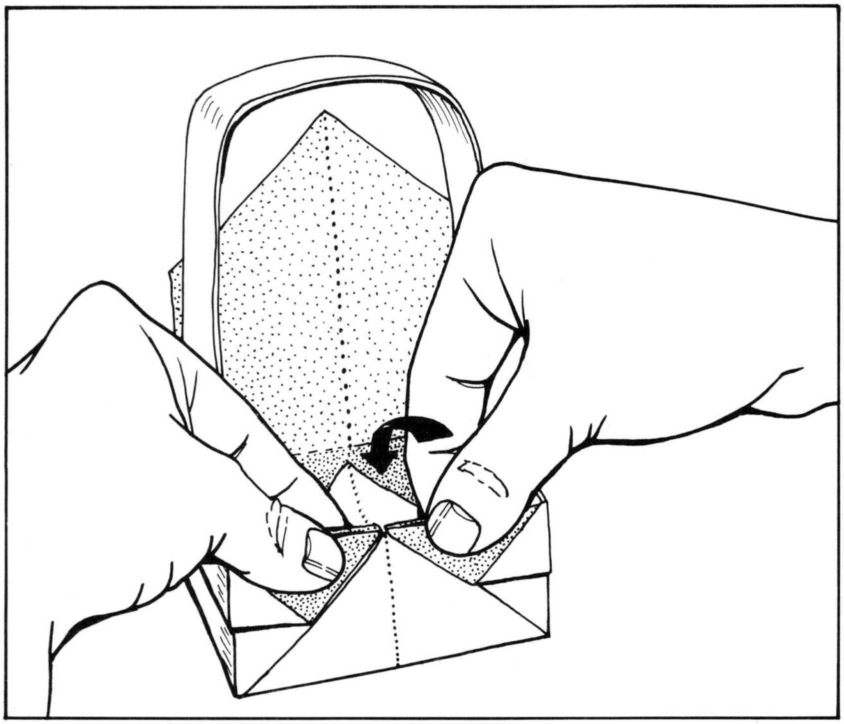

Now take the bottom corner and the end of the handle, and make three rolling folds up towards the centre-middle of the square. Turn the project over and fold in the other end of the handle in the same way. When the handle has been folded in, and still with the handle loop uppermost, fold all four side-corners back and into the model.

FINISHING

With all four sides tucked in, folded and creased, take the model in both hands, hold it with a pinching action at the base of the handle, then, at one and the same time, ease the sides out and the base up. As the sides of the basket come out, so the form will take on its characteristic box shape and you will be able to establish and crease the base.

When you have done this, sit the project on its base, and turn the two tall and pointed flaps in towards the centre of the basket. Finally, wrap the two flaps over the basket sides, crease them so that they sit on the basket bottom, and the job is done.

AFTERTHOUGHTS

If, at any stage, you have doubts as to the next step, then have a try-out with a scrap of paper – in fact it might be as well if you are a beginner to have several pieces on the go at the same time, then you could make all your mistakes on one of the secondary models.

When you are buying origami paper, make sure it isn't rolled; in fact make a point of telling the shop assistant that you want it flat.

PROJECT ELEVEN

HARLEQUIN JUMPING JACK

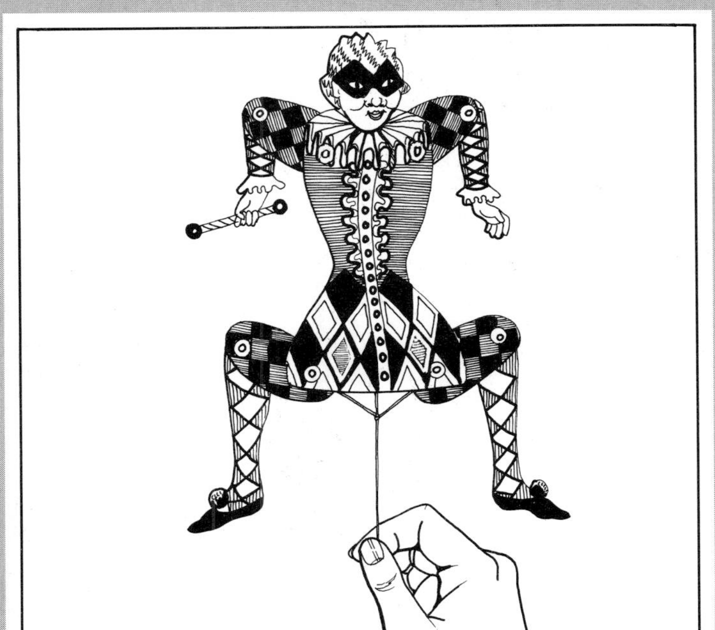

PROJECT PICTURE
The jumping jack in action, see how at the pull of a string the jointed arms and feet swing upwards.

INSPIRATIONAL
Classic clown figures taken from a woodcut dated 1856.

INTRODUCTION

THOUGHTS ON THE PROJECT

The Jumping-Jack is an archetypal international toy; a toy that in its many forms, from monkeys and clowns through to folk-tale figures, has been made in places as far apart in time and space as ancient Egypt, nineteenth century Maori New Zealand, Europe, and Central America. Of course from country to country, he goes by many names, for example in West Germany he is known as Hampelmann, in East Germany he is called Zappelman, the Mexicans think of him as Polchinelle, and so I could go on ad infinitum. However, perhaps the best known and most loved of all jumping-jack types is the eighteenth

INSPIRATIONAL
Traditional English and European jumping jacks.

century French pantin. Made from cut and painted cardboard, these string-operated figures traditionally took the form of Harlequin, the foppish lover of Columbine, or celebrities and political figures decked out in diamond patterned multicoloured tights and a black mask so as to look clownish. Playthings of this type became very popular in eighteenth century France, so much so that famous artists were commissioned to design forms that could be used at court and soirée satirical puppet show entertainments.

Design wise, pantins or jumping jacks are characterized by having a one piece head-and-body, arms hinged at the shoulders and elbows, and legs hinged at the hips and knees. In use the toy is held on a stick or hung from the wall, and at the pull of a string, the limbs jerk up so that the figure looks to be grotesquely dancing.

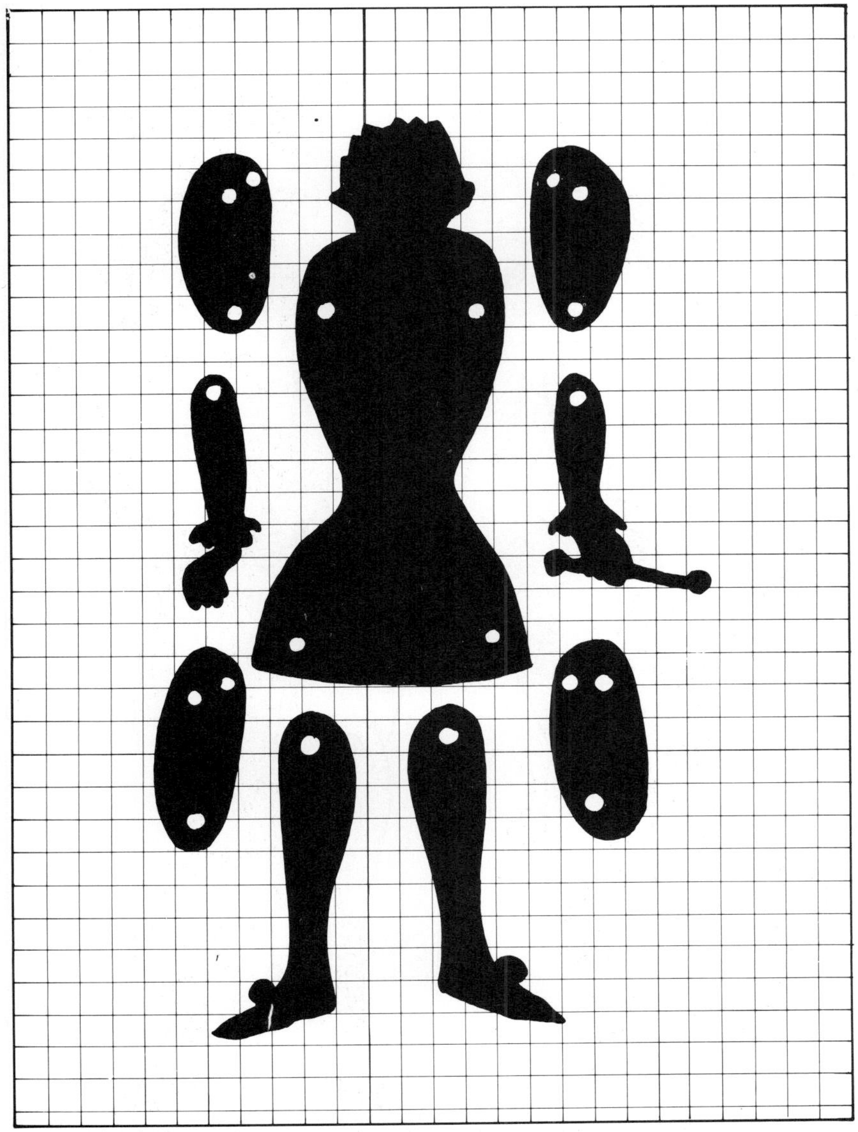

WORKING GRID
The scale is about four grid squares to 1 inch. Note the position of the pivot and string holes – these may need to be repositioned if you modify the design.

CONSIDERING THE PROJECT

Have a look at the drawings and see how the jumping-jack works, that is to say, see how the various limbs are pivotted and how, at the pull of a string, the arms and legs swing up and jerk out. Note especially the placing of the limb-to-limb cord linkage. When you have analized just how the toy operates, then visit a suitable museum and have a look at eighteenth and nineteenth century European pantins and the various ethnic and folk jumping-jack types. When you get to see a traditional cardboard French pantin or maybe one made in Germany or Switzerland, make a series of detailed drawings. Note the characteristic imagery, the powerful forms and the use of bold colour.

Have a look at our various inspirational drawings and decide just

WORKING GRID
The scale is about four grid squares to 1 inch. When you come to tying in the strings, make sure the limbs are in the 'at rest' position.

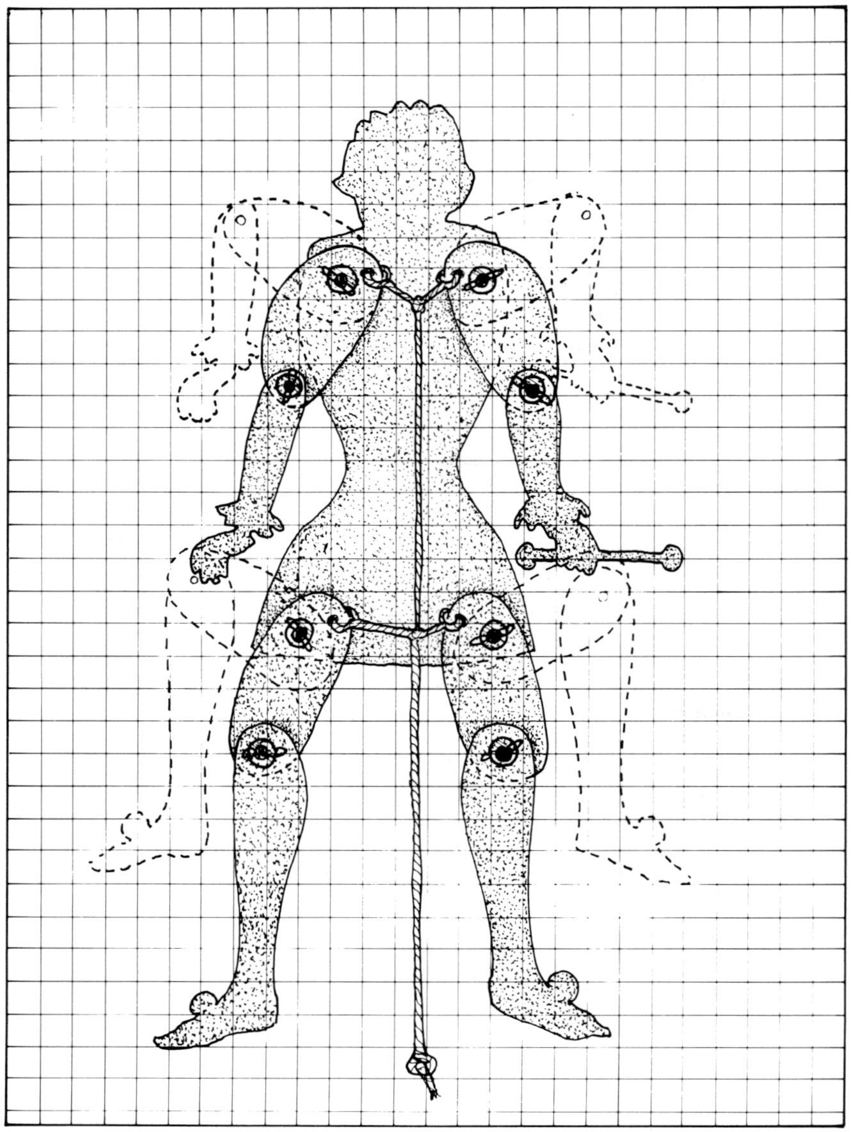

how you want your figures to be – for example are you going to make a traditional figure, or are you going to modify the project and have say a figure in modern costume? Note how we have chosen to use a stout white-faced art board and coloured pencil crayons. Finally, draw up your materials list accordingly.

TOOLS AND MATERIALS

For this project you need, a sheet of stout white or tinted art board, meaning a thick mounting board that has one smooth working face, a drawing board, a cutting board, tracing paper, pencils, coloured pencil crayons, a pen and black ink, scissors, a large craft knife, a fine-point scalpel, a heavy duty card punch, a hammer and block, about

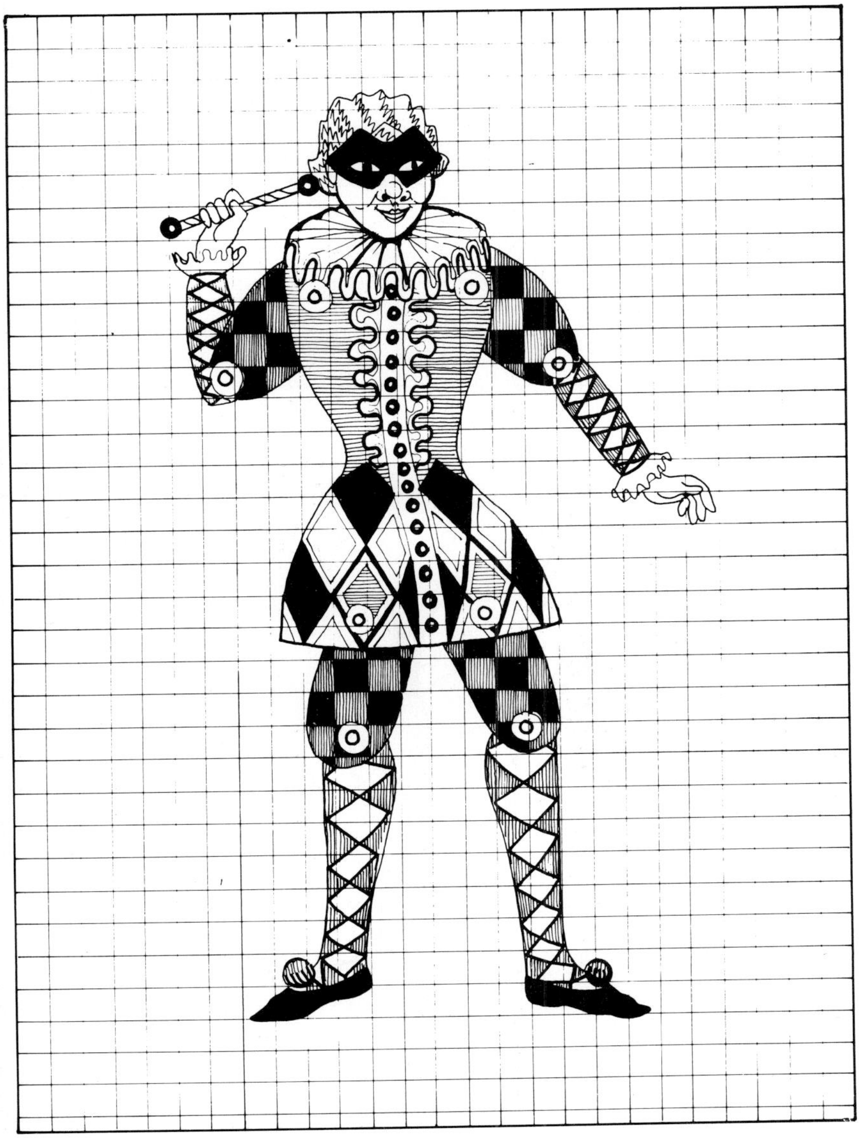

COLOUR GRID
The scale is about four grid squares to 1 inch. When you have coloured in all the design areas, pick out and emphasise the details with a pen and black ink.

Once you have transferred the lines of the design, support the card on a work board and cut out the shapes with a fine-point knife.

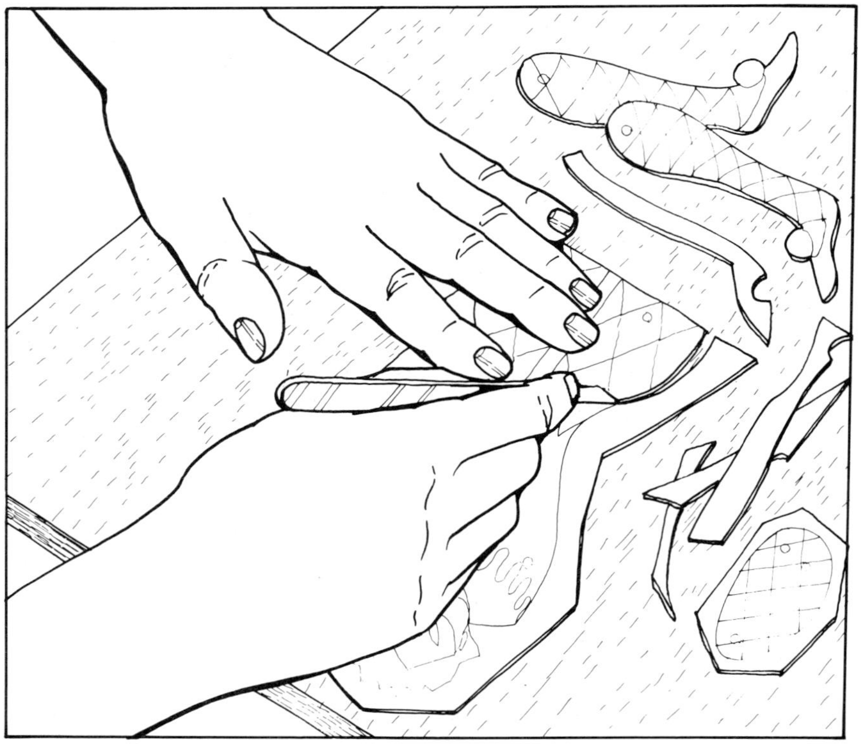

Establish the position of the various string and pivot points, then chop out the holes with a punch.

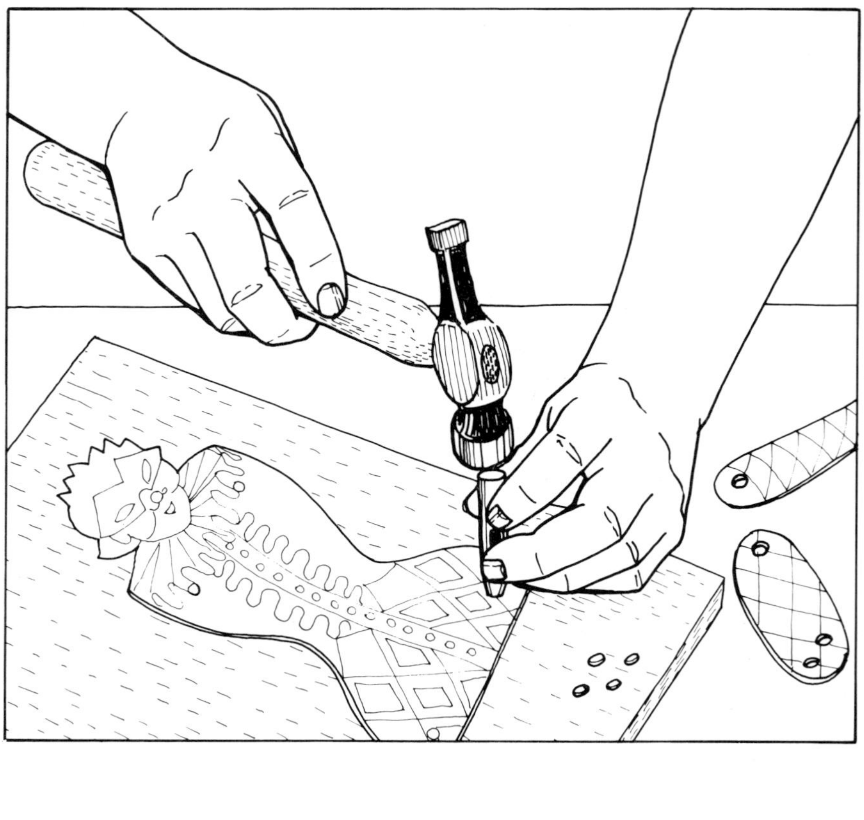

24 inches of fine strong cord, eight brass pivotal clips, the type with washers and fold-back tabs, a sketch book and a quantity of scrap card.

DRAWING UP THE MASTER DESIGN

When you have studied the working drawings and considered how the arms and legs are placed in relationship to each other, and the cord linkage, then take your sketch book and draw out a series of possible figures. Don't in the first instance worry too much about the strings and pivots, just aim to draw a well proportioned, nicely costumed figure. This done take a tracing and then pencil press transfer the various parts of the figure through to your scraps of card.

Now set about making a full size working prototype, that is to say experiment with limb sizes, proportions, and possible pivot points, until you have a jumping jack that operates smoothly. When you have achieved a good working model, re-adjust your working drawings to fit, take another tracing, and finally pencil press the lines of the tracing through to the working face of the mounting board.

CUTTING THE BOARD AND PUNCHING THE HOLES

When you have pencil press transferred the traced lines, position the board on the cutting surface and take up the large craft knife. Start by roughly separating the nine elements that go to make up the total

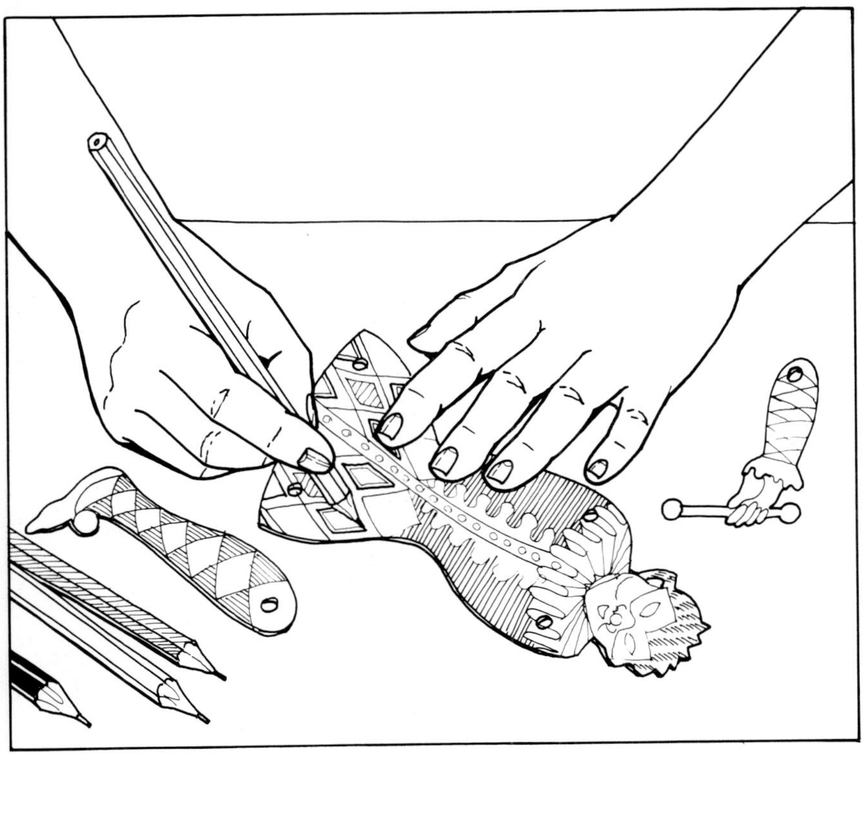

Use coloured pencil crayons to block in the design.

Emphasise the design details with black ink; use either a pen and indian ink or a felt tip pen.

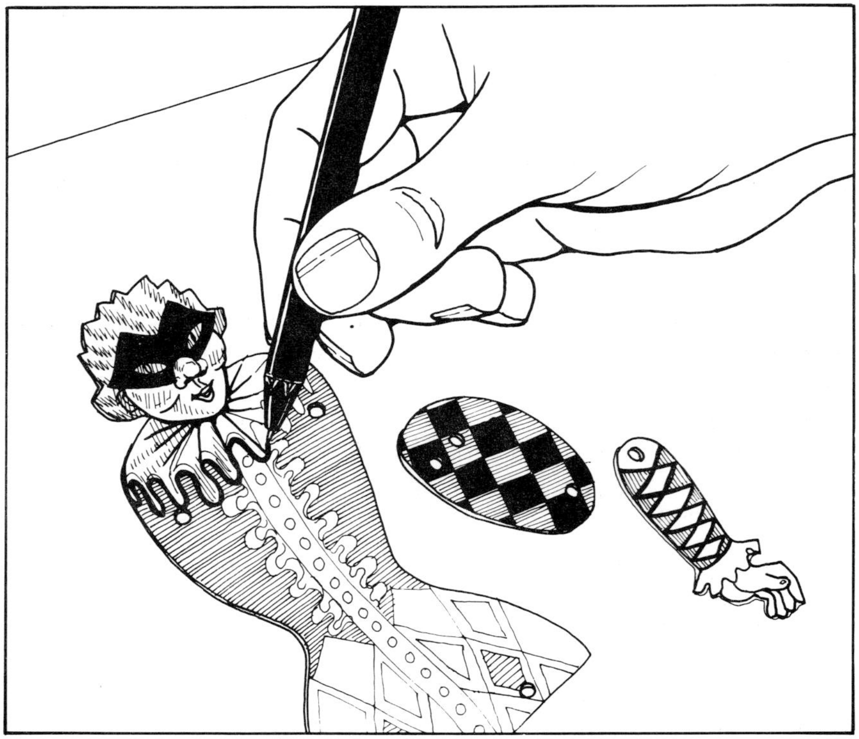

Pivot the limbs with brass tab fixings and clear plastic washers.

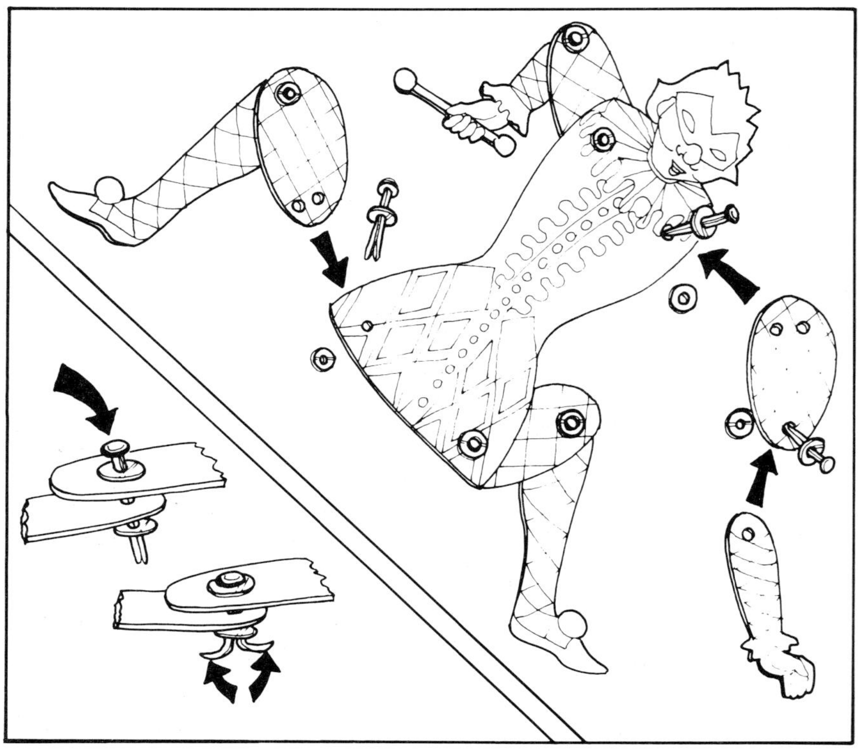

figure, meaning cut out the head-and-body, the two upper legs and the two lower legs. This done clear away the main bulk of unwanted card.

Now take the smaller fine point scalpel, one with a short stout blade, and proceed to trim up to the drawn lines. Watching out for your finger tips, manoeuvre the card with one hand and follow through with the scalpel. As you are cutting, take such factors into account as the thickness of the card, the size and sharpness of the scalpel blade and your strength. Don't try to cut through the card with a single stroke, but rather aim to work the forms with a series of repeated little-by-little cuts. Don't twist or force the blade, and try to leave the cut edge crisp and clean. When you have cut out all nine forms, take a pencil and establish clearly the position of the twenty string and pivot holes. Finally, piece at a time, take the hammer and punch, support the card on the cutting board and work the holes.

COLOURING AND INKING IN

Have a good look at your master design, then trace and pencil press transfer the various costume and motif details through to the individual pieces of card. Go over the transferred lines with a pencil, then set about blocking in the details with the pencil crayons. Work a subtle multi-colour textural effect by over-working the colours one on top of another. So for example, if you want a green, then lay down an interwoven mesh of blue and yellow crayon lines, lines that describe

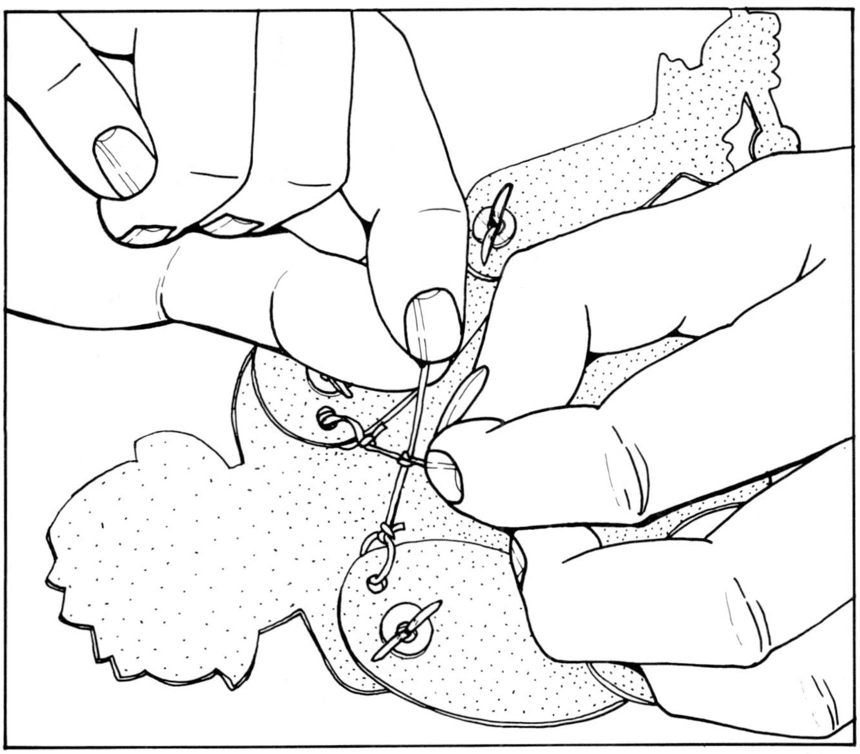

Finally, place the jumping jack face down and in the 'at rest' position and knot in the 'pull' strings.

the form. Working in this way it is possible to achieve a design that has a delicate, subtle, antique texture. And so you continue, over-working the colours until you have a characteristic pencil crayon patina.

Finally take the fine-point pen and the black ink, and pick out and emphasise what you consider to be the most important costume and detail features.

THE PIVOT CLIPS AND STRINGS

When you have cut, punched and coloured all nine pieces of the jumping-jack, lay them out on a clean worksurface. Now have another look at the working drawing, just to see how the various limbs are layered and placed, then locate the brass pivotal clips, slide on the washers and bend back the tabs.

When you have done this and all the limbs look to be securely fixed but free moving, turn the jumping-jack over so that he is face down, and then set about tying in the cord linkage. Have the arms and legs in the 'at rest' position, and then, using two short lengths of cord, link arm to arm, and leg to leg, as illustrated. Finally tie in the long piece of cord so that it runs from the two short linkages and becomes the 'pull' cord.

Note – the cord linkages must be tied when the figure is in the 'rest' position.

AFTERTHOUGHTS

To cut costs you can use scrap carton card faced with white cartridge paper – if you do this, either use paste and let it dry before you do the colouring, or use quick-dry paper-to-paper adhesive.

If you only want to make a quick throw-away toy, then you can use button-and-thread pivot points.

You could modify the project and use paints or inks.

You could embellish the figure with brass bells, beads or trim.

PROJECT TWELVE

VICTORIAN VUE D'OPTIQUE

PROJECT PICTURE
A traditional boxed and glazed shadow box, inspired by a Victorian fashion print.

INTRODUCTION

THOUGHTS ON THE PROJECT

Découpage Vue d'optique or shadow-box découpage is the art and craft of cutting and working two-dimensional prints or pictures, and then mounting them under glass in such a way that they look realistic and three-dimensional. Although it is possible that the origins of the craft go back a long way, (I've seen a little Persian box that was made in the early fifteenth century), it was during the late nineteenth century that the craft really became popular. Victorian and Edwardian, artists and hobbyists, encouraged by the great magazines of the period, 'The Girls Own Paper', and 'The House, The Journal of Home Arts and Crafts,' took to the craft in a big way. They selected prints, drawings

WORKING GRID
TOP *The scale is about four grid squares to 1 inch.*
BOTTOM *Not to scale. Note – the cross hatched areas on the bottom plan detail show the position of the figures in relationship to the backdrop.*

and illustrations, flowers, birds, classical figures, fruit, feathers, and the like, and by cleverly colouring, tinting, cutting and gluing, they created the most beautiful shadow box scenes.

The best works of the period are characterized by having a slightly bizarre quality, with the découpeurs favouring melodramatic, almost sinister subjects like little bedroom and parlour scenes, infamous murder tableaus, butterflies with the most amazingly realistic wings, bowls of fruit, exotic insects, animals and birds. It has been said that some of the best boxes of the period have about them a Wellsian, 'held in time' quality. These glass encapsulated illusions of reality, are thought by many to be the forerunners of Victorian and Edwardian peep-shows, tableau vivant magic lanterns, and of course, much later, television.

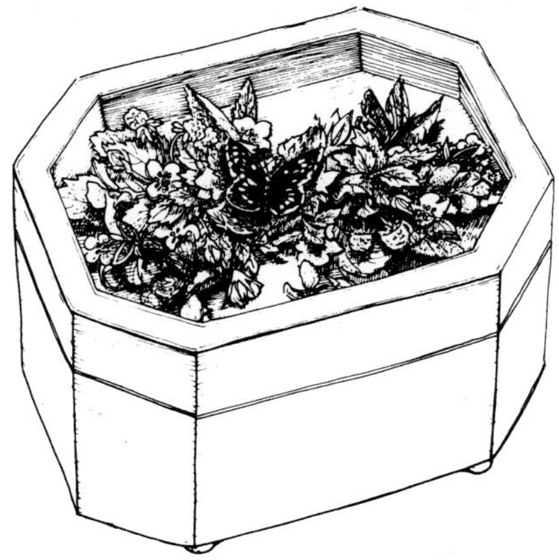

INSPIRATIONAL
A Vue D'optique set within a glazed box lid.

CONSIDERING THE PROJECT

Before you put scissors to paper, visit a museum of Victoriana, and get to see as many shadow box découpages as possible. Under-glass pictures, cut paper backdrops to sand box toys, paper pulp fruit and flower, boxes with under-glass scenes in their lids, all need to be studied. Don't settle for a quick glimpse, but rather ask if you can have a close-up look. Spend time seeing how the scenes have been made from printed cut-outs, printed fashion plates, clips from magazines, pen drawn and colour wash illustrations, and so on. Note how variously the cut-outs have been modelled, overworked and then mounted on little pieces of cork. If you look closely you will see that not only are the little figures actually mounted in front of each other so as to give the illusion of space and perspective, but many of them have costume details that have been cut and worked so that they really stand out, and colours that have been toned so that objects within the scene appear to be in more shadow than they actually are.

When you come to working the project, have a good look at the drawings and the inspirational illustrations, and see how we have chosen to use pen illustrated figures, rather than printed cut-outs, and how we have used the pinprick technique to give the illusion that the lace trim has a delicate structure and depth. Note – if you prefer, you can cut and work a period print.

TOOLS AND MATERIALS

For this project you need, two illustrations or prints, one for the background, and one for the figures or objects in the foreground, a quantity of card, a clear instant glue, a small fine-point knife or scalpel, a really sharp pair of fine-point nail scissors, a pair of tweezers, a small tea spoon, a couple of corks, a felt pad, brushes, water colours, or coloured pencils, a hat pin or needle, a cutting board, paper paste, a glass fronted box, or a picture frame with a deeper than normal rebate, and finally, you also need all the usual workshop items.

INSPIRATIONAL
A traditional romantic gazebo scene.

Note – you can of course build a shadow box with mitred picture

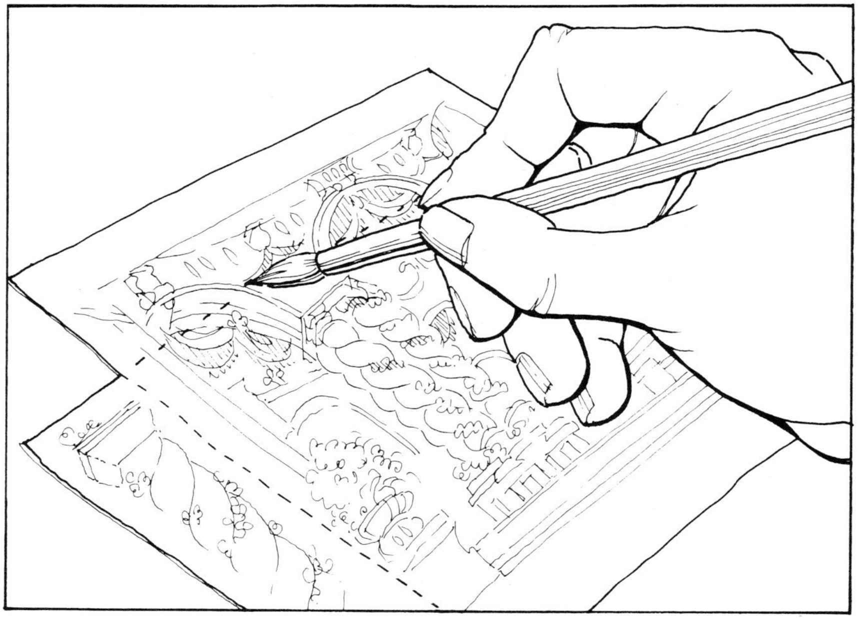

When you have chosen your background scene/print, tint it with delicate water colour washes.

framing and glass, or you can use a 'found' ready made box. I've seen shadow boxes that have been built into old wooden clock cases, glass topped cigar boxes, glass topped coffee tables, and glass fronted wall niches. This project is a good excuse for searching around in attics and junk shops.

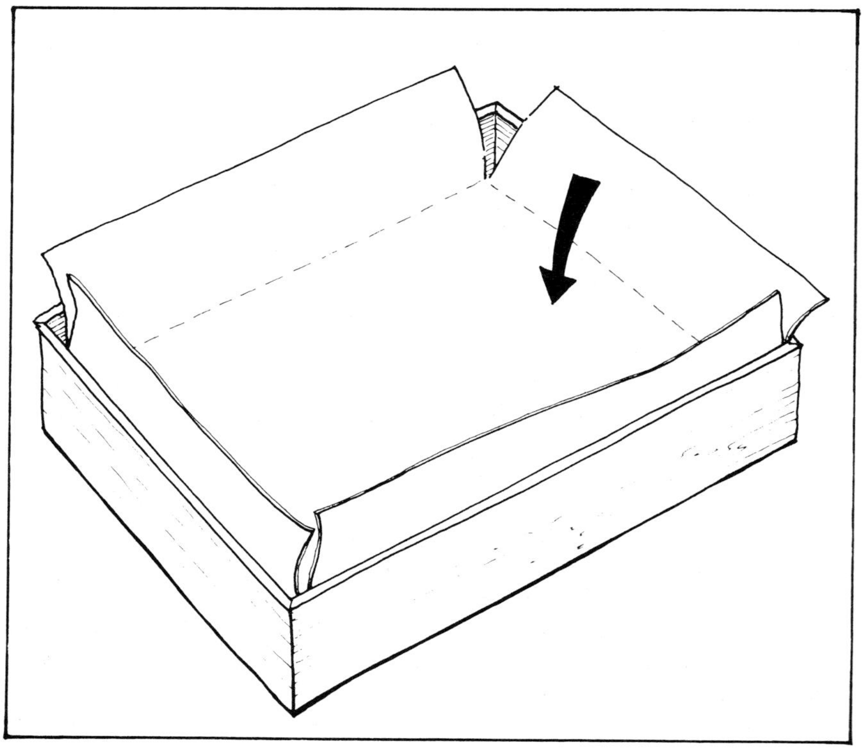

When the paints are dry use the scene to line out the box.

Take your chosen print and establish the cutting lines.

PLANNING THE SCENE

Set out your chosen illustrations, your tools and materials, and make a series of detailed study sketches. Using tracing paper and scrap paper, decide how you want the figures to stand in relationship to the background; generally play around with the material until you have a clear image in your minds eye of just how your shadow box scene will be. If necessary, draw up a scaled 'stage set', and have a trial placing.

COLOURING, CUTTING, AND PREPARING THE BOX

Take your illustrations, and colour them in with the paints or crayons. Try not to be heavy handed, but rather apply the colours sparingly and go for thin washes or tints. When this has been done, take your background print, and then with a pencil and ruler, mark it out so that it fits your chosen box. Have a look at the various working drawings and see how the background print needs to be coloured, folded and cut, so that all five faces of the box are lined. This stage can be tricky, so measure and double check before you start cutting.

THE FIGURES

When the box has been well prepared, cut out all the figures and objects. Use the fine-point scissors, and with great care, remove the figures either completely or partially from their background. Note how our figures were inspired by a Victorian fashion plate, and see also, how we have lifted them out of their rural scene, and how we have altered the placing and set them against an architectural backdrop. If you have any doubts at all as to the possible placings, experiment

Cut, work, curl and pin-prick the cut-outs so as to give them three-dimensional form.

with unwanted magazine pictures. Aim to achieve a three dimensional illusion by cutting out foreground figures and then moving them so that they are actually physically nearer the front of the box.

CURLING

When you have cut out all your figures, and have decided where they are going to stand, then you can start curling. Let's say, that you want the body of a dress to curve away from the viewer and appear

Using a spoon and pad curl the cut-out so as to give roundness to the skirt.

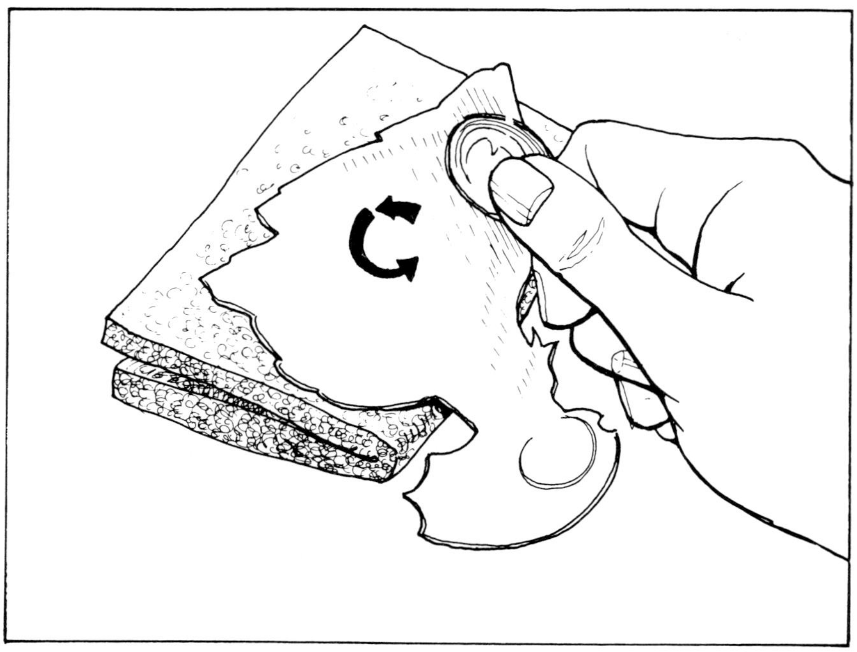

rounded. All you do is to lay the cut-out face down on the felt pad or cork, and then to gently rub it with a burnisher – we use the back of a small tea spoon. Continue gently stroking and rubbing, until the fibres expand and the card curls. If you want a tighter curl, then use a smaller burnisher, something like the end of a pen.

PRICKING

When you have achieved a collection of figures, some curved and some flat, then decide whether or not, some part, parcel or detail, needs to be pin pricked. Have a look at the project and see how we have chosen to raise and emboss the dress trim. The technique is pretty straight forward – simply select an area to be worked, and this might be anything from a bunch of flowers to a bush, then place the cut-out face down on the cork and pierce it repeatedly with a small pin. Don't stab at random, but carefully start by defining the area with a pin-pricked outline. This done, systematically fill-in with pin holes, until the fibres of the thin card stretch and part. Continue pricking until the front of the flowers, lace or whatever, domes and blisters. By working in this way, it is possible to achieve the most beautiful minute raised details that look to be delicate and feather light.

PUTTING TOGETHER

Clear the worksurface, set out the lined box and the various pricked and curled cut-outs, and then arrange the figures and objects so that

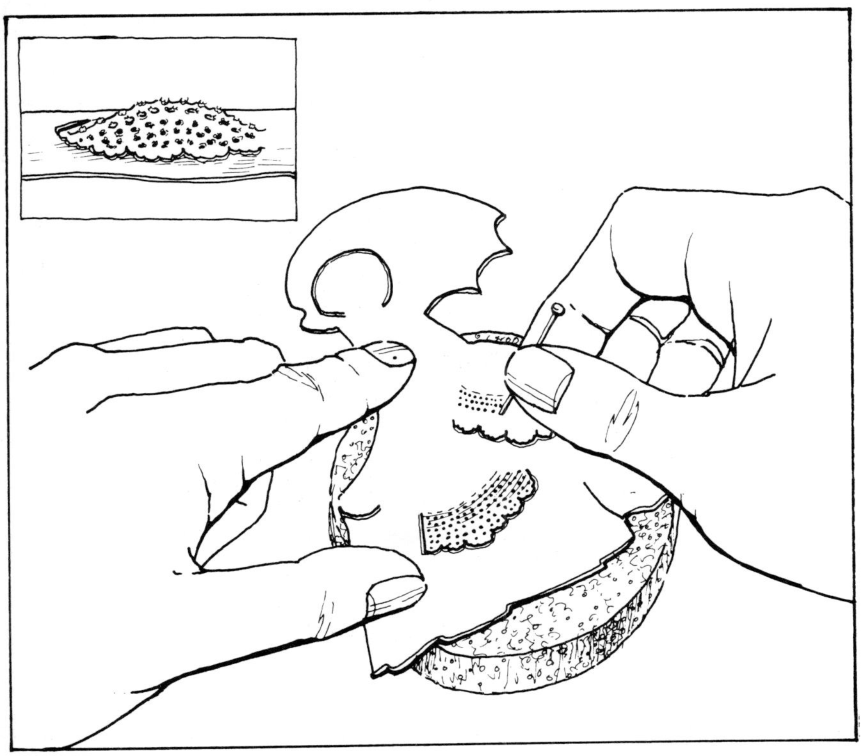

Using a pin and a cork mat, prick areas so as to give a lacy effect.

they form the little tableau. Check that all the elements are correctly placed in relationship to both the front and the back of the box, and with each other, then, when you are happy with the placing, start mounting the figures.

Working from the back of the box to the front, cut small pieces of cork, then with care, mount the cut-outs on the backdrop, and/or on the base. Using the instant glue, the tweezers and a deal of patience, gradually build up the scene until all the elements are in place.

Finally when the glue is dry and you are sure that all the 'behind the scene' supports are secure, then brush out all the small waste fragments of cork and card, bang the box to make sure everything is secure, have another last check that all is correct, then fix the glass with pins and tape.

AFTERTHOUGHTS

If, as you are building up the tableau, you find that a piece of support cork is visible or badly placed, then add another 'bush' or a piece of 'furniture'. Note – see how we have covered up a badly placed cork support with the piece of 'stone'.

If you are going to purchase say a Victorian facsimile print, a card or whatever, then buy two, just in case you make a blunder.

Before you fit and fix the glass, make sure the paste, paint and glue are completely dry; if in doubt, let the box dry out for at least twenty four hours before glazing.

Finally, use small pieces of cork to support and mount the cut-outs against the backdrop – try to achieve a convincing 3–D effect.

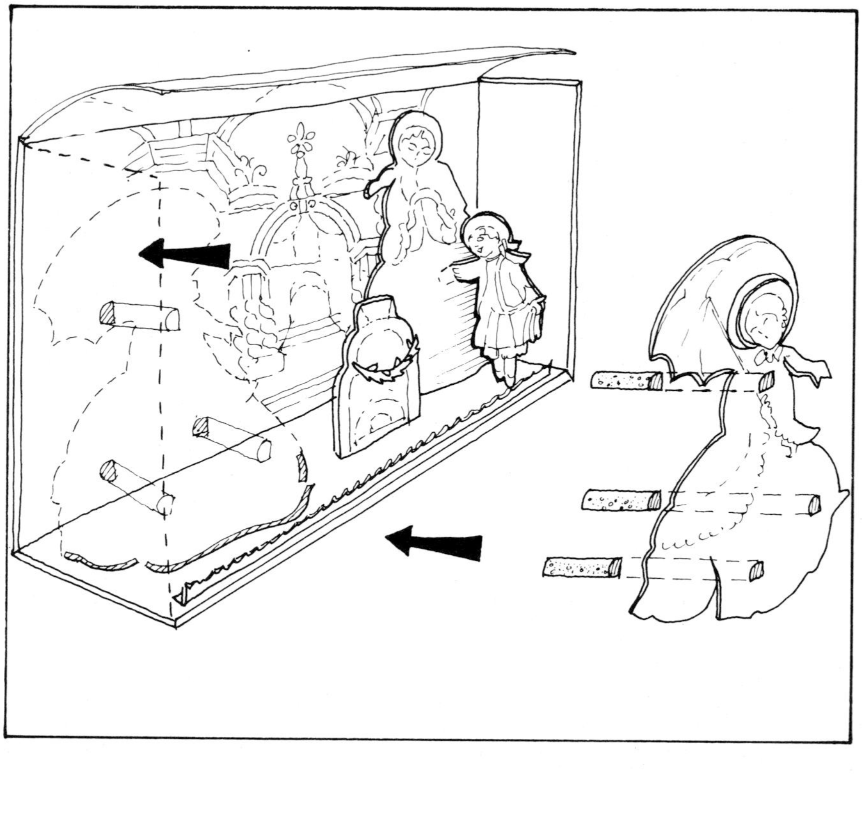

PROJECT THIRTEEN

DECORATING A PICTURE FRAME

PROJECT PICTURE
A quilled picture frame, note the traditional use of the quilling and the quartered symmetry.

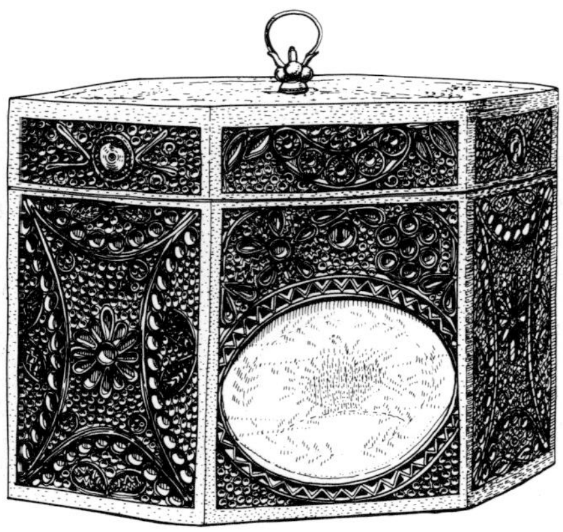

INSPIRATIONAL
TOP *English quilled motifs, thought to be seventeenth century.*
BOTTOM *An early nineteenth century tea caddy with inset quilled panels.*

INTRODUCTION

THOUGHTS ON THE PROJECT

Quilling is the craft of rolling thin strips or ribbons of paper and then mounting and displaying them in such a way that the paper is seen edge-on. No one can say with any degree of certainty where the craft originated, or even how long it has been practiced, all we really know, from surviving examples, is that in England it was worked as early as the fifteenth century.

With these early quillworks, usually rather formal heraldic pictures, the paper strips are of many different widths, and the resultant cones and coils are mounted in such a way that they look to be boldly three dimensional and sculptural. That said, eighteenth century quillings, variously termed, quillworks, mosaic quillings, or even filigree paper pictures, are characterized by being all worked at the same level, by being built up so that the motifs are densely packed, and by being mounted and protected under glass.

It was during the Georgian period, say between 1730 and 1830, that the craft became really popular. In fact, quilling became so fashionable, that ladies of leisure were taught by professional quilling teachers, and paper patterns and articles were published in journals and magazines. Cabinetmakers of the Georgian period produced all manner of little boxes, frames, caskets, screens and small pieces of furniture especially for quillers; the idea being that the cavities and recesses could be lined with pretty papers and delicate fabrics, and then filled with quillworks and glazed. As to how the craft came to be called 'quilling', it is thought that it took its name either directly from the old English term 'to quill', meaning to press flutted folds into a ruff, or from the term 'gofer quill' meaning to imprint a thin wafer or biscuit with a delicate filigree pattern.

CONSIDERING THE PROJECT

Quilling is, at one and the same time, inexpensive, visually exciting and intricate, and yet it is also a craft that is very easy to do. The actual paper rolling techniques can be mastered in a few minutes; the end of a narrow paper strip is inserted into the tip of a split-end tool, the tool is rolled between the fingers, and then the resultant paper coil is either, allowed to fall free, glued tight and removed, or variously squashed and shaped. The quillings, the hoops, coils, rolls and lozenges, are set, arranged and confined within a paper or card design grid, and then finally the whole arrangement is framed and glazed. The art is not so much in the actual making of the individual coiled and rolled quillings, but rather in the placing and the total design arrangement.

That said, before you start work on this project, visit one or other of the many museums that specialize in eighteenth and nineteenth century drawing room arts and crafts, and get to see examples of Georgian, Victorian and Edwardian quilling. These works might take the form of wall-hung pictures, locket miniatures, decorative features on or in such small items as tea trays and cigar boxes, or they might even be built into small pieces of furniture.

When you get to see examples of the craft, note how although in broad terms the designs look to be symmetrical, most of them are in fact built up from many individual and asymetrical elements. That is to say, the total grand designs are usually balanced, but within these balanced designs, quillings and groups of quillings are quite individually placed. Have a good look at museum exhibits, and see how variously, works are made up from different colour papers, embellished with beads, trimmed with sequins, set against fabric and foil grounds, and so on. Finally, make a series of motif and pattern sketches, and take note of all the individual quilled forms.

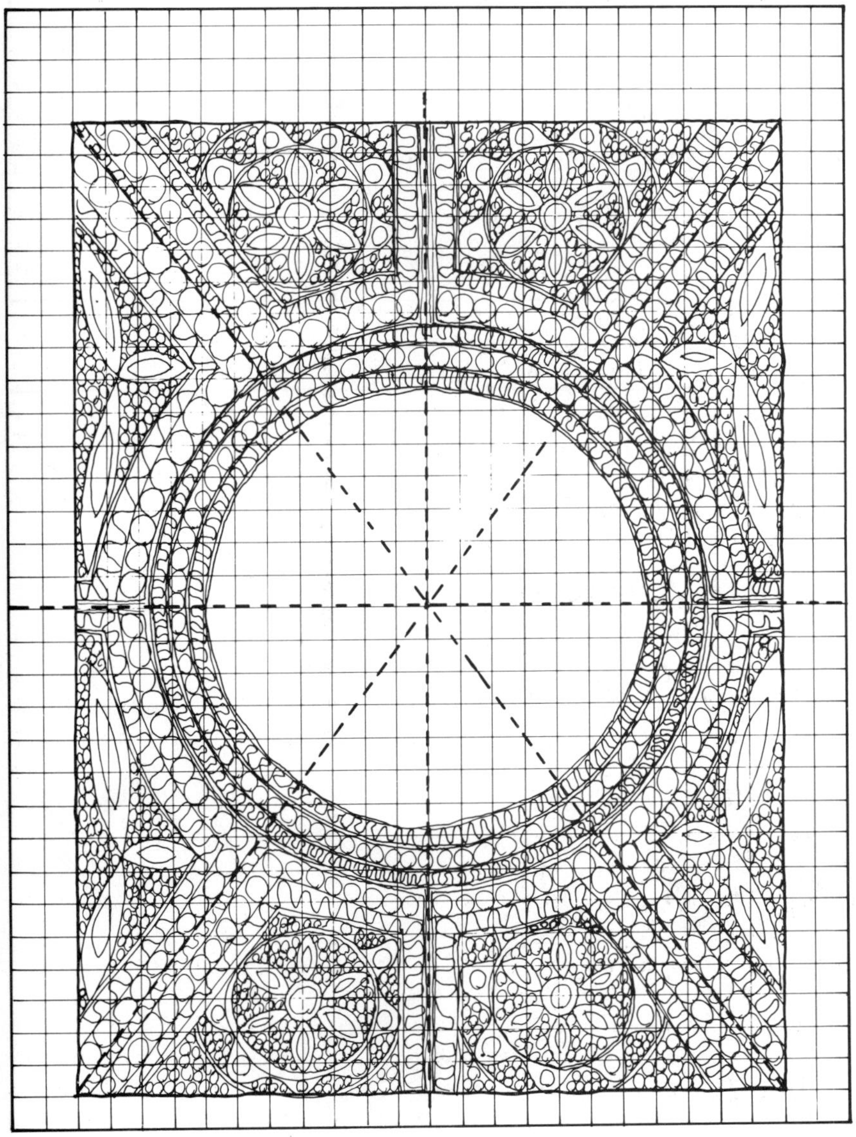

WORKING GRID
The scale is about four grid squares to 1 inch. Note the quartered symmetry, and see how the various subdivisions each contain quilled infill of a slightly different design and character.

Trace off your master design and then trace and pencil press transfer the traced lines through to the picture ground paper.

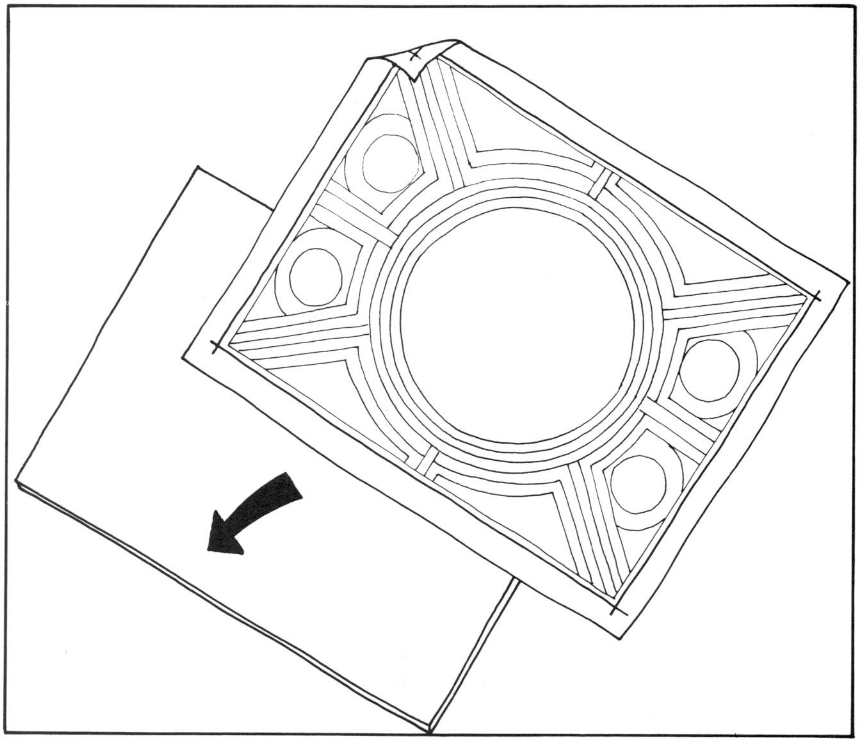

Place the ground paper on the working board, and then use strips of grocery carton card and pins to build a temporary wall/frame.

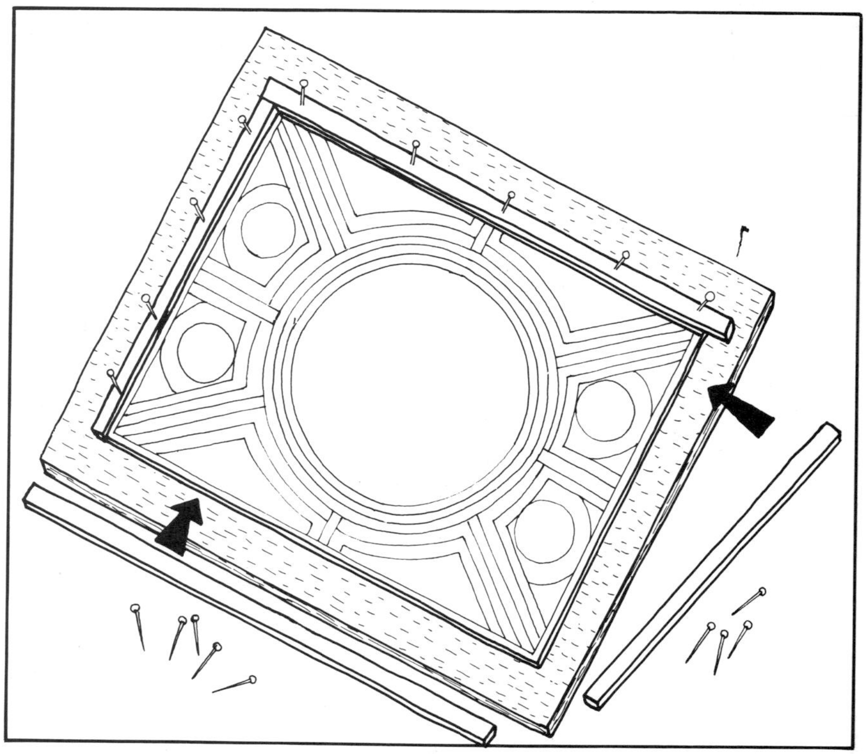

TOOLS AND MATERIALS

For this project you need, a sketch book, a pencil and measure, a supply of coloured paper or thin card, a sharp craft knife, a pair of tweezers, a 'safety' metal straight edge, a wooden cutting board and jig, a collection of split-end rolling tools, (these can be made from goose quills), knitting needles and such like, a collection of formers, empty cartons and, cardboard tubes, a special paper-to-paper adhesive, a clear quick-dry model makers glue, tracing paper, a small deep-rebated and glazed picture frame, a backing card to match the frame, a supply of long bead-end dressmakers pins, and finally you will need such items as scrap card and scissors.

DESIGNING

When you have studied as many museum quillworks as possible, then take your chosen picture frame, and draw up a suitable design grid. Meaning, measure the frame, decide on the shape and placing of the central display window, then draw the design out to size. Now have a look at our working drawings and see how we have quartered and sub-divided the available space so that the overall design is symmetrical. Note also how the sub-divisions have been broken down so that the entire frame has been reduced to a series of quill-encircling retaining walls.

When you have considered how you want your design to be, and have decided on the size, colour and character of the quill in-fill, then take a tracing of the master design. Finally pin up the master design so that it is in view.

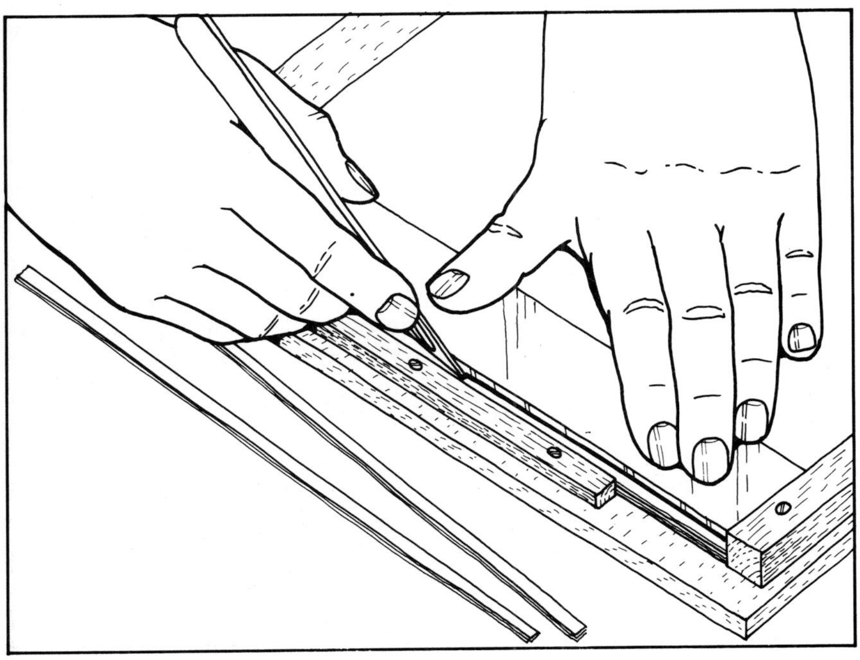

Use a metal straight edge, a sharp knife and a cutting board to cut the quilling strips – note the home made batten jig.

Set the main design structure out by building 'boxed' areas, use formers to achieve the various different size circles.

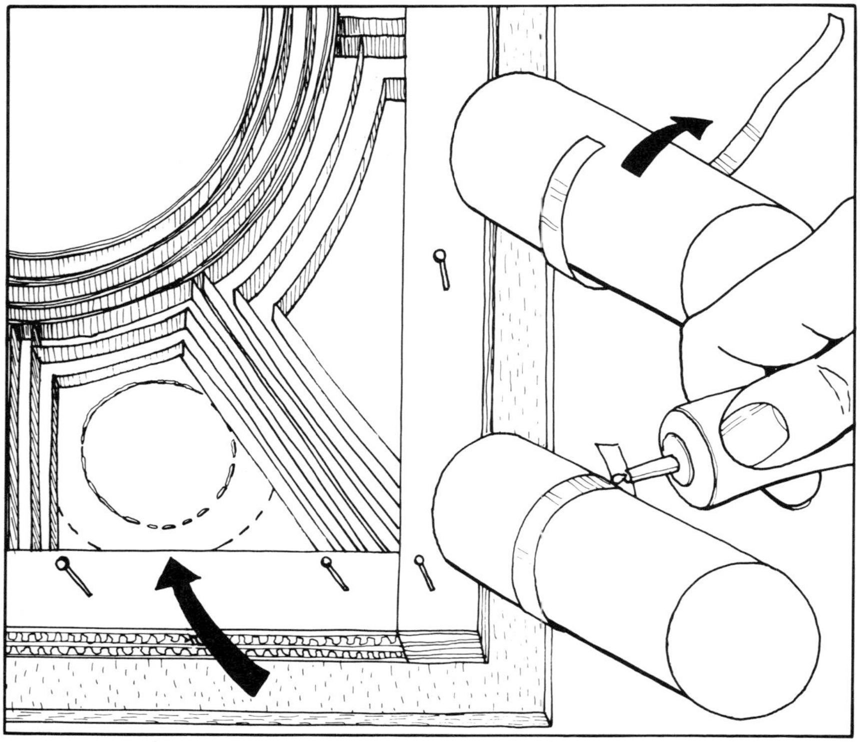

BUILDING THE FRAME

When you have drawn to size and traced what you consider to be a good design, take the picture frame backing board, and then with a little paper-to-paper adhesive, cover it with your chosen ground paper. This done, take the tracing and pencil press transfer the lines of the design through to the working face of the decorative paper.

Now, using scraps of grocery carton card and long bead-headed pins, build a temporary frame round your design, and then pin the frame and the design securely to the working board. Note – make the temporary cardboard frame slightly smaller than the picture frame rebate.

CUTTING THE QUILLING PAPER

When you have established the size of your frame then take your various coloured papers, metal straight edge, cutting board and craft knife, and start cutting out a supply of quilling strips. The papers can be, 1/8 inch 1/4 inch or even 1/2 inch wide, no matter, as long as they are all the same size. For this particular project, we favour strips that are 1/4 inch wide. Set the battens on the jig, as illustrated, so that the desired strip width can be cut, check that the battens are at right angles to each other, and then proceed to cut a supply of strips. The actual cutting is pretty straight forward – half a dozen or so sheets of paper are set up in a stack against the jig battens, the papers are aligned, and then, with knife and a 'safety' straight edge, the strips

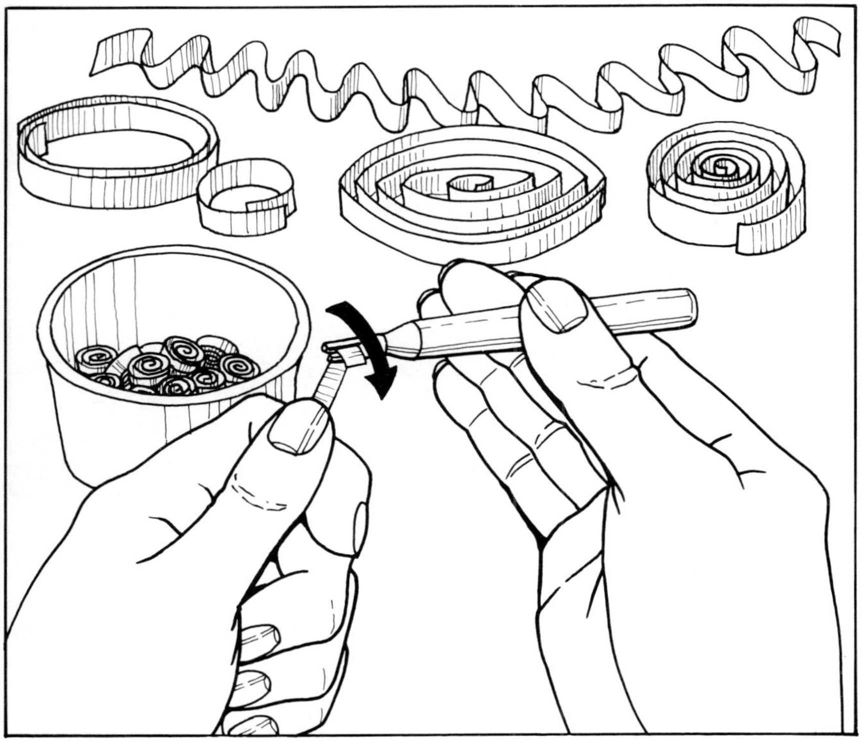

Model the various quillings by winding and pleating the paper strips with the small forked tool – shapes can be made in odd moments, and put by until they are needed.

are cut. Note – cut your strips so that they relate to the size and depth of your picture frame rebate – don't forget to take into account the thickness of both the backing board and the glass.

BUILDING THE DESIGN GRID

Have a look at the working drawing and see how the design has been set out and divided so that there are a number of main frames, frames that have themselves been sub-divided. For example there are four central circles, and then radiating out from the circles there are a number of arms. Note how the arms quarter the design and fix the position of the circles. See also how, within the various sub-divisions there are secondary features – circles, petal lozenges and such like. These 'boxed' areas not only set out the design, but are, as it were, structural retaining walls that contain the quilling.

Measure the various circles, search around for suitable formers, then start to build the frames. You might for example build the main circles around the bottom of coffee mugs, the secondary circles around cylindrical grocery packagings, and so on. The actual building is simple enough, you just wrap the quilling paper round and round your chosen former until you have a hoop, then the end of the paper strip can be fixed with a dab of adhesive. As to how many wraparounds you need, this will of course depend on the thickness of the paper and the size of the hoop. And so you continue, until you have worked all the primary forms.

Using tweezers, a small stick or probe, and quick dry glue, fill in the various boxes areas, best to glue the underside of the quillings.

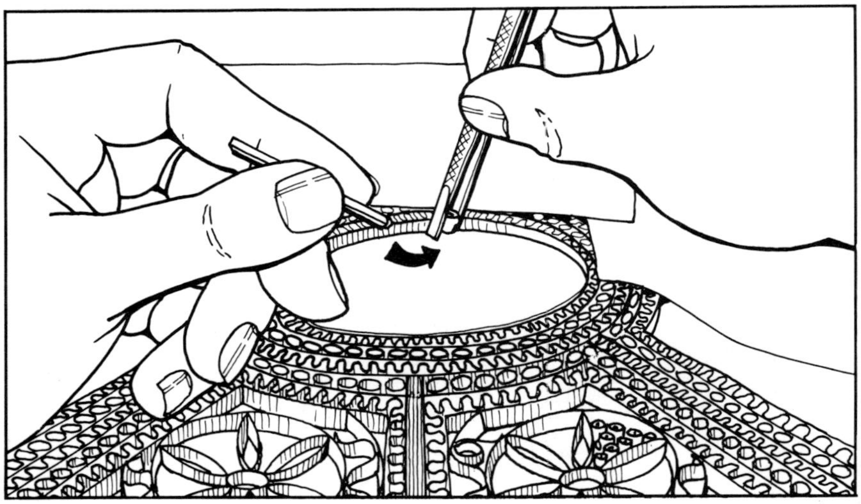

This done, set the various hoops and strips out on the design grid and trim them to size. Finally, starting at the centre and working out, glue, place and pin the main forms onto the backing board. Use dabs of quick-dry clear glue, and continue until you have made the main box grid.

FILLING IN THE DESIGN

When you have made the grid, then take up your tweezers, the quick-dry model makers glue and the stockpile of quilled shapes, and then start filling in the various boxes. Start with the main hoops and then work out from the centre gradually filling in as you go. Select such and such a quilled shape, try it for size, then touch it with the smallest dab of glue and then set it in position. Working in this controlled way, you will soon build up a quilled design that is both stable and strong. When you have achieved what you consider to be a good design, make sure all the quillings are secure, then remove all the pins and lift the quillwork from the workboard.

Finally, position your chosen display piece, a photograph, illustration, embroidery or whatever, clean the glaze, locate the whole project in the picture frame, tack and tape the backing board in place and the job is done.

AFTERTHOUGHTS

Woodworkers and turners still make recessed and glazed items to order – small items like writing boxes, lidded cylinders and paper weights.

When you are covering the backing board with a decorative paper, be sure to use a special paper-to-paper adhesive.

For an ultra rich effect, quillings can be sprayed with metalic paints.

When you are working difficult to handle small quillings, use tweezers, a small stick and clear quick-dry glue.

As you are working, protect finished areas with a sheet of paper.

PROJECT FOURTEEN

CHINESE DRAGON KITE

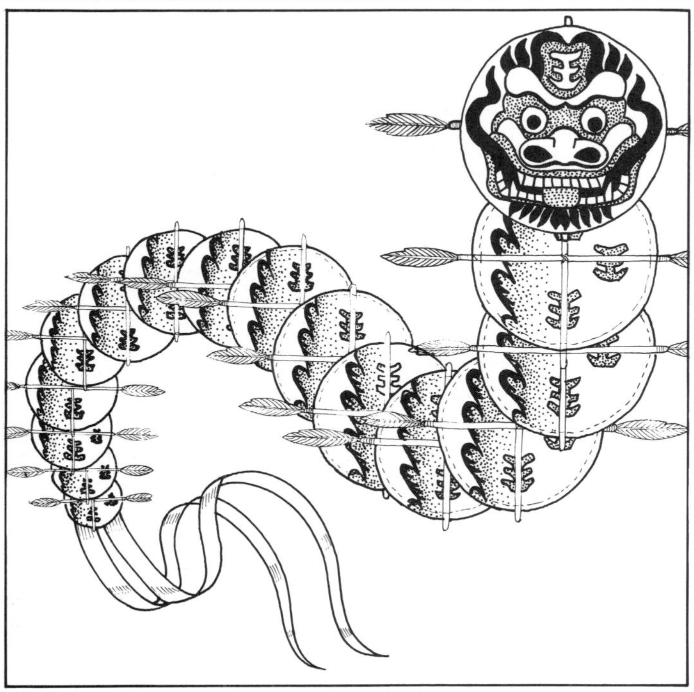

PROJECT PICTURE
The dragon kite in flight, note how the hoops/discs are graded in size, see also the important and functional feather stabilizers.

Traditional Chinese dragon motifs

a paper cut design.

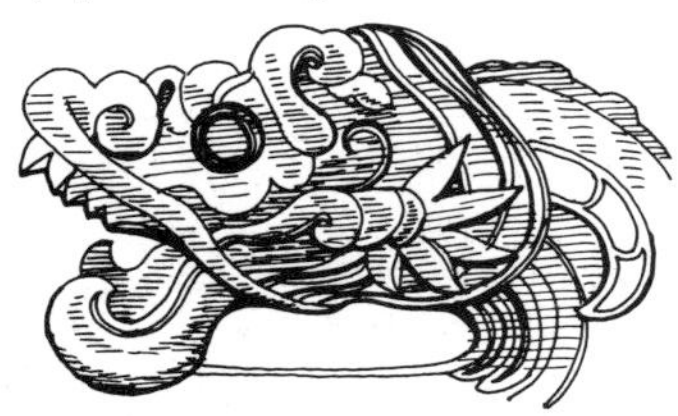

a wood carved head.

a lacquered chest motif.

INTRODUCTION

THOUGHTS ON THE PROJECT

Did the Chinese invent the kite? who can say – all we really know for sure, from ancient illustrations and written accounts, is that kites were being flown in China may centuries before they were introduced to the West. Certainly the Chinese have created, and are still creating, some of the most beautiful, the most imaginative, and the most spectacularly dramatic kites. At first, they were made from expensive silks, and only flown on prestigious occasions, in religious ceremonies, and such like, so it must be supposed that the whole activity was restricted to a privileged few. However, that said, when paper was invented in China around about 100BC, then kite making, and kite flying became

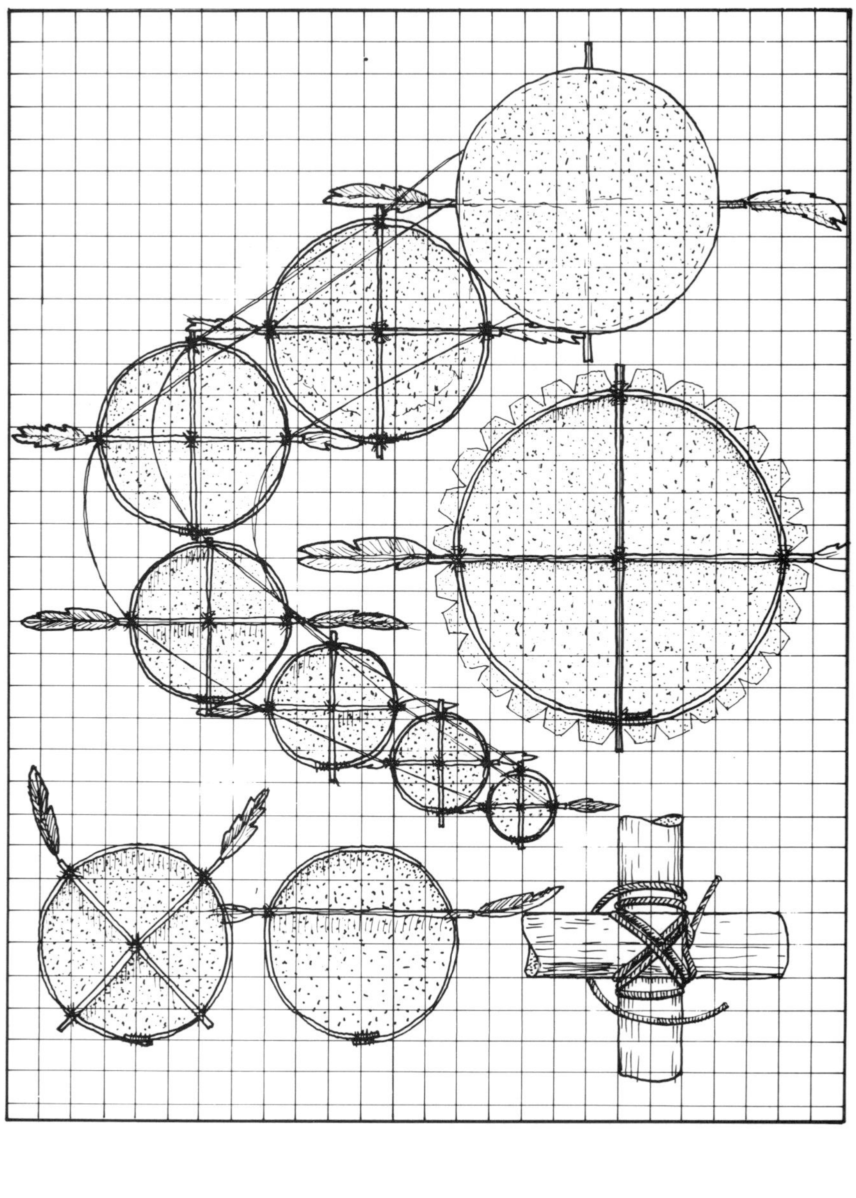

WORKING GRID scale to suit – reckon on the largest hoop being about 24 inches in diameter. Note the cross binding and, at the bottom left, the two possible strut modifications.

a popular activity. There are many Chinese folk tales that tell of robbers using kites to steal treasures and then making a flying get-away, of spys and generals sending signals, and so on; kites are a deeply rooted part of the Chinese persona. Today in China, the craft of making and flying kites is so widespread, that it has become a national pastime.

Kites are flown everywhere – at festivals, during birthdays celebrations, on good luck days, and as a competitive sport. In China, as in Japan, the craft is culturally important, so much so, that the kites are considered to be an art form, and kite makers are treated as personalities, rather like poets, painters and potters. Both modern and traditional Chinese kites are characterized by having lightweight rattan and cane frames, tissue paper sail-covers, silk flying lines and brightly painted designs that are inspired by mythical flying beasts.

a porcelain dragon.

a classic Chinese figure kite.

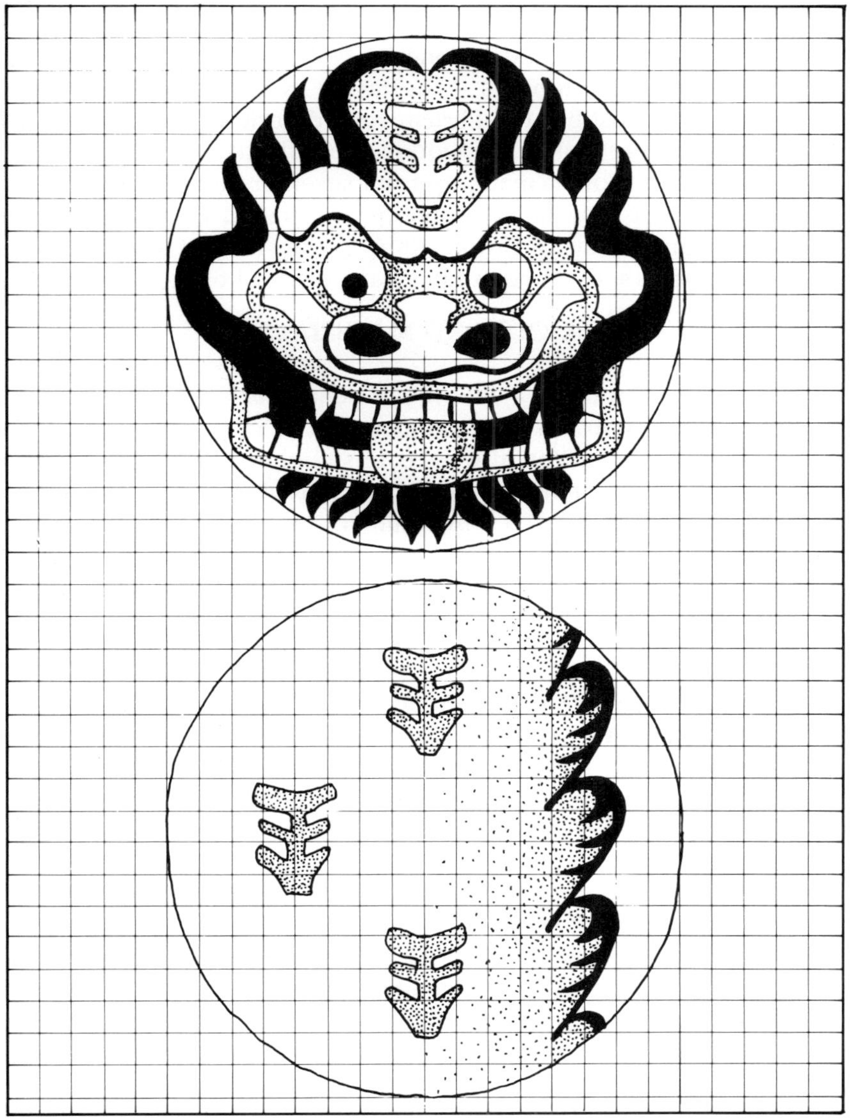

COLOUR GRID

The scale is about four grid squares to 6 inches. Go for bright colours and big bold hard edged motifs.

CONSIDERING THE PROJECT

Flying a shop bought kite is certainly an exhilarating experience, but flying a kite that you have created – a delicate, beautifully built Chinese type kite, is altogether a more gentle and mind soothing activity. What could be more fun than making your own kite out of rattan, tissue paper and coloured inks, and then watching your creation as it soars up into the great blue yonder. The dragon kite isn't a high performance record breaker, but rather, by its very nature is a beautiful gesture, a piece of transient art. In fact this kite is so beautiful, that like a picture, he can be strung from the ceiling, or hung from the wall.

Before you start this project, have a good look at the working drawings, then take a trip to the nearest museum or ethnic craft centre, and get to see examples of Eastern kites, kites that have been made in China, Japan, Korea and Indonesia. Note the lightweight, strong and decorative characteristics – the rattan frames, the tissue paper covers, and the most beautiful brushworked designs and motifs. This done, have another look at the working specifications and the details, and note how this kite is made up from seven or more paper covered rattan hoops. See also how the hoops are graded in size, from the largest at about 24 inches in diameter, to the smallest at 6 inches in diameter. Note – some dragon kites have discs all of the same size.

TOOLS AND MATERIALS

For this project you need, a quantity of pencil thick rattan cane – note how the largest hoop has a circumference of 72 inches plus, and then buy your cane to suit. You also need 14 straight bamboo canes, again of a size to suit, a quantity of good wet strength, colour-fast tissue paper, a number of chicken wing feathers, fine cotton thread, water based paste, a small amount of resin glue, coloured inks, varnish, brushes, a sharp craft knife, scissors, and a pencil and ruler.

BUILDING THE HOOPS

First of all estimate the circumference of the various discs, allow for an overlap of about 2–3 inches, then cut the rattan to size and leave it soaking overnight in a bath of water. Now take the longest length of soaked and flexible rattan, and carefully bend it into a full circle. Cut and overlap the ends, as illustrated, then take a length of dampened cotton twine and bind the overlap.

Now place the hoop on the worksurface, and cut and position the two thin bamboo cross-spars. Make sure that these canes cross at the centre, check that their ends stand proud of the rattan hoop, then take some more lengths of dampened twine, and bind the five cross points; that is to say bind the central cross and the four circumference crosses. And so you continue, until you have made at least seven hoops.

Finally when both the cane and the cotton bindings are completely

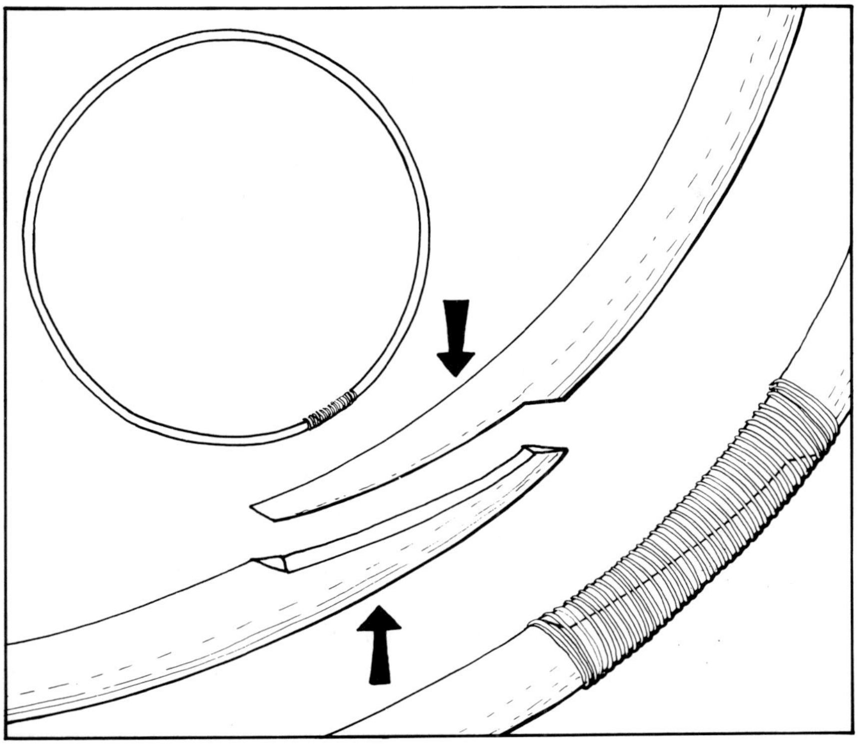

Overlap the dampened rattan, cut a nicely fitting half lap joint, and then bind with the dampened cotton twine.

dry, dribble a little resin glue over all the knots and lashings, just to make sure that all is secure. Note – When the twine dries, it will shrink and pull the hoop ends together.

MAKING THE TISSUE PAPER SAIL COVERS

Clear the worksurface, then set out the tissue paper and the seven cane hoops. Now, disc at a time, place a hoop on the tissue, mark out a circle, making sure that there is a 1 inch circumference margin, cut the tissue to size, and finally cut V-notches around the overlap margin. This done, spread the tissue over an easy-to-clean worksurface, then sponge it down with a generous amount of water. Wait for a few minutes for the tissue to expand, then position the hoop on the tissue, paste the 1 inch V-notched margin, and with great care go round the hoop, working the tissue over the cane. Try to achieve a nicely rolled wrinkle-free edge.

Finally, when you are pleased with your efforts, put the disc to one side to slowly dry out, and then repeat the procedure with the other six hoops.

PAINTING THE DRAGON

Take the large tissue covered disc, place it frame-side-down on the worksurface, then set out your sketch book, inks and brushes. First have a look at our various inspirational designs, then take your sketch

TOP *Cross the canes, tie the twine to one cane and then wrap it figure-of-eight fashion round the cross.*
BOTTOM *Bind round the cross by going over and under the spokes.*

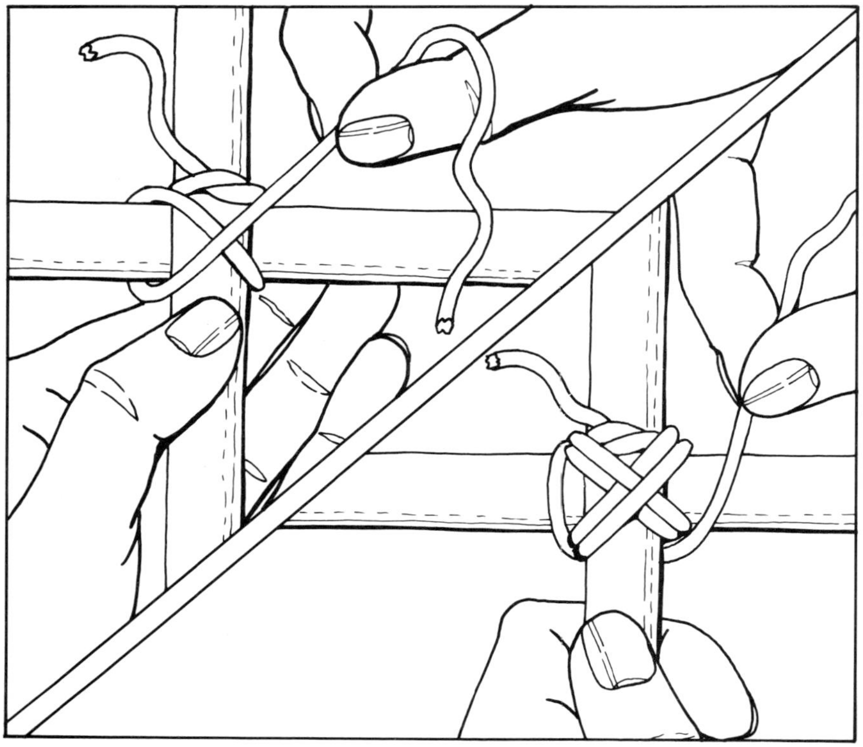

TOP *Now turn the partially tied crossed spars over and tie off the ends.*
BOTTOM *Finally, when the twine is dry dribble glue over the knot.*

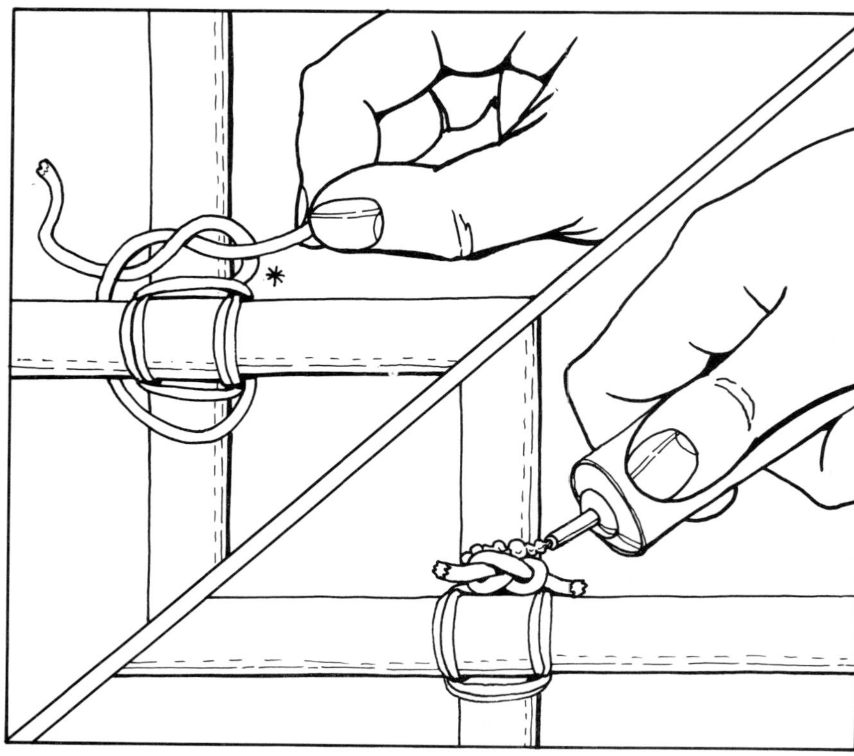

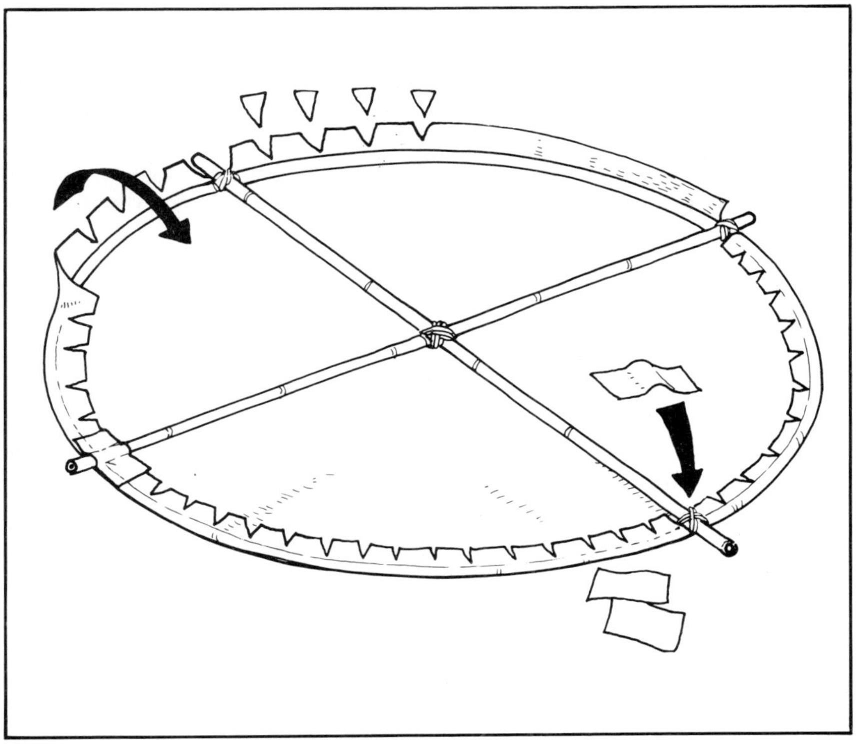

Trim the tissue so that it is larger than the hoop and cut the V-notches, now dampen the tissue, paste the notched margin, finally place and position the hoop, and wrap the pasted tissue over the cane.

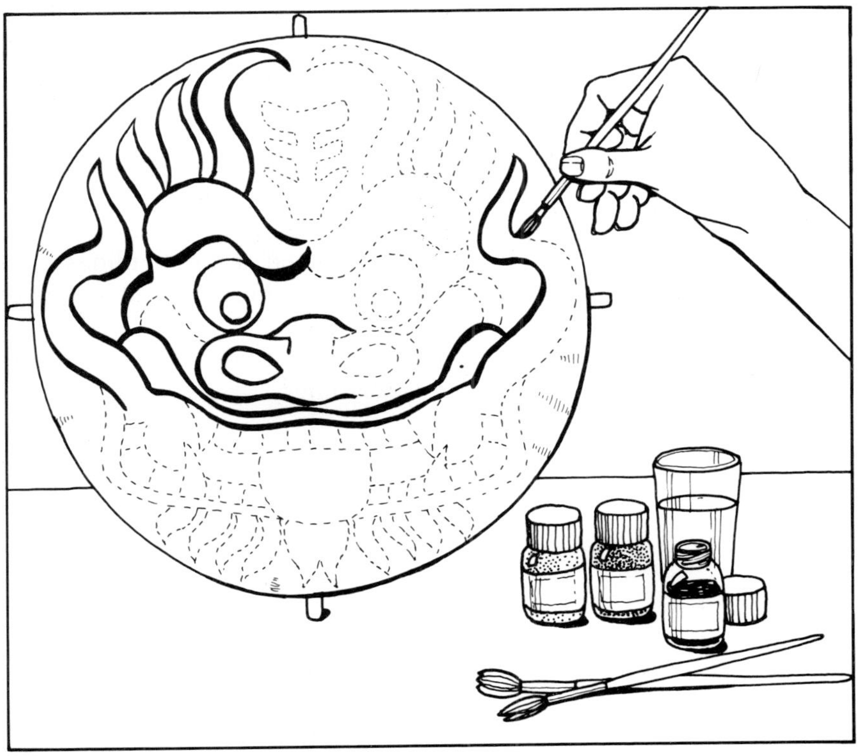

Finally, when the tissue is dry, use inks and long haired brushes to achieve the Chinese dragon imagery.

book and make a series of brush and ink roughs. Aim to use the brushes and the inks in a free-wristed way, meaning, go for big shapes, bold fluid motifs and strong direct colours. Don't fuss around trying for subtle details. When you have worked a fair number of sketch designs, and have achieved a confident feel for the tools and materials, then go straight in and start painting the dragon. When you have blocked in the main areas of colour, lined in the details, and generally worked a powerful motif, then put the large hoop to one side, and decorate the smaller hoops in like manner. Finally, when the inks are dry, lay on a couple of coats of a clear spirit varnish or an acrylic glaze.

GETTING IT TOGETHER

When the hoops are all dry, take your chosen flying line, and link the hoops with three lines, top-to-top and side to side, as illustrated. Reckon on having the first two discs set about 12 inches apart, then tie on the other discs, each time successively decreasing the spacing by say 1 inch. Now take your clutch of chicken feathers, trim them up so that they are more or less the same size and weight, then bind them onto the ends of the horizontal spars, as illustrated.

Finally, decorate the feathers with a splash or two of coloured ink, join a flying bridle onto the top and bottom of the largest disc, attach a tissue paper streamer to the smallest disc, get yourself a good length of flying line, and then you are ready for the great outdoors. This kite is best flown in a light to moderate breeze – if in flight the kite bucks or staggers, try adjusting the bridle-to-line link and if the kite falls to one side, then trim up the stablizer feathers.

AFTERTHOUGHTS

When you are making the hoops, be sure to have the rattan overlap at the bottom of each of the discs.

When you are buying your twine, ask for cotton; the shrinkage characteristics of a natural fibre makes for good secure bindings.

The resin glue ensures that all knots and lashings stay put and gives the whole kite an extra measure of stability.

Finally, never fly your kite in rain, and most important of all, stay clear of busy traffic and overhead power lines.

PROJECT FIFTEEN

WELCOME GARLAND

PROJECT PICTURE
A paper rose and ribbon 'Welcome' wreath or garland.

INSPIRATIONAL
The paper roses might be used with feathers, dried leaves and lace to make exciting swags, garlands, wreaths and 'trees'.

INTRODUCTION

THOUGHTS ON THE PROJECT

Garlands and wreaths, as worked and displayed in America are a traditional way of saying, 'Welcome'. Made variously of cultivated flowers, foliage, wayside flowers, fir cones, embroidery, fabrics, painted card, ribbons and, perhaps best of all, festoons of handmade paper flowers, they have come to symbolize goodwill greetings, festival celebrations and friendship. As to where the American craft of making welcome garlands originated, the various immigrant groups each had their own garland and paper flower making crafts, so it's as likely as not, that the wreaths are, as it were, a coming together of all the Old World folk and ethnic flower making traditions. For example

the Pennsylvanian Germans made and painted paper flowers, the Polish immigrants made huge ceiling-hung hoops all decorated with bouquets of crêpe flowers, the Swiss made very delicate pen decorated flower cut-outs, the Scandinavians made flowers from paper and curls of wood, and so on. The Russians, Czechoslovakians, Hungarians, Fins, English, Japanese, Chinese, all contributed their own unique flower making designs, techniques, motifs and skills.

And so it is that the craft of making garlands and wreaths decorated with paper flowers, a craft that many consider to be uniquely American, is in fact a craft that draws its inspiration from just about every corner of the globe.

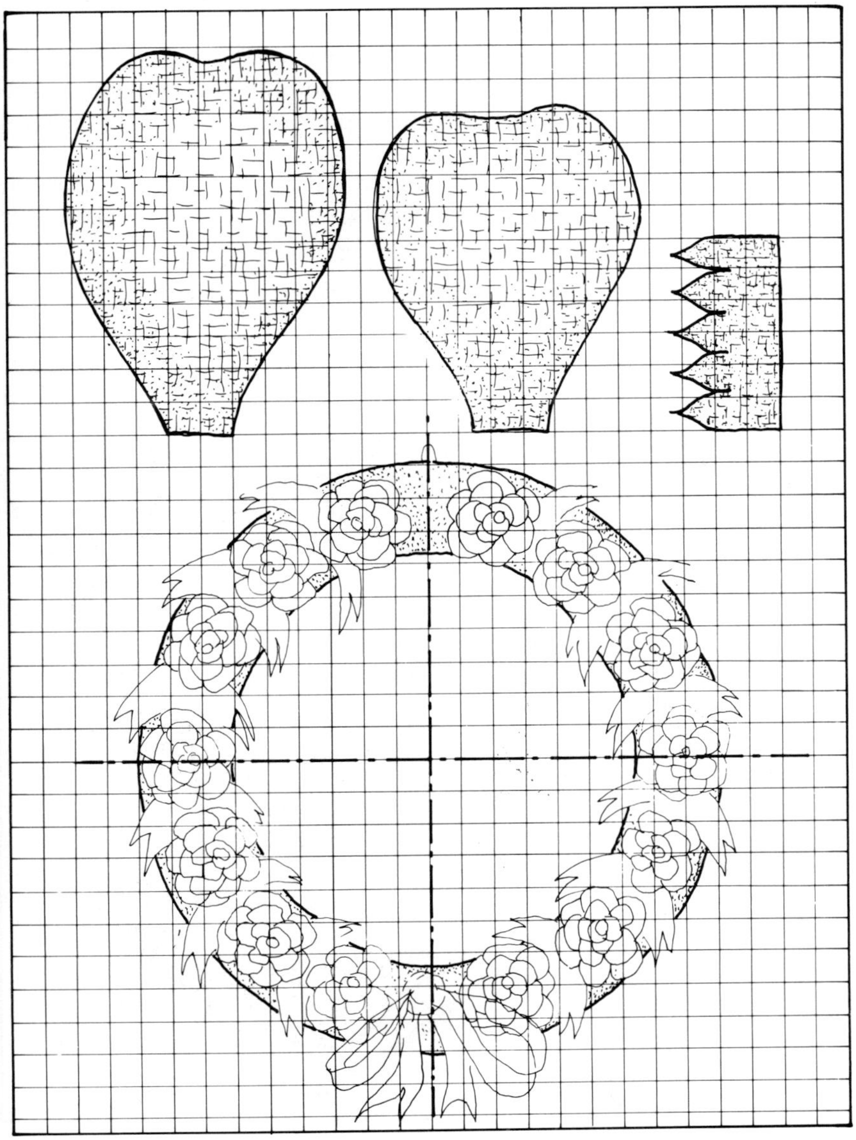

WORKING GRID
TOP *Three templates, two for the petals and one for the calyx, the scale is four grid squares to 1 inch.*
BOTTOM *The scale is three grid squares to 2 inches, the wreath is about 12 inches in diameter, note the symmetrical placing of the flowers.*

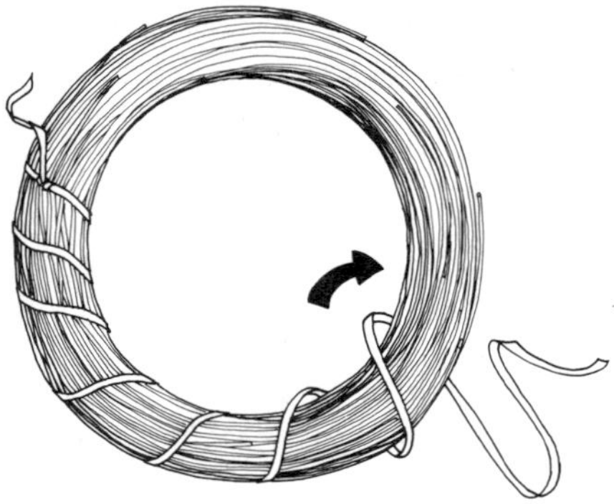

Make a plump straw hoop and bind it with raffia.

CONSIDERING THE PROJECT

Before you start snipping and cutting have a look at the working drawings and see how this project concentrates on making a straight forward door 'Welcome' wreath, that is to say a straw hoop decorated with crêpe paper roses. Of course if you like the overall idea of making a welcome wreath, but would rather decorate it with say Chinese paper-cuts, Polish paper cuts or whatever, take note of the initial hoop-making stages, then look to the other projects. Now take a trip to the nearest museum or a gallery that has on display traditional European folk crafts and get to see as many examples of paper flower making as possible. With a sketchbook and coloured pencils, work a series of reference illustrations.

Now have a look at the project details and see how we have placed the emphasis not so much on the hoop, but rather on the making of a number of identical very realistic Old Fashioned Roses. Note the full, slightly ragged edges of the petals, the blob-end stamens at the centre of the flower and the green wrap-around calyx that encloses the base of the petals.

Finally, take your sketch book, search out one good rose, a rose in full bloom, and make a single detailed illustration of what you consider to be the most important colour and form characteristics.

TOOLS AND MATERIALS

For this project you need, a quantity of single thickness crêpe paper for the petals – go for a delicate pastel colour, a quantity of green

Build an eight-thickness stack of crêpe paper, then use the two templates to achieve the petal profiles, pin the stacks, chop out manageable shapes with the large scissors and use the fine scissors to cut out the petal detail.

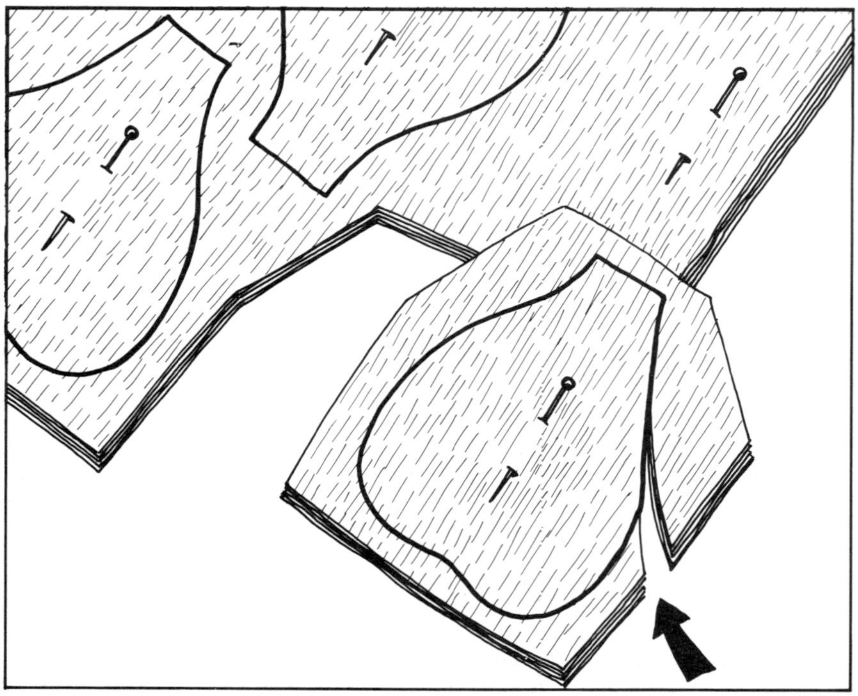

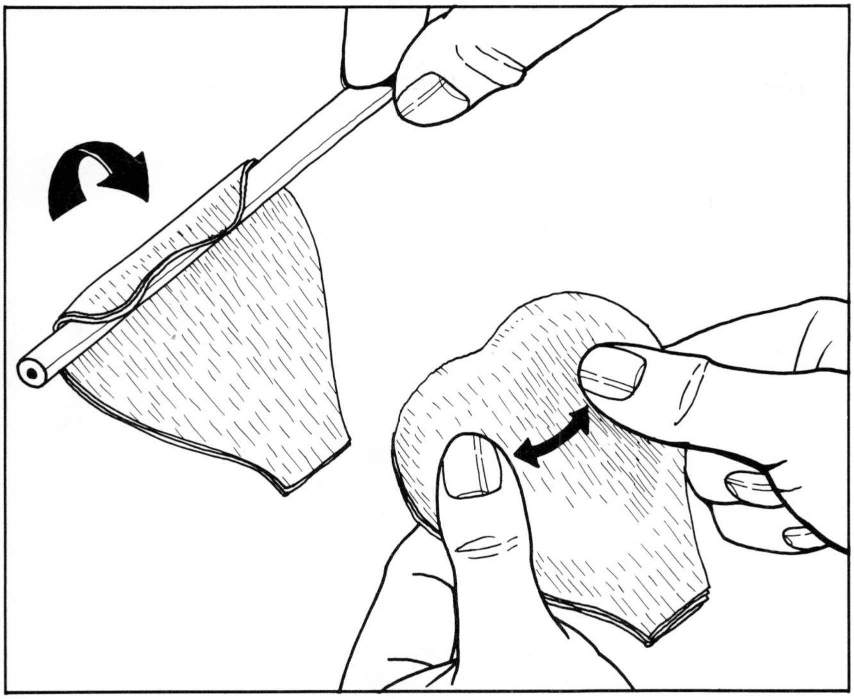

Roll the petals round a pencil and then stretch them at the centre to make the characteristic rose petal forms.

crêpe paper, a roll of straw, thin basket cane, rush, or some such for the hoop, a quantity of raffia, of a colour to suit, a roll of wire for the stems – best to use 18 gauge, a roll of fine florists wire, a quantity of cut and chopped yellow wool, a small roll of paper string, PVA glue, a quick dry clear tube glue, a cutting and work board, a pair of wire snips, a pair of long-nosed pliers, a pair of scissors, a pencil, tracing paper, a small amount of template card, a craft knife, a pack of dressmakers pins, and finally of course you will need some workout paper and a pack of coloured pencil crayons.

MAKING THE HOOP

Have a look at our working drawings and the making stages. Note that our wreath is about 12 inches in diameter, 36 inches in circumference, and is made up from about fifteen roses, then decide how large you want your particular wreath to be. This done, take your chosen hoop material, straw, cane or whatever, and arrange it on the worksurface to shape and size. Now take the raffia and very carefully go round and round the coil binding, easing and arranging as you go. Aim for a nice plump well formed hoop, and to this end take the binding round the circumference at least twice. This done, put the hoop to one side and set out the other tools and materials.

MAKING AND PREPARING THE PETALS

First of all smooth the crêpe paper out and fold it so that there are about eight thicknesses. Now look at our working drawings and note

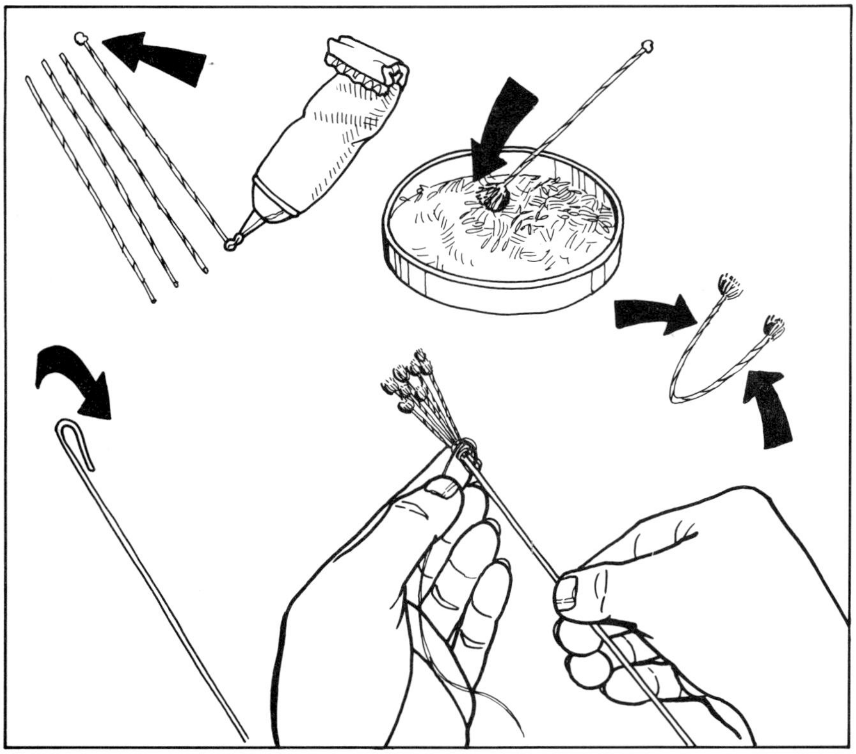

Making the stems and stamens, cut the brown paper string into 2 inch lengths, dab the ends with glue and dip them in the cut wool, fold the stamens in half, hook the stem wire and then bind the stamens to the hook with the fine wire.

the two petal shapes and the need for about 30 or so petals for each rose – twenty small and ten large. Trace off and maybe modify the two petal forms, and make two cardboard templates. This done, take the templates to the folded crêpe paper and draw out as many petal forms as possible, arranging the templates so that they make the best and most economical use of the paper.

Now pin through the crêpe so that each petal stack is contained, and when this has been done, take a large pair of scissors and roughly chop the crêpe up into individual petal stacks. Now, stack at a time, cut out the eight thickness petals, remove the pins, and then put them aside in a box or on a tray. And so you continue until you have reduced the crêpe paper to two heaps of petals.

Finally, take little petals stacks, say four or five petals at a time, and variously roll them around a pencil and stretch them at the centre so that they take on the characteristic rose petal form. There are really no hard and fast rules as to how you should work this stretching and rolling – our considered advice is to study a single rose petal and then, with the tools of your choice, anything from a spoon, the back of a knife, through to your fingers, experiment with rolling and stretching until you have got it just right. Note – when crêpe paper has been stretched and curled, it stays stretched and curled – the process cannot be reversed.

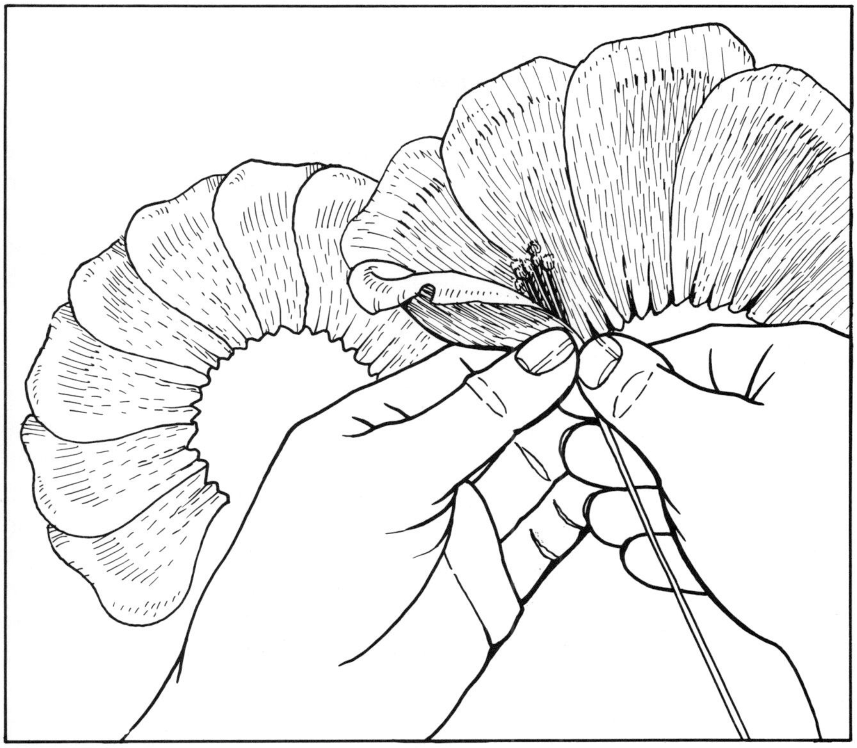

Overlap and glue the petals, then gather them slightly and wrap them round the stem.

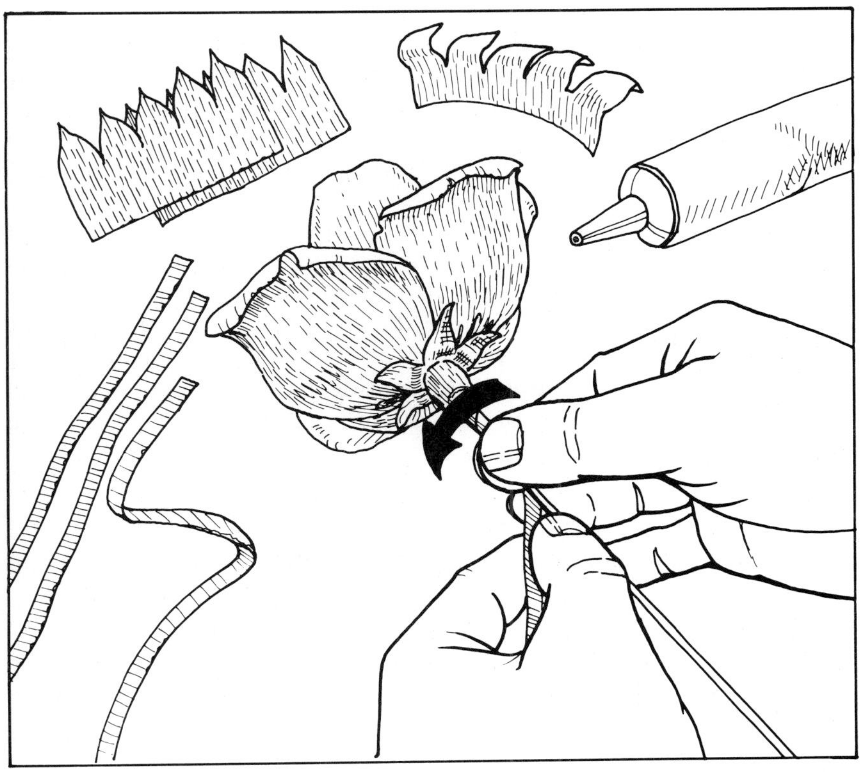

Stretch, shape and wrap the calyx strip round the base of the flower, secure it with a dab of glue, and then finally wrap a strip of green crêpe round the wire stem.

MAKING THE STEMS AND STAMENS

Take the brown paper string, and cut it into 2 inch lengths, reckon on having four such lengths for each flower. Now, take the yellow wool, all finely chopped, and length at a time, dab the ends of the string with quick dry clear glue and dunk them in the wool. When you have made a little stock pile of yellow ended stamens, take a length of stem wire, bend one end over on itself, then use the fine wire to bind the stamens in place, as illustrated. Make one such stamen-ended stem for each flower.

BUILDING THE FLOWER HEADS

Now flower at a time, arrange the petals, left to right, so that there are twenty small petals and ten large. Overlap from left to right so that the second petal overlaps the first, the third overlaps the second, and so on. Now glue the overlaps with the small amount of glue so that you have three ten-petal chains. When the glue is dry, take a flower stem up in one hand and a linked chain of small petals up in the other, and then very carefully wrap the petals around the stamens. First work the small petals and then the large until you have achieved the characteristic full rose head.

Now bind the petals in place with the fine wire, and then spend time easing and shaping the petals until you have got it just right. This done, cut little crown shaped strips and ribbons from the green crêpe paper, as illustrated. Now stretch and shape the calyx strip round the base of the flower, stand back just to make sure everything looks to be about right, then secure it with a small dab of glue. Finally take a strip of green crêpe and bind the stem.

PUTTING TOGETHER

Clear away the clutter and set the raffia covered hoop and the roses out on the worksurface. Establish the top and the bottom of the hoop, maybe fix a wire hanging loop at the top and a bow ribbon at the bottom. Now working down from the top of the hoop, first on one side and then on the other, push, fix and position the flowers so that they run from top to bottom in a considered overlapping sequence. Finally add another ribbon or two, perhaps a little 'Welcome' card and the job is done.

AFTERTHOUGHTS

If you want to tint and tone the paper petals use a little oil paint and white spirit – apply the paint with a fine soft haired brush.

You might use double thickness crêpe paper, if you can find a supplier that is.

You can use powder paint or flock for the stamens.

When you are working with crêpe paper, make sure that your hands are clean and dry.

PROJECT SIXTEEN

PAPER LAMPSHADE

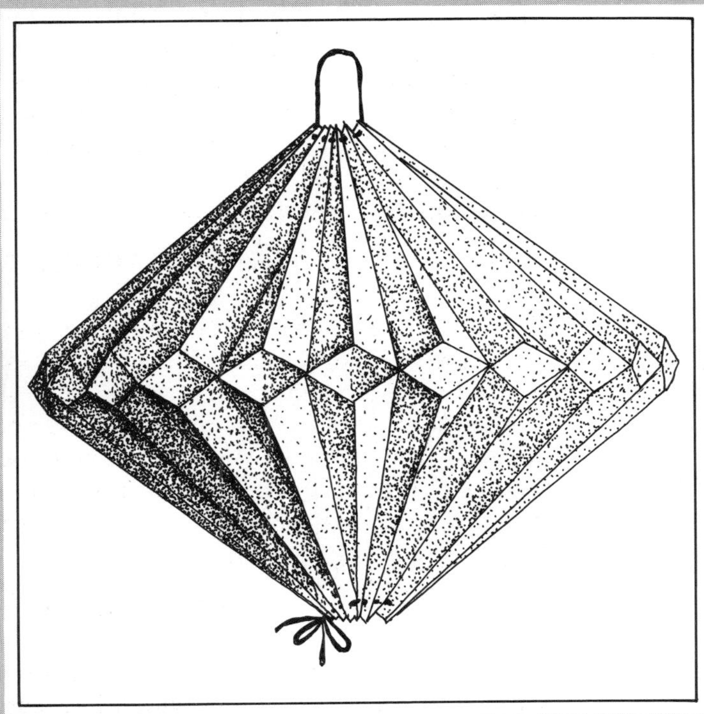

PROJECT PICTURE
A deceivingly simple traditional Japanese paper sculpture lampshade.

INTRODUCTION

THOUGHTS ON THE PROJECT

The Chinese may well have invented paper in or around the year 100 AD, and certainly there is evidence that suggests that a Chinese man called Tsai Lun perfected the paper-making process. However, having said that, it is just as certain that it was the Japanese who first realised the full sculptural potential of the material. Understanding that, once folded, a two dimensional piece of paper becomes three dimensional and sculptural – this is an inherent and integral part of Japanese culture and of the Japanese art and craft tradition. As to when and where in Japan folded papers were first made into ordinary domestic

INSPIRATIONAL
Traditional Japanese lampshade forms.

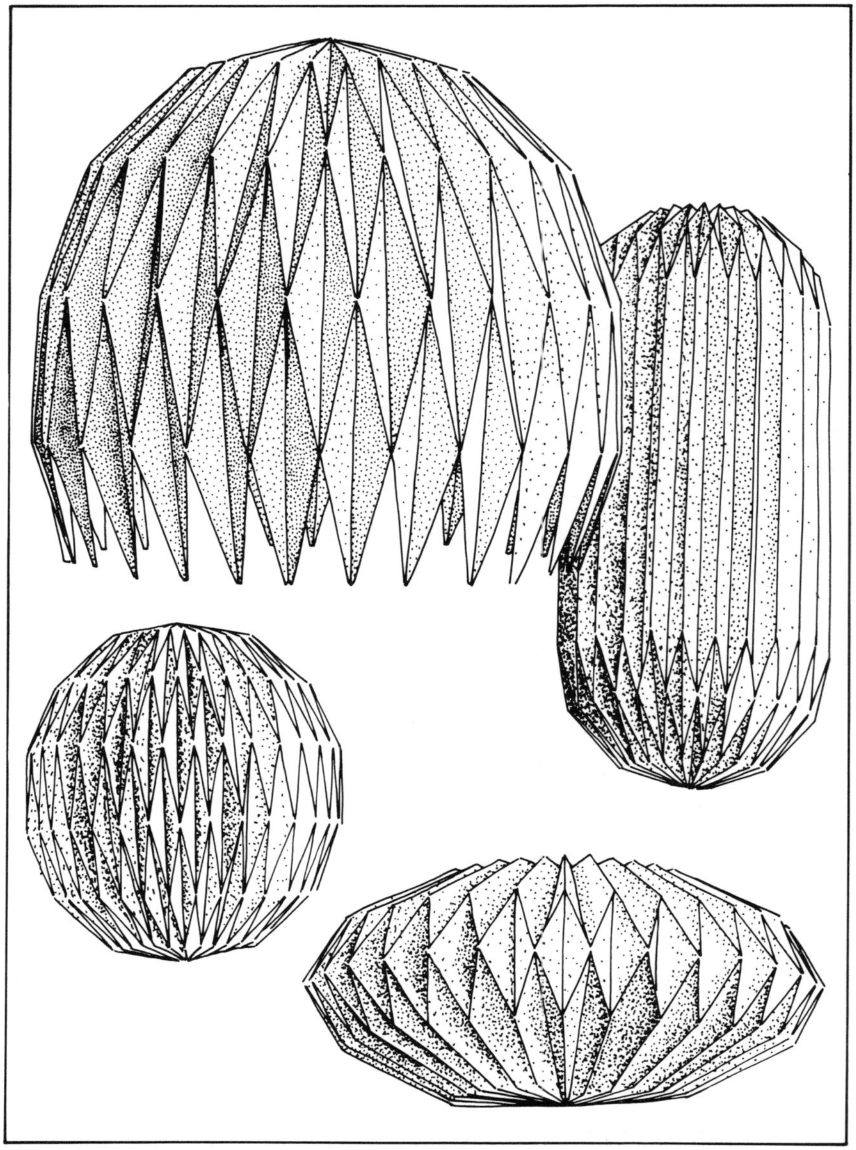

sculptural objects – everyday objects like umbrellas, screens, kites, fans and clothes, who can say; enough to know that paper in its many abstract and functional sculptural forms is still an important part of the Japanese way of life. In many ways the Japanese have developed the craft of paper folding to a point where they consider it to be an intellectual and spiritual accomplishment, with the various folds and creases being likened to valleys and mountains, and paper fold sculptures being presented on special religious and ceremonial occasions. Of course the Japanese also have many naive folk crafts that involve decorative paper sculpture, and this project relates to one such craft . . . that is making paper lampshades and lanterns.

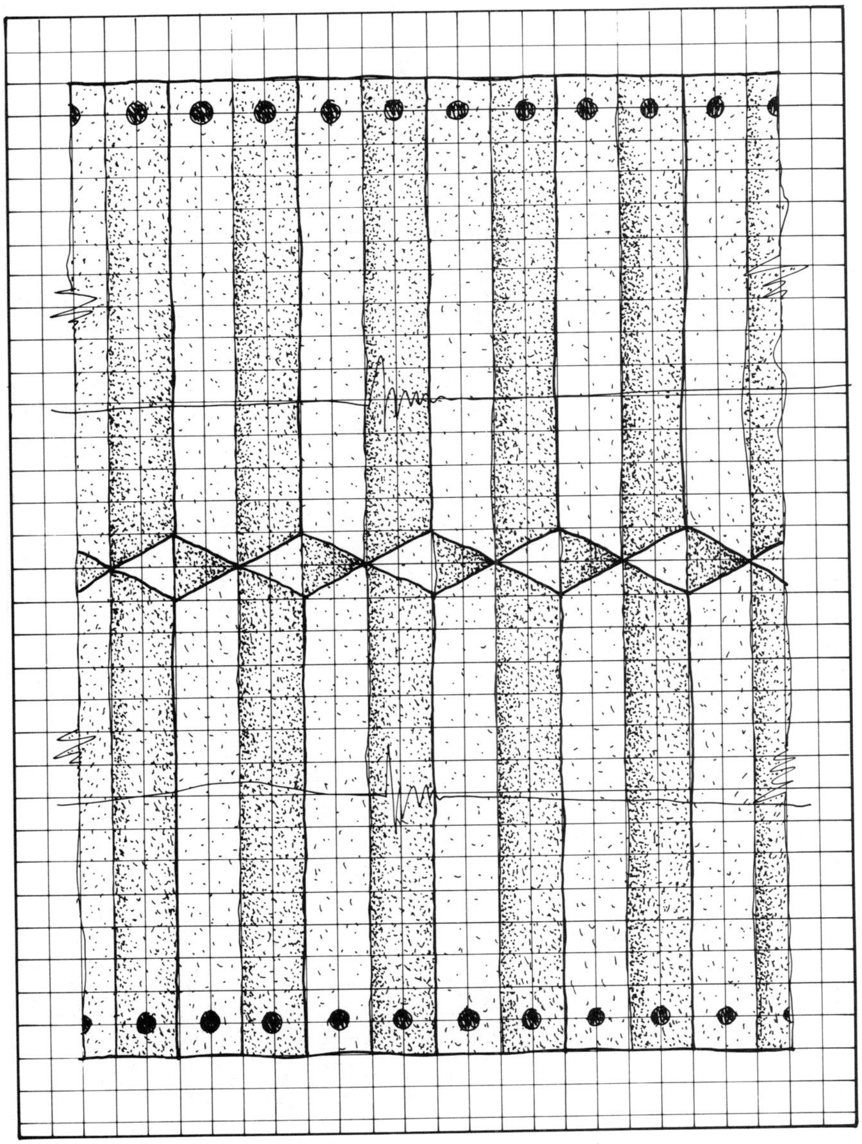

WORKING GRID
The scale is four grid squares to 1 inch. This project uses five 8.¼ × 12 inch sheets of cartridge paper, see the placing of the string holes, and note that the heavy black lines indicate 'mountain' folds, while the medium lines indicate 'valley' creases.

Fix the paper to the drawing board with tabs of masking tape, then use a T-square, a set-square, a ruler and the back edge of a scalpel to draw out the fold and crease lines.

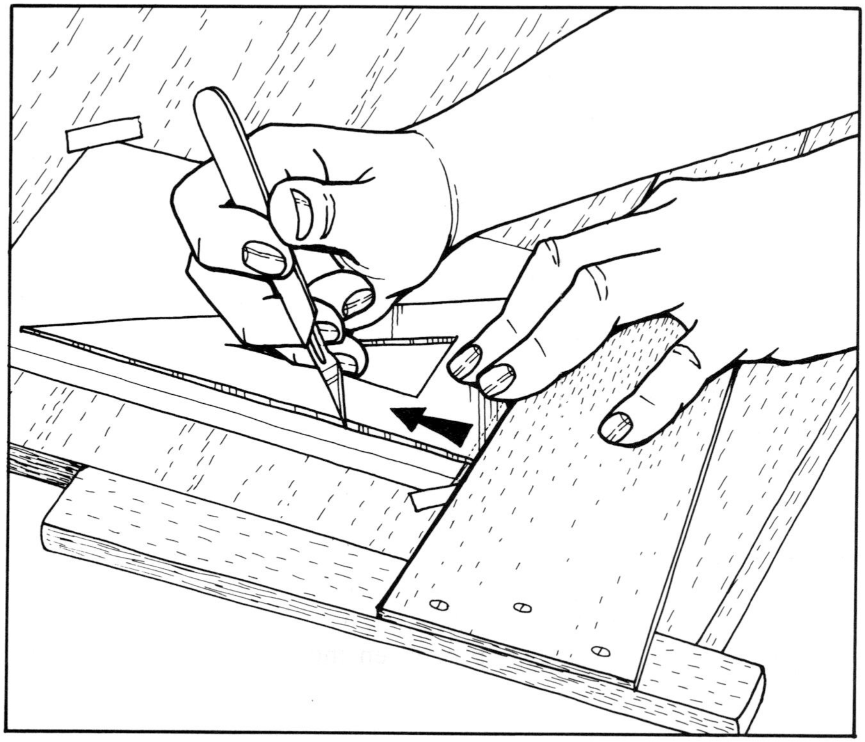

Fold the scored paper so as to make a concertina fan. Note – the diamond criss-crossing also needs to be scored.

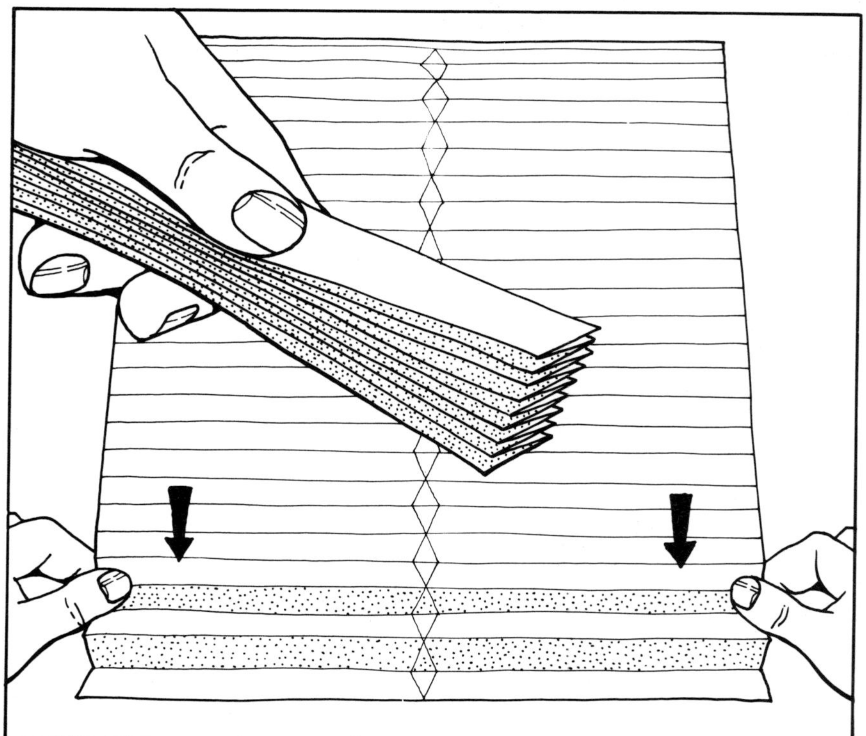

CONSIDERING THE PROJECT

Before you start this project, take a trip to the nearest museum and/or an ethnic craft shop, and get to see folk arts and crafts that have been made in Japan. Don't in the first instance look only at the paper crafts, but also let your gaze wander over the pottery, the textiles, the wood carving, and the block prints. See if you can, as it were, absorb and appreciate some of the qualities that make an item uniquely Japanese. All-in-all I think it fair to say that characteristically Japanese folk crafts have about them qualities that are at one and the same time, uncluttered, subtle and sophisticated. And so it is with a piece of good Japanese paper sculpture, although the overall form looks to be beautifully pure and direct, this very directness is in a way deceptive because it relates to techniques that are complex and sophisticated.

Once you have some inkling of what this project involves, take a few sheets of scrap paper and make a prototype. See how by varying the length of the paper in proportion to the width it is possible to change the size and proportion of the lampshade. Note – although you can modify the size of the shade by having a larger or smaller sheet of paper, it is best to stay with the same size grid, meaning don't change the ½ inch relationship between the folds and the diamond lozenges.

TOOLS AND MATERIALS

For this project you need, a drawing board, a T-square, an adjustable set-square, a hammer, a hole punch, a pair of scissors, a craft knife, a blunt-tip knife for scoring, an instant paper-to-paper adhesive, a

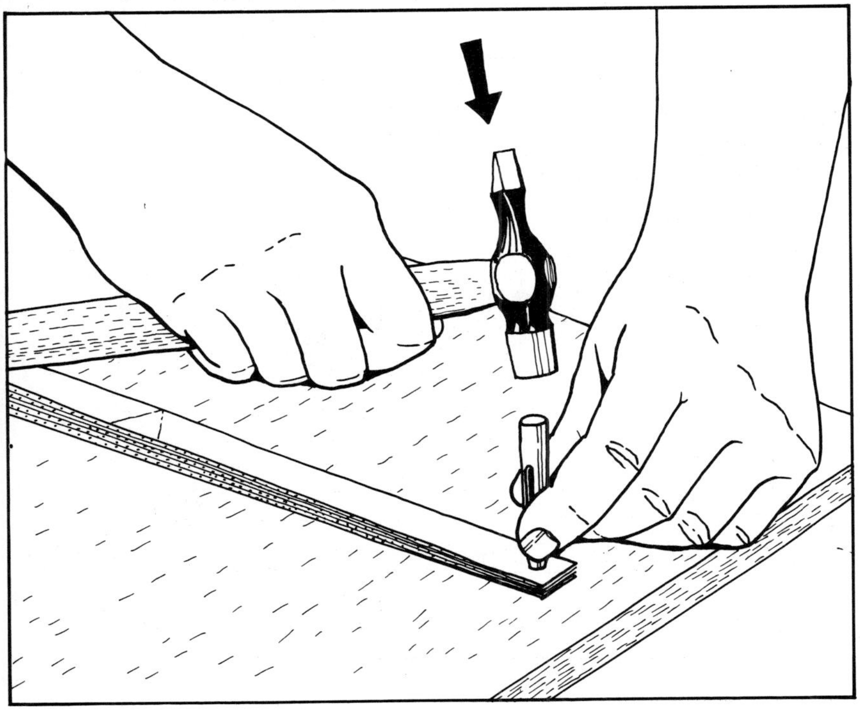

Punch holes through the concertina at both top and bottom.

handful of paper clips, a roll of masking tape, a workboard, a measure, about 24 inches of soft cord, and finally of course you need your paper. Note this project uses five 8.¼ × 12 inch sheets of best quality white machine made cartridge type paper, (see the Tools Materials and Techniques glossary).

MEASURING AND MARKING OUT

Take your paper, sheet at a time, position it on the drawing board so that the 8.¼ inch side is at the top, square the paper with the T-square, then secure it with four small tabs of masking tape. This done have a look at the working drawing grid and see how the paper has been set and spaced so that the folds and creases are parallel and ½ inch apart. Note also how each of the ½ inch wide, 1 inch long diamond lozenges is positioned on the centre line, then take the blunt-point knife and the ruler, and mark off your paper accordingly.

When you have what you consider to be a well set out and accurate grid, use the T-square, the set-square and the knife to score in all the creases and the folds. As you are working, make sure that each and every crease and fold is carefully scored with a single run of the blunt-point knife. Don't press so hard that you cut through the paper – if you have any doubts as to just how hard you should press, have a trial run on an off-cut. Note – if you are using a stout paper, then you might need to score the folds on one side, and then turn the paper over and score the folds on the other side. (see the Tools, Materials and Techniques glossary).

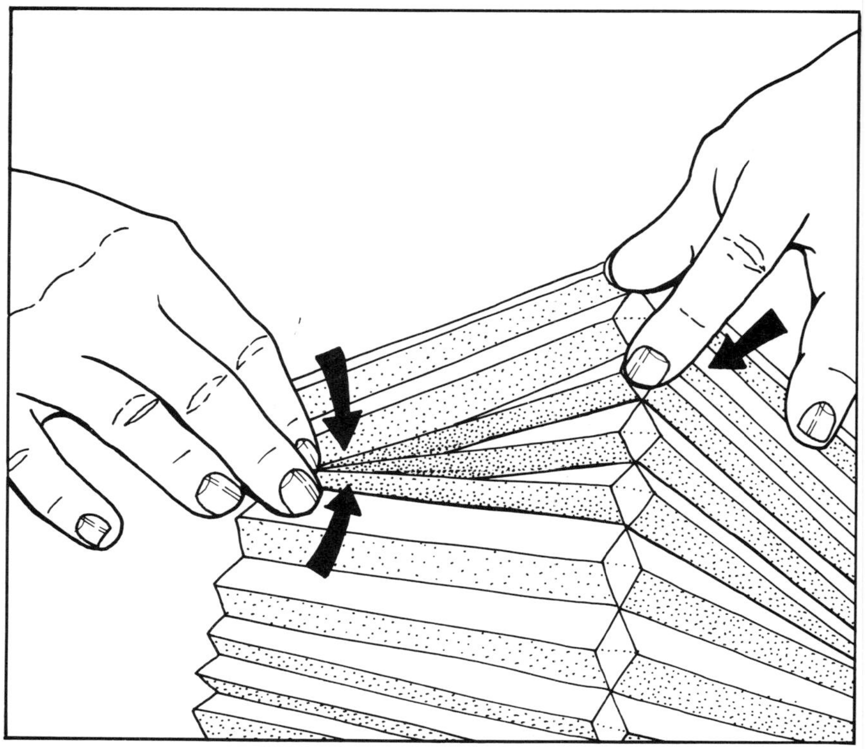

With care and caution pinch the concertina into the shade shape, gently dent and shape the lozenges with the fingers of the other hand.

FIRST FOLDS AND HOLE PUNCHING

When you have marked out and scored the five sheets of paper, clear the worksurface of all clutter, make sure that your hands are clean and dry, note the crease and fold sequence, and then start the concertina folding. Work the sheet of paper a fold at a time, meaning fold the paper along a score line, then turn the paper over and fold the next score line, and so on until you have a concertina gathering. Finally take the hammer and punch, position the folded paper on a block or a rough cutting board and then work the bottom and top cord-holes. Do this with all five sheets of paper.

FOLDING THE DIAMOND LOZENGES

This part of the project is tricky, so take your time, and aim to get it right the first time around. Hold one of the folded and punched pieces of paper between thumb and forefinger, spread it out so that you have a fan, then with the thumb and forefinger of the other hand, feel out and establish the form of the diamond lozenges. Now, with a gentle persuading action, very carefully bend and hinge the paper at the lozenge. At one and the same time, as you bend the paper, run your finger tips over the diamond lozenges so as to maintain their crispness. This part of the project relies on delicate, confident finger-to-paper control. If you are less than confident, practice with a sheet of marked out scrap paper. And so you proceed, working all the lozenges on all five sheets of paper.

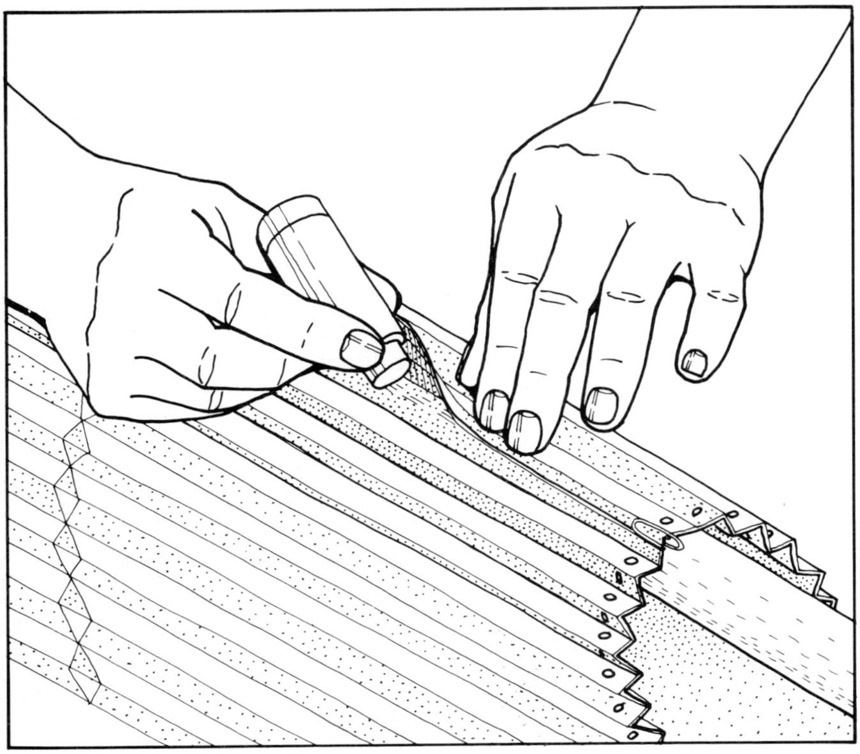

Once you have scored and folded the five sheets of paper, glue them together so as to make the lamp shade cylinder.

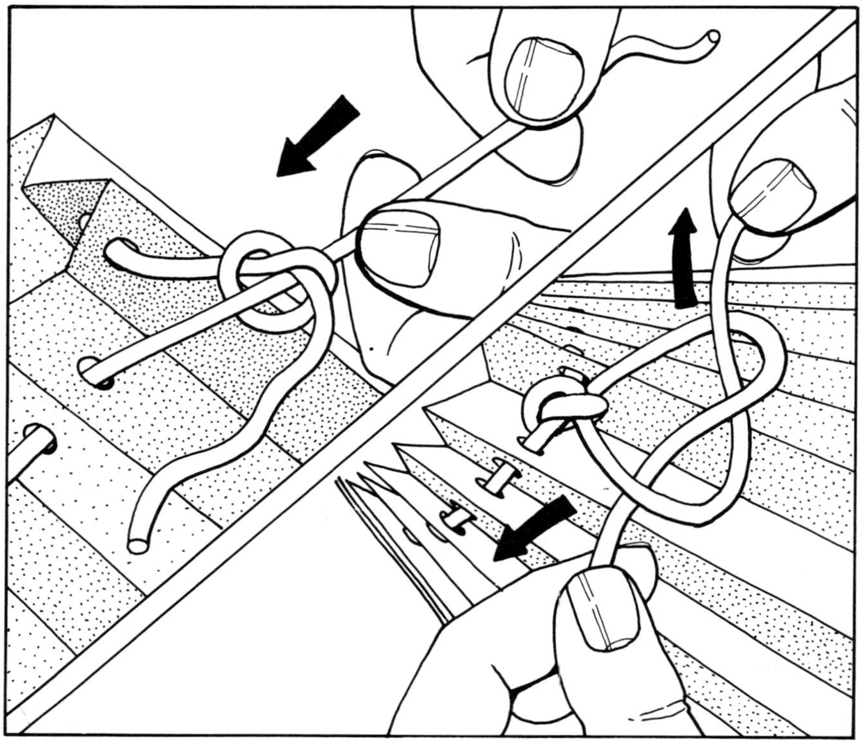

TOP *Take the two cords and thread one through the holes at the top of the cylinder and the other through the holes at the bottom of the cylinder, make slip knots.*
BOTTOM *Finally, shape the shade by adjusting the slip knot, then tie the knot and trim off the ends.*

PUTTING TOGETHER

When you have established all the creases and folds that go to make up the project, take the paper a piece at a time, carefully spread adhesive on the edge-tab, align it with its neighbour, and then press and clip-hold until the glue is dry. Do this with all five sheets of paper until you have built the cylinder. Now take the cord, pass it through the holes at one end of the cylinder, tie a slip knot, and then gather work the other end of the cylinder in like manner. As you pull the cord tight, ease the creases and folds into place. Now adjust the total form by loosening or tighting the two slip cords, have a last check just to make sure that all is as described, then tie off the slipknots. Finally, dab the cords with a spot of adhesive and the job is done. Note – see how one cord needs to be looped and tied so that it can be knotted on the light flex.

AFTERTHOUGHTS

With this project it is vital that each and every line be perfectly placed; use a T-square and a set-square – measure twice and mark once.

Make sure that your hands are clean, do all the marking with a blunt-point knife, and do not use a pencil.

Some paper sculptors prefer to only score folds, so they score in all the folds on one side of the paper and then turn the paper over and score in all the folds on the other. Note – a fold on one side of the paper is of course a crease on the other.

INDEX